# A RESTATEMENT OF RABBINIC CIVIL LAW

# A RESTATEMENT OF RABBINIC CIVIL LAW

## VOLUME II

### LAWS OF LOANS

Emanuel Quint

*Jerusalem Institute of Jewish Law*

Jason Aronson Inc.
Northvale, New Jersey
London

Production Editor: *Gloria L. Jordan*
Editorial Director: *Muriel Jorgensen*

This book was set in 11 point Bramley by Lind Graphics

It was printed and bound by Haddon Craftsmen in Scranton, Pennsylvania

**Library of Congress Cataloging-in-Publication Data**

Quint, Emanuel B.
    A restatement of rabbinic civil law.

    Adaptation of: Hoshen mishpat / Joseph ben Ephraim
Karo.
    Includes bibliographical references and indexes.
    Contents: v.1. Laws of judges, laws of evidence
— v. 2. Laws of loans.
    1. Jewish law. I. Karo, Joseph ben Ephraim,
1488–1575. Hoshen mishpat. II. Title.
LAW          340.5'25694          89-18546
ISBN 0-87668-799-0 (v. 1)
ISBN 0-87668-678-1 (v. 2)

Manufactured in the United States of America. Jason Aronson Inc. offers books and cassettes.
For information and catalog write to Jason Aronson Inc., 230 Livingston Street, Northvale, New
Jersey 07647.

To my wife Rena

Then was our mouth filled with laughter,
And our tongue with singing (Rena).

*Psalm 126:2*

# CONTENTS

## Chapter 39

## THE WRITING OF NOTES OF INDEBTEDNESS
### 1

## Chapter 40

## GRATUITOUS ASSUMPTION OF OBLIGATIONS
### 12

## Chapter 41

# LOST OR DESTROYED
# INSTRUMENTS
## 16

## Chapter 42

# LANGUAGE CONSTRUCTION
# IN WRITTEN INSTRUMENTS
## 23

## Chapter 43

# INCLUDING THE DATE OF EXECUTION
# OF THE INSTRUMENT
## 27

## Chapter 44

# THE FINAL LINES
# OF THE INSTRUMENT
## 38

## Chapter 45

# THE SIGNING OF THE INSTRUMENT
## 43

## Chapter 46

# AUTHENTICATION OF INSTRUMENTS
## 53

## Chapter 47

# THE CREDITOR IMPUGNS
# HIS OWN INSTRUMENT
## 72

## Chapter 48

# PRE-PREPARATION
# OF LEGAL FORMS
## 76

## Chapter 49

# WITNESSES MUST RECOGNIZE
# THE PARTIES
## 80

## Chapter 50

# AN INSTRUMENT THAT DOES NOT CARRY THE NAME OF THE OBLIGEE
## 88

## Chapter 51

# NOTES WITH ONLY ONE SUBSCRIBING WITNESS
## 92

## Chapter 52

# INSTRUMENTS WITH INTEREST PROVISIONS

# TORN INSTRUMENTS
## 99

## Chapter 53

## PROHIBITION AGAINST EXCHANGING
## INSTRUMENTS OF INDEBTEDNESS
### 103

## Chapter 54

## WRITING RECEIPTS OF PAYMENT
### 106

## Chapter 55

## PARTIAL PAYMENT
## AND ESCROWING INSTRUMENTS
### 113

## Chapter 56

# LAWS OF ESCROW
## 118

## Chapter 57

# THE PROHIBITION
# AGAINST RETAINING PAID INSTRUMENTS
# OF INDEBTEDNESS
## 125

## Chapter 58

# APPLICATION OF PAYMENT
# TO ONE OF MANY DEBTS
## 127

## Chapter 59

## BORROWER ALLEGES PAYMENT, BUT LENDER UNCERTAIN
### 132

## Chapter 60

## LIENS ON PERSONAL PROPERTY CONTRACTS PROPER PARTY NOT NAMED
### 137

## Chapter 61

# MISCELLANEOUS LAWS REGARDING INSTRUMENTS OF INDEBTEDNESS
### 155

## Chapter 62

# THE WIFE WHO MANAGES THE HOUSEHOLD
### 163

## Chapter 63

# A HOLDER WHO REQUESTS THE FORGERY OF AN INSTRUMENT
### 169

## Chapter 64

# LEVY MADE BY A CREDITOR/BAILEE ON INSTRUMENTS IN HIS POSSESSION
## 172

## Chapter 65

# FOUND INSTRUMENTS AND RECEIPTS
## 174

## Chapter 66

# ASSIGNMENT OF INSTRUMENTS OF INDEBTEDNESS
## 190

## Chapter 67

## LAWS CONCERNING *SHEMITAH* AND *PROSBUL*
### 205

## Chapter 68

## DOCUMENTS EMANATING FROM GENTILE COURTS
### 219

## Chapter 69

## WRITTEN EVIDENCE OF LOANS
### 225

## Chapter 70

## LAWS OF ORAL LOANS, AND LENDER'S INSTRUCTIONS REGARDING REPAYMENT
### 231

## Chapter 71

## CREDENCE GIVEN TO THE LENDER'S ALLEGATIONS BY THE BORROWER
### 237

## Chapter 72

## COLLATERALIZED LOANS
### 248

## Chapter 73

# TIME ALLOWED FOR REPAYMENT
# OF A LOAN
## 280

## Chapter 74

# PLACE AND MANNER
# OF LOAN REPAYMENT
## 292

# PUBLISHER'S NOTE

The series of volumes entitled *A Restatement of Rabbinic Civil Law*, by Rabbi Emanuel Quint, of which this book is the second, is a restatement of the fourth part of R. Joseph Karo's *Shulhan Aruch*. This fourth part, called *Hoshen haMishpat* ("Breastplate of Judgment"), codifies such laws as court procedure, torts, contract law, agency, inheritance, theft, destruction of property, and labor. Volume I covered Laws of Judges and Laws of Evidence and the present volume covers the Laws of Loans. Subsequent volumes in this series follow chapter by chapter through *Hoshen haMishpat*, and the series includes all 427 chapters of Part Four of R. Karo's work.

The Jewish code of civil law is at once one of the most difficult fields of study for the expert and one of the most compelling for the lay person. Based on biblical injunction, reinforced by Rabbinic enactments and by thousands of Rabbinic court rulings, Jewish civil law is a sophisticated legal system, built upon meticulous moral standards.

The Jerusalem Institute of Jewish Law, founded by Rabbis Adin Steinsaltz and Emanuel Quint, is dedicated to the study of Jewish civil law through two of Judaism's seminal legal texts, the Talmud and the *Shulhan Aruch*. While other portions of the *Shulhan Aruch* have been greatly explicated and popularized, *Hoshen haMishpat*, the section dealing with civil law, has been regarded as a closed book to all but the most scholarly. Yet, especially in today's complex commercial environment, the study of Jewish business ethics should be an urgent reminder that Jewish law governs all areas of life.

In order to clarify and simplify the law and render it more certain, the first step must be the preparation of an orderly restatement of the common law, including in that term not only the law developed solely by judicial decision but also the law that has grown from the application by the courts of generally and long-adopted statutes.

The function of the courts is to decide the controversies brought before them. The function of the Jerusalem Institute of Jewish Law is to state clearly and precisely in light of the decisions, principles, and rules of common law. The sections of the Restatement express the result of a careful analysis of the subject and a thorough examination and discussion of pertinent cases.

# PREFACE

This is the second volume of *A Restatement of Rabbinic Civil Law*, a restatement of *Hoshen haMishpat*, the fourth part of the *Shulhan Aruch*. The first volume (*A Restatement of Rabbinic Civil Law—Volume I: Laws of Judges, Laws of Evidence*, Jason Aronson Inc., 1990) contains two parts on procedural law: Chapters 1 through 28, which discuss the laws of judges and the beth din system, and Chapters 29 through 38, which discuss the laws of evidence.

Volume II begins with Chapter 39 and deals with the next thirty-six chapters of *Hoshen haMishpat*, having to do with the granting of loans and their designation as oral or written loans. In a sense, these chapters are also procedural in nature, since the emphasis in this volume is on the written note of indebtedness, which in essence is a document of evidence to prove to beth din the terms of the loan and the fact that the lender did lend money to the borrower.

With the possible exception of sales, loans are probably the most common business transaction in the world. Banks derive most of their income from loans to businesses or to individuals. Governments lend money to other governments and international loan agencies have become commonplace. There are also many (interest) free loan societies. When a government or a corporation sells its bonds, it is borrowing money. Very often when a person purchases a home he borrows money from a bank to pay for it.

## STRUCTURE OF THIS VOLUME

The topics are sequentially arranged according to the *Shulhan Aruch*, with very little deviation. The *Shulhan Aruch* arranges this subject matter into thirty-six chapters, from Chapter 39 through Chapter 74. I have arranged the chapters into twelve topics, and, to facilitate the reading of these chapters, I list here the topics and the chapters within each topic.

1. Creating the indebtedness: chapters 39 and 40.
2. Creating the instrument evidencing the indebtedness: chapters 41–45, 48–51, and 61.
3. Validity of the instrument of indebtedness: chapters 46, 52, 53, and 68.
4. Liens created by the instrument of indebtedness: chapters 60 and 64.
5. Defenses to the instrument of indebtedness: chapters 47, 63, and 67.
6. Receipts of payments, partial payments, and escrowing of the instrument of indebtedness: chapters 54–57, 62, and 71.
7. Dispute as to whether the loan has been paid: chapters 58, 59, 65, and 69.
8. Transferring instruments of indebtedness: chapter 66.
9. Loans not evidenced by instruments of indebtedness: chapter 70.
10. Collateral security for loans: chapter 72.
11. Time for repayment of loans where no time specified: chapters 73 and 74.
12. Formation of contracts: chapter 60.

## THE LOAN TRANSACTION

The loan transaction is very often a simple one. It consists of the lending of money to the borrower upon certain terms for repayment. There may be witnesses to the loan. There may be a writing evidencing the loan. The writing may create a lien on the realty of the borrower. If a third party purchases the realty on which the lender has a lien, and if the borrower does not have assets to repay the loan, the lender may trace the realty to the purchaser.

The loans contemplated in this volume are interest-free loans. What is written about loans can apply equally to any kind of credit transaction, such as sales and contracts for services, which are interest free. Business loans bearing interest are discussed in *Shulhan Aruch, Yoreh De'ah.*

As will be seen in this volume, the Torah requires one Jew to lend money to another Jew who is in need. Therefore, if a lender has the ability to make the requested loan and there is reasonable likelihood that it will be repaid, he really has no option but to make the loan.

The lender is admonished to make the loan in the presence of two persons and, better still, to have the two witnesses reduce their testimony to a document called a note of indebtedness, signed by the two witnesses, which will remove all questions regarding the loan and the terms thereof, and will also create a lien in favor of the lender on the realty then owned by the borrower.

# ACKNOWLEDGMENT

Thou openest Thy hand,
And satisfiest every living thing with favor.
*Psalm 145:16*

It is with great pleasure that I express my thanks:

Once again to my dear friend Marvin Klitsner for his great help.

To Arthur Kurzweil, Gloria Jordan, Nancy Andreola, and the staff of Jason Aronson Inc., who once again produced a book from a mere manuscript.

To Leah Globe, the greatest mother (in-law), grandmother, and great-grandmother in the world.

To my children and grandchildren, who bring Rena and me so much happiness:
Menucha, Ezra, Odeliyah, Moriyah, Eliyana, Chamutal, and Carmi Chwat
Naomi, Ruven, Eliyahu, Shoshana and Michal Sara Silverman
Jodi, Daniel, and Elad Patt
Rachel, David, and Zipporah Quint.

Our age has been especially faithful to the enterprise of making Jewish sources available to nonexperts. It has proven to be a boon not only for non-Jews who are curious about Judaism, but also for Jews who lack the language skills, scholarly background, and general training to study the sources of their tradition in the original Hebrew.

The latest and most welcome of these efforts is Emanuel Quint's *A Restatement of Rabbinic Civil Law*, Volume II, Laws of Loans. The author, an ordained rabbi and a member of the bar who has distinguished himself both in talmudic scholarship and the law, is eminently qualified to undertake this exposition of *Hoshen haMishpat*, the Standard Code of the Halachah's civil law.

What we have here is not a translation, but something better—in the sense of more comprehensible as well as more comprehensive— a "restatement" of *Hoshen haMishpat*. The language is clear and, despite the complexity of the issues involved, unencumbered by unnecessarily technical jargon. The work is at once lucid and authoritative.

The general reader will find this restatement of rabbinic law enlightening. And lawyers, especially those interested in comparative law, will find this a mine of relevant information.

Dr. Norman Lamm

The magnificant world of Torah is closed for so many people, not only due to linguistic and external difficulties, but largely because it contains means of expression and ways of thinking that are very different from those prevailing in the Western world today.

Rabbi Quint's work is paving a way; it is a means of orientation with which a contemporary person can find his way in the great sea of Jewish Law, thus training and inspiring the thought of the student and the reader.

Rabbi Adin Steinsaltz

# LAWS OF LOANS

# Chapter 39

# THE WRITING OF NOTES
# OF INDEBTEDNESS

## INTRODUCTION

With Chapter 39 we enter into a new topic: laws of credit. In the *Shulhan Aruch*, Karo refers to these laws as "laws of loans." It should be remembered that it is a Torah commandment and the responsibility of every Jew to lend money to those who are in need, even if the needy person is wealthy.[1] Such loans may be intended for personal or household needs, business needs, or any other legal purpose.[2] Indeed, it is considered base and ignoble to refuse to lend money to someone in need.[3] (What we say about loans will also apply

---

1. In the phrase "If thou lend money to any of My people" (Exodus 22:24), the word "if" is not fully permissive. It permits the lender the right to refuse only if he is not in a position to lend. If he can lend, however, he must surely do so. Rambam enumerates this as positive commandment 197, one of the 613 commandments.

2. The Midrash, in discussing the verse "Woe unto them that join house to house" (Isaiah 5:8), cites the statement of R. Yohanan, who said that the verse refers to those who make a loan on a man's house and field with the intention of taking them from him.

3. See Deuteronomy 15:9, "Beware that there be not a base thought in thy heart, saying: 'The seventh year, the year of release, is at hand, and thine eye be evil against thy needy brother, and thou give him nought.'" Rabbeinu Yonah adds: "If we have been exhorted not to desist from lending at the approach of the seventh year for fear

to other forms of credit, such as those used in sales, contracts for construction or labor, and the like.

According to halachah, all loans and extensions of credit are to be interest-free.[4] Business investments are discussed in *Shulhan Aruch, Yoreh De'ah,* and not in *Hoshen haMishpat,* since laws regarding permissible business investments and the prohibition of taking of interest are there discussed.

The Sages have advised all lenders and extenders of credit to refrain from lending or extending credit unless there are witnesses present; better yet, the loan or extension of credit should be evidenced by a formal note of indebtedness. The note should be drawn by a competent lawyer, who should see to its drafting, execution, and delivery. A properly drafted, executed, and delivered note of indebtedness creates a lien on the real estate owned by the borrower on the date of the loan.

This chapter discusses the writing of the note of indebtedness. I have suggested herein that the beth din in every community have an index of all such notes of indebtedness loans that can be examined by prospective purchasers or mortgagees who wish to determine whether an impending transaction is subject to any note of indebtedness loans. In those places where a central indexing system is in place, the holder of the note of indebtedness will be able to have it registered. This will remove any temptation on the part of the debtor to deny the loan, whether honestly or not. The lien of the note of indebtedness loan does not extend to personalty; such an extension would have the effect of preventing ordinary trade.[5]

The purpose of the note of indebtedness loan is to afford protection to the creditor. Therefore, if there was a mistake in any of the terms of the note of indebtedness, it would generally be ascribed to an error made by the scribe who drew up the note. The creditor would then be

---

of the institution of release, how great must be the sin of one who refrains from lending when there is no danger of his suffering such a loss."

4. Rabbi Samson Raphael Hirsch, in his commentary on Exodus 22:24, states: "So the duty of lending money without interest is one of the rocks of that granite base on which Jewish social life rests. Carrying out this duty is at the same time one of those great acts of acknowledgment by which God wants our allegiance to Him to be sealed by acts of sacrifice in our daily life."

5. Mortgages on personalty are discussed in Volume IV, Chapter 117.

permitted to ask the beth din to have the note of indebtedness corrected.

The beth din must in all cases weigh the conflicting claims of the parties. In the absence of witnesses to testify as to what transpired, the beth din is relegated to relying on the note of indebtedness. The party named in the note may offer any of a variety of defenses in order to disclaim liability. He may contend, for example, that the note was a forgery, or that it was a note of trust to be held by the creditor in trust on a loan that was never made, or that the note was paid, and/or anything else which the debtor asserts to disclaim liability.

The Glossary at the end of this book will help the reader to understand some of the terms used in this chapter.

# TEXT

## The commandment to lend money

The Torah requires all Jews to lend money to those in need. However, this obligation is not enforceable in beth din, even if the proposed lender promised the borrower, and even if a *kinyan* was made to lend the money.[6] If the borrower incurred expenses, such as those to have the note of indebtedness drawn, and the lender reneges, then the lender must reimburse him.

If the lender instructed the borrower to furnish a pledge, then the moment the lender takes hold of the pledge, he is obligated to complete the loan.[7]

When a loan is made, the borrower must pay the expenses of the

---

6. This is the case because moneys cannot be acquired by a *kinyan*. See Chapter 195.

7. The picking up of the pledge immediately acts as a barter exchange, since objects are acquired when they are picked up. The moment the creditor acquires a security interest in the pledge, the borrower acquires an interest in the money to be loaned to him. The barter exchange would not have taken place if the borrower had picked up the money first, since money cannot be acquired by *kinyan*. Picking up the money first would not give the lender any security interest in the pledged item. Although this was the intent of the parties, their intention would be frustrated until the creditor picked up the pledge.

borrowing, such as the fees of the scribe and witnesses, if any,[8] and recording fees, if any. If the lender loses the note of indebtedness or the note of admission, he must pay to have a duplicate drawn.[9] When the loan is repaid and the lender does not have the note of indebtedness to return to the borrower, the lender must pay for having a receipt drawn.

## The writing of the note of indebtedness

The creditor may refuse to make the loan or extend credit unless the debtor instructs the writing, signing, and delivery of the note of indebtedness to him.

A note of indebtedness may not be written until the debtor instructs the person drawing the note of indebtedness to do so and the subscribing witnesses to sign the note and deliver it to the creditor. There is an opinion that even if the debtor gave the instructions to write and to sign, he must once again instruct the scribe to deliver the note of indebtedness to the creditor; otherwise he may not do so. Similarly, any document that changes the legal relationship of a person or a thing, such as a deed for property, a deed of gift, a release, or an admission, may not be drawn without the specific instruction of the person to be charged. In deeds of gift or marriage contracts, the donor or the bridegroom should be asked a second time before the delivery of the gift to the donee, or the marriage contract to the bride.[10] If the creditor, in the presence of the debtor, instructed the scribe to write the note of indebtedness and the witnesses to sign, and the debtor remained silent, it is taken as a sign of his assent to the procedure, and the note of indebtedness is then written, executed, and delivered. If a note of indebtedness is drawn up without the instructions of the debtor, then it is treated as a memorandum of the event and is not considered a note of indebtedness.

The note of indebtedness may be written and delivered even

---

8. See Chapter 34 in Volume I regarding when fees may be charged by the witnesses.

9. Lost notes are discussed in Chapter 41.

10. In the cases of marriage contracts and deeds of gifts, there is an undertaking by the obligor of his own money; in the case of the loan, however, it is rather a return of the lender's money.

without specific instructions from the debtor if a *kinyan* was made.[11] This is the case even if the witnesses to the writing were not present when the *kinyan* and/or the loan was made, if the debtor admitted to them that the loan was made and a *kinyan* took place.[12] Some authorities hold that if the *kinyan* took place after the loan, it is effective as authorization only if there was a promise to repay the loan within a specified time. If no time of repayment was specified, then the entire *kinyan* is ineffective because the *kinyan* did not enlarge the obligation of the borrower.[13]

At any time after the *kinyan* was made, the creditor may request that the note of indebtedness be drawn, executed, and delivered to him. Some authorities limit the time for such writing to 30 days after the indebtedness was incurred. The author prefers the first opinion. Some authorities hold that the note of indebtedness may not be drawn up if the time for payment of the loan has passed because the loan may have been repaid on the due date.[14] If the due date has not yet passed, then the persons writing, executing, and delivering the note of indebtedness need not fear that the indebtedness was paid in the interval.[15] The date of the making of the *kinyan* is inserted in the note of indebtedness. If the note of indebtedness is drawn at some time after the *kinyan* was made and the date is not remembered, then the note of indebtedness states that the date of the writing is being inserted because the witnesses do not remember the date of the *kinyan*. If a *kinyan* was made, the note of indebtedness may be written

---

11. The *kinyan* acts as a sort of power of attorney, enabling the recipient of the rights to act in the stead of the obligor in giving instructions to prepare the note of indebtedness. A *kinyan* enables the recipient of the rights under the *kinyan* to have the document set to writing.

12. Other witnesses may have testified that a *kinyan* was made, or the debtor may admit to these two witnesses that a *kinyan* was made.

13. As was stated in the Introduction to this chapter, the best way to make a loan or to extend credit is to have a competent person, preferably a lawyer, draw, execute, and deliver the proper instruments.

14. It is presumed, however, that a note of indebtedness is not paid before its due date. (See Chapter 78 in Volume III.)

15. If the debtor knows that there are witnesses to the *kinyan* or to his admission, he would be foolish to repay the loan unless he received a receipt. He knows that the creditor may at any time request that the note of indebtedness be drawn up, executed, and delivered to the creditor. If he has a receipt, the debtor does not take the risk of having to pay twice.

even if the debtor or the creditor or both have died. The lien clauses may be inserted if they have been omitted because there is a rule of law that a mistake made by the scribe may be corrected. The creditor need not be present when the *kinyan* is made,[16] although there is also authority that he must be present when the *kinyan* is made.

If the debtor is dissipating his assets or is about to leave the community, or if the witnesses to the loan are about to leave the community, then the creditor may ask the witnesses to appear in beth din; the beth din will then write the note of indebtedness and the witnesses will execute it then and there, and the beth din will deliver it to the creditor.

At any time before the note of indebtedness is drawn up, the debtor may instruct the scribe not to draw the note and the witnesses not to execute it. If the note was already drawn and executed, then the debtor may instruct that it not be delivered to the creditor. The debtor may so instruct only if he has not yet received the credit or the loan. There is an opinion, however, that the debtor may render such instruction even if he has received the credit or the loan. According to this last opinion, the creditor has no recourse except to sue for repayment on an unsecured loan.[17]

The debtor may not instruct that the note of indebtedness is not to be written if he has agreed by *kinyan* not to do so. However, there is also an opinion that holds that the debtor may stop the note of indebtedness from being written or delivered even if he has undertaken by a *kinyan* not to stop the writing.[18] If the debtor has already

---

16. The *kinyan* can be made even if the creditor is not present, since the handkerchief need not belong to the creditor. It can belong to a third party, such as the witness. The only restriction is that it cannot belong to the debtor. A *kinyan* made by a minor is a nullity.

17. Before making the loan, the creditor may insist that the note of indebtedness be drawn.

18. According to this opinion, the *kinyan* is not effective in this case because the promise not to rescind permission to write the note of indebtedness is only a declaration of intent, and a declaration of intent cannot be made binding by a *kinyan*. The other opinion, which states that the debtor may not rescind his instructions to execute the note of indebtedness if he has agreed not to do so by *kinyan*, holds that it is a decree of the Rabbis that he may not do so once a *kinyan* has been made. Technically, a principal may rescind the agency of his agent, but the Rabbinic decree prevents him from so doing. This same decree permits the writing after the debtor has died, for the agency should have terminated with the death of the debtor.

received the loan or credit, then in spite of his instructions not to proceed, the scribe and/or witnesses may proceed to write the note of indebtedness unless the debtor has returned the loan or credit to the creditor. There is an opinion that if the debtor has instructed that the note of indebtedness not be drawn, then the creditor must bring the witnesses who witnessed the loan, admission, or *kinyan* to the beth din and then the beth din will write the note of indebtedness. This is the case unless the debtor is leaving the jurisdiction or is dissipating his assets, in which events the scribe and the witnesses may write and execute the note of indebtedness or note of admission without having to go to beth din.

Any note of indebtedness drawn without the instructions of the debtor is not valid as a note of indebtedness if there was no *kinyan*.

In general, all those who have witnessed a matter may testify to it. In the case of the witnesses to a *kinyan*, however, only those designated to be the witnesses may write the note of indebtedness.[19] In the case of an oral loan, all those who were present may testify.[20]

## The writing of the note of admission

A note of admission has the same legal effect as a note of indebtedness with regard to a lien on the real property owned by the debtor when the loan was made.

A note of admission regarding money or personalty may not be drawn up without the instructions of the debtor.[21] In the case of an

---

The *kinyan* referred to here is a *kinyan* not to stop the writing; it is not the *kinyan* obligating himself to pay the loan, which *kinyan* entitles the creditor to have a note of indebtedness executed no matter what the debtor says.

19. If all those who were present when the *kinyan* was made could write the note of indebtedness, then if there were ten persons present when the *kinyan* was made, there could theoretically be five separate groups of two witnesses, each of which could each write a note of indebtedness, and the creditor could then have five notes of indebtedness.

20. In the case of an oral loan there is no danger that the creditor may sue several times and bring different witnesses each time who actually witnessed the loan. The debtor can always either swear that he paid the loan or demand a receipt of payment after he makes the first repayment.

21. The reason for not writing the note of admission is that the debtor may have returned the deposit or the personalty, and the note of admission would subject him

admission regarding realty, the witnesses may write a note of admission even without the debtor's instructions.[22] The note may be drawn up without the debtor's instructions if the debtor admitted the loan before three persons whom he brought together to act as a beth din. If the admission and instruction to draw a note of admission was made before one witness and was later made before a second witness, they may combine to write a note of admission, and the date will be that of the second instruction.[23]

If an appointed beth din, at the behest of the creditor, summoned the debtor to beth din,[24] and the debtor appeared and admitted the indebtedness, then the beth din may draw the note of admission, execute it, and deliver it to the creditor.[25] The beth din may draw a note of indebtedness or a note of admission only if they know the identities of both the creditor[26] and the debtor.[27] There is also an opinion that the beth din need not know the identity of the creditor.

If the debtor's instruction was that the note of admission should not be given to the creditor, then his instruction is to be followed even if given simultaneously with a *kinyan.*

---

to liability again. With regard to realty, however, the same claim cannot be made again, since it is easy to see who is in possession.

22. An example of an admission regarding real property is a case in which an individual admits that the house in which he resides belongs to another.

23. See Chapter 30 in Volume I regarding combining of testimony.

24. A note of admission will not be written if both parties appeared voluntarily before beth din to make this request. It is only when the parties appear in an adversary proceeding that the news of the proceeding becomes known and people become aware of the judgment in favor of the creditor and the note of admission written pursuant to the judgment. In such circumstances, the delivery of the note of admission will serve as notice to all that there is a lien on the real property of the debtor.

25. This follows the opinion that holds that a decision of the beth din is equivalent to an authenticated instrument and the debtor may not allege that he repaid the loan. Just like a written note of indebtedness, it is a lien on the debtor's realty.

26. The creditor may come to beth din with a fictional name because he may not want his creditors to know that he has an outstanding claim against his debtors. Thus the beth din would be abetting his perpetration of a fraud on his creditors.

27. If the beth din does not know the identity of the debtor, then anyone could come to beth din and claim to be the debtor and admit a debt in the name of some other person. The beth din would then draw up a note of admission with the name of the other person therein as the debtor.

If the admission was that the debtor owed money to two persons or that he borrowed from two persons, then the note of indebtedness or the note of admission names them both as creditors. Even if the note of indebtedness or note of admission is given to only one of the two creditors, the other has the same rights as against third parties.[28] If the admission is for a nonexistent obligation, as described in Chapter 40, then only the person who holds the note of admission may enforce it against third parties, and the second person stands in the position of a creditor who holds an oral loan.[29] If a *kinyan* was made, however, then the second person may also enforce his rights as against a third party.

## Presumption of regularity

Both the note of indebtedness and the note of admission have a presumption of validity. If the note fails to state that it was drawn up at the behest of the debtor, in those instances where his instructions are required, it is presumed that he gave such instructions. When questioned by the beth din the witnesses are believed to state that the debtor gave such instructions. However, the note is not presumed valid if it also contains another defect,[30] such as a statement of execution before a beth din in a note that contains only two signatures.[31] The note is valid, however, as an oral loan.[32]

---

28. The third party might be someone who purchased realty from the debtor after the date of the note of admission and that the debtor owned on the day on which the note of admission was executed. The creditor who does not hold the note may proceed against the third party.

29. This may be enforced only out of the unsold property of the debtor.

30. If the note of indebtedness or note of admission states that it was executed before a beth din and signed by two witnesses, and the authentication by the beth din states that one of the judges did not sign, it is still a valid note of indebtedness or note of admission.

31. A beth din must have at least three persons. Thus a note of indebtedness or note of admission is deemed invalid if only two persons signed it. If the note also failed to state that it was executed pursuant to instructions from the debtor or by a *kinyan*, then the presumption of validity is lost.

32. It is valid as affects the borrower unless he contests it, as he can contest any oral loan. It is not valid as against purchasers of the borrower's real estate.

## Allegations of payment

During the period of time between the *kinyan* and the writing of the note of indebtedness, the debtor is not permitted to allege payment.[33] There is a difference of opinion between R. Karo and Ramo as to whether the debtor may assert a defense of payment against a judgment on the debt. R. Karo holds that it may not be asserted,[34] whereas Ramo holds that such a defense is admissible.[35]

## Predrafting a note of indebtedness before making the loan

A debtor may request that a note of indebtedness be drawn up even if the creditor is not present.[36] However, this may be done only if a *kinyan* has been made whereby the debtor's realty is liened by the note of indebtedness.[37] It may also be done if the note of indebted-

---

33.  The reason is that the debtor knows that as a result of the *kinyan*, the creditor may have a note of indebtedness drawn. Thus the debtor would not pay the debt unless he received a receipt of payment. If he does not produce such a receipt, his plea of payment is not admitted.

34.  The defense of payment may not be asserted because the judgment of the beth din is equivalent to a note of indebtedness. The beth din will not write a note of indebtedness or render judgment without the debtor's being summoned to beth din. Thus the debtor is aware of the fact that he should not repay the debt unless he has a receipt of payment. Without such a receipt, he may not assert a defense of payment.

35.  According to this opinion, there is a distinction between a judgment of the beth din and a verdict of the beth din. The verdict of the beth din is not equivalent to a note of indebtedness, but rather to a memorandum of the beth din's holding. Thus the debtor can allege that he paid the amount of the verdict. (See *Aruch haShulhan*, Chapter 39, paragraph 16, for the distinction between a verdict and a judgment of the beth din.)

36.  Neither the witnesses nor the beth din need be concerned that a debtor may be putting himself into a vulnerable position because the note of indebtedness may fall into the hands of the creditor without the loan's having been made. The debtor made the decision and it should be followed. A debtor may want to have a note of indebtedness ready in case the lender is in a hurry and will not have time to obtain a scribe and witnesses.

37.  If no *kinyan* has been made, then there is no lien, since the loan has not yet been made. If the note of indebtedness was written on January 1 and the money was loaned and the note of indebtedness delivered to the creditor on February 1, then the

ness states that it creates a lien from the date on which the note of indebtedness is delivered to the creditor in the presence of two witnesses. If there is no *kinyan*, then the note of indebtedness may not be drawn up until the creditor is present and the note of indebtedness is delivered to him. This holds true even if the money has been loaned to the debtor. The note may not be drawn, however, if the creditor objects.[38]

The creditor may not request that a note of indebtedness be drawn up only when the debtor appears; and should the loan not be made then the note may be destroyed. The note may not be drawn up even if the creditor agrees to leave it with the scribe until the loan is made. Some hold, however, that the note may be drawn up so long as the witnesses do not sign.

Witnesses may not sign a blank note of indebtedness or even a completed note of indebtedness with instructions that it be held in escrow until the loan is actually made.

## Indexing notes of indebtedness

It is suggested that every beth din establish an indexing system for all notes of indebtedness and notes of admission so that they will serve as notice of lien, thereby protecting purchasers of real estate as well as lenders and extenders of credit. It is also suggested that when a *kinyan* is made, the witnesses reduce the fact of the *kinyan* to writing. This writing should also be included in the index. The index system should also provide that the lien be removed when the debtor presents a receipt of payment of the debt.

---

lien should be effective as of February 1, although it appears from the note of indebtedness that the lien commenced on January 1. If the debtor sold realty to a third person on January 15, then the property would be subject to the lien as appears from the date of the note of indebtedness. In truth there was no lien in effect on the debtor's property until February 1.

38. The creditor may object because he does not want the loan to appear on his statement as an asset. He may have two reasons for this. First, it is not yet actually an asset. Second, the creditor may be deliberately seeking to minimize his net worth because he is concerned that his wealth will become widely known and he may then be asked to pay higher taxes or to make charitable contributions beyond his means.

# Chapter 40

---

# GRATUITOUS ASSUMPTION OF OBLIGATIONS

## INTRODUCTION

Chapter 39 discussed notes of indebtedness and notes of admission, which have the effect of placing a lien on the realty of the debtor. In this chapter, Chapter 40, ways are described in which a person may obligate himself to pay someone else money when in fact no money is owed. This writing, the note of confession, also gives rise to a lien on the real property of the obligor.

Witnesses in halachah may be of several types (see Volume I, Chapter 35). For example, witnesses may be present to give effect to the act. Such is the task of witnesses to a betrothal. Unless the witnesses are present, the betrothal is of no effect, even if both bride and groom admit that a betrothal took place. In commercial law the function of the witness is to testify in beth din in the event that differences arise between the parties. Sometimes these witnesses, by their signatures, can make an otherwise promissory note into a note of indebtedness, which effects a lien on the realty of the debtor. Thus, in Chapter 39, even when the lien was created by a *kinyan*, there was nevertheless the expectation that the debt would be reduced to a note of indebtedness. In addition to witnesses who sign an instrument, there should be witnesses to the delivery of the instrument, who may or may not be the same witnesses who signed the document. Indeed, it is the witnesses to the delivery of the promissory note to the creditor who, by their witnessing the act, effect a lien on the realty of the debtor. There is also the opinion that the witnesses, by signing the note of indebtedness, create the lien. This opinion is not generally accepted, however.

Similarly, a person may obligate himself as a guarantor on a debt even though he is not indebted to the creditor.[1] Although the guarantor has no direct financial obligation to the creditor, his mere acceptance of responsibility obligates him to the creditor. Similarly, in this chapter, the debtor accepts an obligation to pay the creditor even though prior thereto he was not obligated to him. This fact is known to the creditor, the debtor, and the witnesses.

The person who accepts the obligation is designated the *debtor*, and the person to whom he obligates himself is designated the *creditor*. Whenever the term *witnesses* is used, it will refer to two eligible witnesses unless the text states otherwise.

The indexing system suggested in Chapter 39 can also be used to index notes of confession.

# TEXT

## Undertaking a gratuitous monetary obligation

A person may obligate himself to pay money to someone even when he is not legally obligated to him. The obligation must be unconditional, and the debtor did not create the obligation merely because he mistakenly believed that he was indebted to the creditor.[2] Consider some examples:

---

1. When the guarantor is named in the note of indebtedness and the witnesses sign the note after the name of the guarantor, then he is bound, even if no *kinyan* was made to bind him. This is true even if he is named after the loan has been made and there is no consideration for him to be bound. (See Chapter 129 in Volume IV.)

2. If the obligation was assumed in error, and the error was later discovered, then the entire transaction is a nullity. It may have been witnesses or the creditor himself who later called the error to the attention of the debtor.

1. The debtor asks the witnesses to witness the fact that he owes money to the creditor. This obligation does not effect a lien on the realty of the debtor.[3] There are authorities who hold that this does not even effect an obligation against the debtor, since mere words cannot create a current obligation; an obligation can be created only by a *kinyan* or a writing. If the declaration stated that the debt was already in existence, then even these authorities would agree that the obligation is binding on the debtor.

2. The debtor writes a note stating that he owes the creditor money, but no witnesses have signed the note.[4] This confession does not effect a lien on the realty of the debtor. If the note was delivered to the creditor in the presence of witnesses, it has all the requisites of a note of indebtedness and effects a lien on the realty of the debtor.[5]

3. The debtor declares in the presence of witnesses that he is already obligated to the creditor in a note of indebtedness. The debtor did not, as in example 1, ask the witnesses to act as witnesses.[6] This confession does not give rise to the placement of a lien on the realty of the debtor.

4. The debtor prepares a promissory note that is unsigned by witnesses. He then delivers it to the creditor in the presence of two witnesses.[7] If the note is in the handwriting of the debtor, and if the witnesses to the delivery read the note, then it is a note of confession and effects a lien on the real property of the debtor.[8] Some authorities hold that the debtor must ask the witnesses to sign that they witnessed the delivery; this may be done on another writing.

5. In examples 2 and 4, which deal with notes, the obligation to the

---

3. It cannot effect a lien since no witnessed writing was delivered to the creditor.

4. Some authorities hold that the note referred to in this second example must be either written in the handwriting of the debtor or signed by the debtor. If neither of these situations obtain, then there is no obligation on the part of the debtor.

5. This example seems identical to example 4, which R. Karo wrote in a separate paragraph. This author therefore believes that the first part of the statement is the preferred view. In that law, there is no lien on the realty of the debtor.

6. The debtor's mentioning an obligation in a note is equivalent to asking them to be his witnesses.

7. This is because the witnesses to the delivery of a document give it effect.

8. The witnesses to the delivery of the note of confession give it effect as a lien on the realty of the debtor. They publicize the obligation to the same extent as they would the delivery of a note of indebtedness signed by two witnesses.

debtor becomes effective when the note reaches the creditor. If the debtor gave the note to an eligible person,[9] he may ask that person to act as an agent to obtain the asset for the creditor.

Similarly, a creditor may, in writing, confess to the debtor that he received a payment of an outstanding debt, even if he did not in fact receive such payment.[10]

---

9. Giving the note to a Gentile or a minor would not suffice.

10. The result would be the same if the creditor orally stated that he received payment.

# Chapter 41

# LOST OR DESTROYED INSTRUMENTS

## INTRODUCTION

Chapters 39 and 40 focus on the writing of notes of indebtedness, notes of admission, and notes of confession. This chapter discusses instruments (whether notes of indebtedness, admission, or confession) that have been completely or partially obliterated, destroyed, or lost. R. Yosef Karo concludes this chapter with a discussion of the effect of the loss of an instrument. Some of these effects can be ameliorated by the indexing system suggested in Chapter 39. In addition, modern methods of paper and ink production make it easier to preserve and to prove the making of the instruments.

The Hebrew word *kiyoom* has been translated here to mean "authentication." An authentication is accomplished before a beth din and generally means that thereafter the creditor need no longer prove the genuineness of the note of indebtedness or of admission, but may proceed, whether at a trial or in another manner, to enforce his note. In such trial or enforcement procedure, the genuineness of the note will not be questioned.

# TEXT

## Decaying instruments

The creditor who sees that his instrument is decaying and may become obliterated may bring witnesses to beth din to testify to the genuineness of the instrument. These witnesses may be the original subscribing witnesses who signed the instrument or others who recognize the signatures of the subscribing witnesses on the instrument and who know the contents of the instrument.

If the beth din can make out the writing on the instrument, then beth din may on its own write a new note of indebtedness or of admission and place an authentication thereon.

Even if the instrument is entirely obliterated, then the witnesses may testify as to its contents and the beth din will write an instrument and place an authentication thereon.[1] When beth din writes a duplicate instrument, it should destroy the original instrument.

The authentication states the names of the three judges of the beth din, the name of the creditor, the name of the debtor, the date of the original instrument, the amount of the instrument, the fact that the instrument was obliterated, the names of the subscribing witnesses on the original instrument, and the names of the witnesses who testified as to the authenticity of the signatures of the subscribing witnesses. If beth din also examined the witnesses as to the genuineness of the instrument, beth din adds such fact, and the instrument need not be authenticated again. If beth din did not state that the witnesses were examined, then the signatures of the witnesses to the original instrument must still be authenticated at a later time. There is an opinion that beth din should add that the original instrument was destroyed.[2] The three judges of the beth din sign the new instrument and the authentication.

---

1. The lien created is effective as of the date of the original instrument (note of indebtedness, admission, or confession) and not as of the date of the authentication.

2. If the original instrument is not destroyed, the danger exists that the creditor may repeat the procedure before another beth din and thus end up with more than one duplicate instrument on which he can collect.

The witnesses may testify even if the debtor is not present.[3] However, one opinion holds that this may be done only if the instrument is not entirely obliterated.[4]

The witnesses to the instrument may not write a duplicate instrument, even if the original was obliterated in their presence.[5] They are permitted to rewrite the instrument only if they have permission from both the debtor and the creditor. In such a case, the instrument must be copied from the original letter by letter, and it must state that it is a copy.[6] The instrument is valid even if two relatives copied it, as long as the two were not the only signatories to the copy. If there were more than two signatories and two of them were not related to each other, the instrument is still valid.[7]

## Obliterated deeds of gift[8]

A new deed of gift may be written without the necessity of destroying the original. The witnesses on the original deed of gift may write the duplicate, the date for which is the same as that on the original deed.

If the deed of gift contained a warranty, the original must be destroyed.[9] Deeds of sale must also be destroyed when a duplicate is

---

3. See Volume I, Chapter 28, where it is stated that the beth din may not accept the testimony of witnesses if the party against whom the witness is testifying is not present. The procedure permitting such conduct in this chapter should be carried out only if the creditor will be prejudiced by waiting for the debtor (if, for example, the witnesses are about to leave the city).

4. This opinion may hold that in cases of obliteration of deeds of conveyance of realty, the witnesses may testify even if the seller is not present, since the purchaser is in possession of the realty.

5. Once they have signed the instrument they have completed their agency and may not commence it anew. If, however, there was a mistake made on the original instrument, they may correct the mistake, because until the instrument is completed legally, the witnesses' agency has not terminated. If the debtor agrees that the witnesses may write a duplicate instrument, then they are, of course, permitted to do so.

6. Beth din will compare the copy to the original before it authenticates the copy.

7. It is valid if it appears that the two relatives did not sign as witnesses but rather to complete the empty space on the copy. (See Chapter 45.)

8. The deed of gift states that the donor will give a gift to the donee or else is itself the deed to the property that is being given.

9. For the grantor to be liable, the warranty must be in the deed. If a deed of gift does not contain the warranty, then it is presumed that the warranty was intentionally

written. If the original is not destroyed, the duplicate must state that the instrument is not valid as a lien on the property of the grantor and is being given only to confirm the grantee as the holder of the property.

## Blotted or blurred instruments

If an instrument was blurred but the writing is still discernible, then the creditor may produce the witnesses in beth din in order to authenticate the instrument. However, this can be done only if the creditor can prove that the instrument became blotted with age, or by wear and tear, or by accident.[10] If this cannot be proved, or if the instrument was left in a place where the writing would be likely to be blotted out, beth din will not authenticate the instrument.[11]

## Lost instruments

If the creditor comes to beth din and states that he lost the instrument, beth din may not write another instrument for him,[12] even if the original witnesses to the instrument appear in beth din to testify that they signed the instrument and that it was given to the creditor,[13] and even if the creditor came to beth din before the time for payment

---

omitted and is not inserted. In the case of a note of indebtedness, admission, or confession, an omitted warranty is attributed to a mistake by the draftsman and is inserted at a later time, unless it can be shown that the note was not intended to include a warranty.

10. Unless the creditor can prove that it was an accident, the presumption will be that the creditor intentionally blotted out the instrument. This presumption arises by virtue of the fact that the instrument was in the creditor's possession.

11. If the creditor leaves the instrument in a place where it will not be safe, then it is presumed that the creditor did so because the instrument was paid.

12. The fear exists that the creditor may collect on the duplicate written by the beth din, and thereafter produce the original and collect again. It is also of no benefit to the creditor if a duplicate instrument is written that states that it may not be collected from the property of the debtor, for this avails the creditor nothing. This is not similar to the situation in which a deed of realty states that it may not be used to levy on the property of the donor, since in that case it serves the purpose of enabling the donee to remain in possession of the property.

13. A mere statement that the instrument was written is not sufficient in any event, since the instrument may have been written and not delivered to the creditor.

provided for in the instrument according to the testimony of the witnesses. A new instrument may not be written even if there are witnesses that the instrument was lost, since the possibility exists that he will later find it. Some authorities disagree, however, holding that in such a case the beth din may write a duplicate instrument. I prefer the second opinion, since if the duplicate or the original is paid, the debtor should obtain a receipt relating to that instrument and the receipt should also state that a duplicate was written.

It would be wise practice to summon the debtor to beth din and ask him whether he paid the instrument. If he admits nonpayment, then a duplicate could be written along with a beth din document stating that the original bearing a certain date was lost, and that if the creditor produces such an instrument it may not be collected upon but must be destroyed by the beth din to which it is produced. If the debtor alleges payment, the creditor is in no worse position than he was before the allegation.

If witnesses testify that the instrument was in the hands of a third party and there lost, a duplicate may be written.

Duplicate deeds not containing warranties may be written by the beth din when the grantee alleges that it was lost and when the necessity for its being written can be shown.[14]

---

14. If the deed contained a warranty, the danger exists that the creditor may wrongfully collect from innocent third parties.

January 1. Grantor owned three parcels of land, parcel 1, parcel 2, and parcel 3.

January 1. Grantor sold parcel 1 to grantee 1 and the deed contained a warranty. As a result of the warranty, parcels 2 and 3 became liened to grantee 1.

February 1. Grantor sold parcel 2 to grantee 2.

March 1. Grantor sold parcel 3 to grantee 3.

April 1. Grantee 1 loses parcel 1 to Mr. Rightful Owner, who was real owner of parcel 1 (not the grantor). Grantor does not have money to reimburse grantee 1.

April 2. Grantee 1 places a levy on parcel 3 purchased by grantee 3 on the strength of the original deed.

April 3. Grantee 1 places a lien on parcel 2 purchased by grantee 2 on the strength of the duplicate deed.

When grantee 1 made the first levy on parcel 3, he would not give a receipt to grantee 3, and even if he did, it would not become known to or protect grantee 2. But if the deed to grantee 1 specifically stated that it was without warranty, then grantee 1 could not levy against grantee 2 or grantee 3.

If witnesses testify that the instrument was destroyed in a fire or by some other casualty, then beth din may, after examining the witnesses, write a duplicate instrument. Here, too, the debtor should obtain a receipt when he pays either the original or the duplicate, and the receipt should relate to the date and amount of the instrument.

If a testator bequeathed property to several persons, each such person may ask beth din to have a separate instrument drawn for him designating his share of the estate.[15] The executors of the estate may defend on the grounds that they paid the bequest.[16]

If the debtor is a long distance away from the creditor and the creditor is going to the place of the debtor to sue on the instrument and is afraid that he may lose the instrument on the way, he may ask beth din to write a duplicate for him. The original is left with beth din, and only the copy is given to the creditor. The copy must recite all of the events leading up to the writing of the copy. If the creditor receives payment in the place where the debtor resides, then the beth din of that place will notify the beth din that holds the original instrument that it has been paid, and they will destroy the original. If the creditor alleges that he lost the copy, he will receive another copy only if he produces witnesses who testify that he lost the copy.

## Defenses against a lost instrument

If the creditor alleges that he had an instrument and it was lost, and there are no witnesses to either the loss or the loan, then the debtor may allege that the loan never took place. The debtor swears a *hesseth* oath, and judgment will be entered in his favor.

If the debtor alleges that the lost instrument was paid and he swears

---

15. This is so because the instrument provided by the beth din may not be used by the parties to make a levy on property.

16. This law is taken from the glosses of Ramo in this volume's Chapter 41. In Chapter 255, R. Yosef Karo states that the executor is not entitled to assert payment. One explanation for the difference is that Chapter 255 concerns an admission that the testator owed money to someone. In such a situation the executor cannot allege payment unless he produces a receipt. In Chapter 41, Ramo speaks of a situation in which the will contained a series of bequests, in which event the executor may allege payment. Other explanations are also given. This topic will be discussed further in Chapter 255.

a *hesseth* oath, he will receive a judgment dismissing the complaint.[17] This is true even if the creditor produced witnesses to the loan,[18] and even if the time for repayment has not yet arrived. There is also an opinion that states that if the time for repayment has not yet arrived and there are witnesses who testify to the loan, the debtor is not permitted to assert a defense of payment.

If the lost instrument is later produced by a third party, the debtor still has the same defense of payment. If he swears a *hesseth* oath that he repaid the loan and that the instrument was returned to him and he lost it, the complaint is dismissed.

If a depository produces the instrument, then the debtor is not believed if he pleads that he repaid the loan. This is true even if the deposit was not made in the presence of witnesses.

In case of a war in which the city is invaded and captured, if the creditor alleges that the instrument was lost and not paid, then another instrument is drawn for him by the beth din even if the debtor alleges repayment.[19]

---

17. The creditor, having desired a note of indebtedness to evidence the loan, is now in an inferior position if he cannot produce the note of indebtedness. It is presumed that he did not take adequate care of the note or that he destroyed it because the debtor's defense that the note was paid is true.

18. The loan without the instrument, relying as it does on the testimony of the witnesses, is in the category of an oral loan, and the debtor may allege payment swearing a *hesseth* oath as a complete defense. The *hesseth* oath is an oath instituted by the Rabbis and will be discussed in Chapter 87, Volume III.

19. If the original instrument contained a warranty clause, then the duplicate must also contain such a clause.

# Chapter 42

# LANGUAGE CONSTRUCTION IN WRITTEN INSTRUMENTS

## INTRODUCTION

Chapter 42 and some of the following chapters discuss various rules of construction of written instruments (notes of indebtedness, admission, and confession), as well as the type of paper on which they may be drawn, the language in which they may be written, the manner of writing numbers in the instruments, the recapitulation of the terms at the conclusion of the instrument, inconsistencies, presumptions against the holder of the instrument, and the placement of the witnesses' signatures.

## TEXT

### The material on which instruments may be written and the language thereof

An instrument may not be written on paper or other material that is erasable. An instrument written on erasable material is void, even if it is to be paid immediately.[1] Deeds of sale are an exception: they may be written on erasable material if the witnesses to the delivery of the deed know what is written therein.[2] However, an instrument describing a transfer of ownership must be on nonerasable paper.[3]

Authorities disagree on whether an instrument can be considered valid if it differs from the form established by the Rabbis. Ramo prefers the view that it is valid.[4] If there is a custom in the community as to the form of instruments, then such custom should be followed.

The instrument may be written in any language so long as the handwriting is consistent throughout.[5] It is this author's contention that modern typewriting machines may be used in instruments except those that must be specifically handwritten, such as a bill of divorce (*get*).

## Formation of the letters and words

Whether inscribed by hand or by machine, the letters should be formed in such a way that there can be no misunderstanding about

---

1. There is also a contrary opinion that holds that if the instrument is to be delivered immediately and is immediately payable, and the witnesses to the delivery are present, then it is not void. The reason is that none of the dangers that are sought to be protected against will be present under these circumstances.

2. If the witnesses to the delivery know what is written thereon, then the grantee will not be able to erase the terms and substitute other terms. The deed's function is completed immediately upon delivery. Transfer of title takes place upon delivery of the deed. If the deed is thereafter lost or destroyed, title is still in the name of the grantee. Thus the deed does not have to have any life beyond the moment of delivery.

3. This document does not effect delivery; rather, it is to be used to prove the transfer of the property. As proof to be introduced into beth din, it is similar to a note of indebtedness and must thus be written with the intent to last until it is required to be used as evidence in beth din should the need arise.

4. There are, however, certain disqualifications that render an instrument *invalid*, such as writing a note as a bound note (that is, writing a line and then folding it over and having the witnesses sign and then binding that part and writing the next line, and continuing in the same manner until the entire instrument is completed). See *Baba Batra*, Chapter 10, on how a bound document is written.

5. The reason for a consistent handwriting throughout is that there should be no alterations in the instrument.

what is written or typed.[6] (Even a typewriter may form a letter in such a way that it may look like another letter.[7])

The letters should be of even height, and the spaces between letters and numbers should be consistent.[8] They should not be crowded in one part and spaces left between letters in another part.

Numbers should not be placed at the end of a line.[9] This author suggests that numbers be spelled out and followed by corresponding Arabic numerals in parentheses—for example, One Thousand Five Hundred ($1,500) Dollars.

The witnesses who review the instrument should examine for flaws in the formation of letters and words. If such flaws are found in an instrument that is before beth din, it should be examined with extra care to see whether any changes have been made in the instrument. Such careful examination may not be required if the debtor admits that the instrument is valid or has raised other defenses. Even if the debtor admits the validity, beth din should carefully scrutinize such flaws if the defendants in the lawsuit on the instrument are the heirs of an estate[10] or if the instrument will be used to effect a lien against a third party who purchased real estate from the debtor. In the latter case, the third party may lose the realty to the creditor and thus the necessity to scrutinize the flaws.

The inconsistencies or ambiguities should be construed against the payee, since he should not have accepted such an instrument.

---

6. If a number can be changed, then the instrument is in the same category as an instrument that is erasable.

7. For example, the arm of the uppercase *G* may be missing so that it looks like an uppercase *C*. In the Hebrew alphabet such mistakes are much more common, especially in the written alphabet or in the letters written by scribes.

8. If spaces are left between letters, it is possible to insert a number to increase the amount of the instrument. Or, a person's initial may be inserted, and thus the obligation may be placed upon a person other than the one intended.

9. For example, if *$100* were to appear at the end of a line, another 0 could be added so that the number would read *$1,000*. Similarly, if the word *four* were to appear at the end of a line, it could be changed to *fourteen*.

10. The heirs of an estate, and for that matter the third-party purchaser for value, will probably not be familiar with the transaction between the creditor and the debtor. If the instrument is flawed, beth din might suspect that there may something wrong with the entire transaction. In the event of such suspicion, beth din should attempt to protect those who need protecting in such a case.

Moreover, the payee has the burden of proof against the person from whom he is trying to enforce collection of the instrument. If a currency is mentioned without the specification of a country, it will be construed to be the currency of the country where the instrument was executed.

If a transaction was completed in Canada between an American and a Canadian, and the instrument stated that it was payable in dollars, and Canadian dollars were less expensive than American dollars, then the instrument is construed as calling for payment in Canadian dollars. If the instrument was executed in neither of these countries, then the creditor takes a *hesseth* oath and his version is believed.

If the instrument states it is payable on February 1, the very next February 1 is meant, and not some other February 1 in the future.

Obvious mistakes are not included in these rules of construction, and an instrument with an obvious mistake should be reformed to give it its intended meaning.

In all of these cases, either party may produce witnesses to testify as to what was intended.

In cases of receipts of payment, the receipt is construed against the payor, since he should not have accepted a receipt that contained inconsistencies.

In cases of arithmetic mistakes, the actual sum of all the items shall be the sum due. An example of such a case would be an instrument in which several sums are mentioned, with an inaccurate sum inserted when the sums are recapitulated.

# Chapter 43

---

# INCLUDING THE DATE
# OF EXECUTION
# OF THE INSTRUMENT

## INTRODUCTION

This chapter continues the discussion of things that are required in an instrument (notes of indebtedness, admission, and confession). The requirement discussed here is that of the date of the instrument. One reason the date is important is that it fixes a time when the witnesses say that they were present and signed the instrument. As was noted (Volume I, Chapter 38), the date and place of signing may leave the witnesses open to a challenge to refute them.

Most important, as was stated in Chapter 39, when the witnesses sign and deliver the note of indebtedness, the effect is to immediately place a lien on the realty of the debtor so that the realty is now pledged to the payment of the debt. If the realty was owned by the debtor on the date of the signing of the note of indebtedness, the lien may be satisfied by levying on the realty sold by the debtor after the date of the note.

The instrument is usually signed on the date that the loan is made and the instrument is delivered to the creditor. Alternatively, the instrument can be assigned the date of the kinyan. Sometimes, however, for reasons known to the creditor and debtor, the note can bear some other date. It can be predated or postdated. If a loan was made on February 1, it should bear that date. If it is dated January 31, it is predated; if it is dated February 2, it is postdated.

A predated note may be used to perpetrate a fraud on the purchasers of realty from the debtor. For example, if the loan was made on February 1, all of the real estate owned by debtor on that date was liened for the repayment of the loan. If the debtor sold some of his realty on January 15, then the property was sold free and clear of the lien of the creditor since the realty was sold prior to the loan and thus prior to the lien. If the note written on February 1 was predated to January 1, then the purchaser would find that the property that he purchased on January 15 was subject to the lien, which was not truthfully the case. The predated instrument is thus a fraud on the innocent purchaser.

If the note of indebtedness is postdated, however, no fraud is usually thereby established, since the lien does not attach to the realty until the later date and the purchase was prior to that date.

The danger of the fraud that could be perpetrated by a predated note of indebtedness was so great that the entire note of indebtedness was declared by the Rabbis to be void as against the purchaser from the debtor. The note of indebtedness was not held to be a valid instrument from the actual date of the loan. Of course, the note could still be enforced as against the property yet in the debtor's hands.

Sometimes a date on an instrument is obviously incorrect. For example, if an instrument is dated October 1 and that was the date on which the Day of Atonement fell (when no notes could be written), that date must be erroneous. Rules of construction had to be made to cover such contingencies.

This chapter also discusses whether the place of the writing of an instrument must be included on the note.

If the indexing system suggested in Chapter 39 is implemented, some of the laws in this chapter may have to be read, or even modified, in that light.

## TEXT

### The requirement for dating all instruments

The date must be inserted in all loan instruments.

Purchasers of realty of the debtor prior to the date of the loan are not subject to a creditor's lien.[1] Purchasers of realty of the debtor on the date or subsequent to the date of the loan are subject to a lien in favor of the creditor. This applies only to land owned by the debtor at the time the loan was made. It may also apply to after-acquired land if the note of indebtedness stated that future land acquired by the debtor would be subject to the lien. Priority of liens on the unsold property of the debtor is also determined according to the dates of the loans.[2]

An undated instrument does not affect the liability for repayment, nor does it affect the ability to collect out of the unsold property of the debtor.

There is an opinion that if a note of indebtedness that was signed by two witnesses is undated but was displayed to other witnesses, then the time of the display is the time from which purchasers take subject to the lien of the creditor. Some question this opinion.[3] This author agrees with the questioners.

---

1. Say, for example, that the debtor sold land to a purchaser on January 1. The debtor thereafter borrowed money from the creditor on February 1. The land purchased is not subject to a lien in favor of the creditor.

2. If the debtor borrowed money from creditor 1 on January 1 and from creditor 2 on February 1, then the lien of creditor 1 has priority over the lien of creditor 2. If the creditors sued on the loans and if the debtor had enough assets to satisfy only one of the debts, creditor 1 would be entitled to priority.

3. The general principle is that the witnesses who sign the instrument and witness the delivery to the creditor give the requisite publicity to the event to alert would-be purchasers of the debtor's realty to be on notice that the realty has a lien on it. The witnesses who say that they saw the undated instrument in the hands of the creditor on a certain date also give the requisite publicity to the would-be purchaser of the debtor's realty that there is a lien on the realty because delivery of the instrument has been made. When the creditor comes to make a levy on the property purchased by the purchaser, and the purchaser defends that he purchased the property before the loan was made, the creditor has no proof that the loan and instrument predated the purchase. The only proof as to a time when the loan was surely made and the instrument surely signed is the date on which the witnesses testify that they saw such a signed instrument in the hands of the creditor. This author assumes that if the creditor produced the witnesses who signed the instrument, and they testified that the loan was made on the date on which they signed and that the instrument was delivered to the creditor on that date, then it would effectively create a lien on the debtor's property purchased after that date. (Some authorities hold that the lien is established as soon as witnesses sign the instrument. The signing produces the requisite notification to would-be purchasers and lenders.)

An instrument signed by the debtor and without witnesses need not contain a date, since it does not effect a lien on the debtor's realty.

A receipt of payment that contains no date of payment is valid.

An instrument is presumed to have been delivered to the creditor on the date of the instrument, unless there was a *kinyan*. In the latter case it is presumed that the date in the instrument is the date of the *kinyan*.

## Flaws in the instrument

If the scribe omitted the first numeral or numerals of the year, then the instrument is valid. For example, if a scribe in the United States wrote *1/1/91* instead of *January 1, 1991*, it is valid. In Hebrew if the year was stated as *751*, or even *51*, instead of *5751*, it is valid. In Israel, if it was written *five thousand fifty-one*, it is valid according to one opinion and not valid according to another opinion.

It is not necessary to include the day of the week in the instrument, although sometimes it is helpful to do so. For example, if an instrument is dated Monday, January 4, and Monday was really January 5, it is valid if it was signed on the 5th.[4] If the day and the date do not coincide, the instrument is nonetheless valid.

The beth din should examine each such situation carefully to determine whether the instrument is predated or validly dated.

## Predated instruments

A predated instrument is invalid as against any purchasers of the realty of the debtor.[5] It is even invalid against those purchasers who purchased after the true date of the loan.[6]

---

4. The instrument is valid because if the loan was made on Monday, the correct date was January 5. If the date were the only matter controlling, the instrument would be considered predated and therefore not valid.

5. If the debt was incurred after the date of the sale of the debtor's realty to a purchaser, but the date of the note of indebtedness states that it was incurred at a date prior to the purchase, the purchaser may find the realty wrongfully liened to the creditor.

6. The invalidity as against purchasers even after the true date of the loan is a penalty against the creditor not to engage in such conduct as may lend itself to fraud.

An instrument is considered predated if (1) the date named therein is prior to the writing of the instrument or (2) it was actually written on the date named in the instrument but was delivered in the presence of witnesses at a later date.

If a *kinyan* was made, the instrument may be written later and dated back to the date on which the *kinyan* was made. If no *kinyan* was made, and the loan was made earlier in the presence of witnesses, but the borrower did not give the instructions to write the instrument until later, then the date of the delivery of the note of indebtedness to the lender must be the date in the instrument.[7]

The predated instrument is valid against the debtor and may be used to levy against the property in the hands of the debtor if the predating was inadvertent.[8] If the witnesses signed knowing that the instrument was predated, it is invalid even as against the debtor.[9] The witnesses are believed if they say that the predating was inadvertent, if it is the type of thing about which witnesses could have been inadvertent.[10]

A predated instrument should be destroyed by the beth din or should have written thereon that it does not constitute a lien on the debtor's realty. If the predated instrument is destroyed by the beth din, a new instrument should be written, signed by witnesses, and delivered to the creditor; the new instrument should be inscribed with the date on which the loan actually took place. The new instrument is valid only against the debtor. If the creditor sued on the original predated instrument and received a judgment against the debtor, such judgment creates a lien on the debtor's realty from the date of the judgment.

The debtor's defense of payment is the same as on any other

---

7. The lien in favor of the lender arises in either of the two times—either from the date on which a *kinyan* was made or from the date on which the instrument was delivered to the lender. It is assumed that there were witnesses in both situations.

8. An example would be a note that was prepared for a loan to take place in January but that, because of unforeseen circumstances, did not take place until February. This practice is not recommended, but if it *is* carried out, the note of indebtedness would be valid as against the debtor only. This also assumes that there was no *kinyan* made on the earlier date.

9. It is invalid even as against the debtor, since the witnesses who signed the instrument are perjurers if they deliberately signed a predated instrument.

10. In case of doubt the matter should be resolved in favor of the witnesses' version of the event.

instrument. If the debtor denied the entire transaction, and the predated instrument and testimony of witnesses was then introduced as evidence to show the making of the loan, then the debtor is considered to be a perjurer. Some authorities hold that the instrument is totally invalid even for the purpose of impeaching the credibility of the debtor.

Predated deeds of gift are invalid. However, the witnesses to the deed, or others who were present when the deed of gift was delivered, may write another deed dated from the date on which they write the replacement deed. Alternatively, the witnesses may testify as to the deed of gift before beth din and beth din will write a new deed of gift from the correct date. The replacement deed of gift may not include a warranty clause unless there was a *kinyan* when the gift was first made. If the replacement deed of gift is to be dated from the date on which the replacement is written, even the original witnesses may write it with a warranty.

If a predated instrument states that it is predated but it was not signed until a later date, it is valid.[11]

If the instrument is written before the date of delivery to the creditor, it should be dated with the date of delivery.

If the predating was intentional, it must be established by independent witnesses; it cannot be established by the testimony of the witnesses who signed the instrument.[12]

## Postdated instruments

A postdated instrument is valid even if it does not state that it is postdated,[13] and even if it was postdated without the consent of the creditor. The creditor in such a case may, however, enforce collection

---

11. This is the case provided that the loan was actually made on or before the later date; otherwise it is still a predated instrument.

12. A person may not admit to an act that would be a transgression of a Torah or Rabbinic commandment. In this situation, if the witness is believed that he signed a predated instrument with intent, then he admits that he perjured himself, and this he is not permitted to do.

13. It is valid because it weakens the position of the creditor, who cannot enforce his lien against purchasers of the realty of the debtor except from the date of the instrument. Thus the creditor has lost the lien against realty sold by the debtor between the actual date of the loan and the date of the instrument.

against the debtor from the date of the loan. A postdated note of indebtedness should not be written in the first instance, especially if it is done without the consent of the creditor.[14]

A note of indebtedness is effective as a lien against the realty of the debtor from the date of the instrument, if the postdating was done with the consent of the creditor.

A postdated instrument is valid if it states that it encumbers the realty owned by the debtor at the time of the instrument and also any after-acquired realty. If it encumbers only realty owned at the time of the note of indebtedness, it is not valid, unless the note of indebtedness states that it is a postdated.[15]

A postdated deed of sale or deed of gift is always invalid, unless it is stated therein that it is postdated.[16]

## Other discrepancies in dates

If an instrument is dated on the Sabbath or on a Holy Day, it is

---

14. It should not be written in the first instance because it would appear to be fraudulent.

15. Say, for example, that the debtor borrowed money from the creditor in January. He purchased realty in February and sold it in June. If the note of indebtedness is dated January, then the realty is not under the lien, since it was not owned at the time when the loan was made. If, however, the instrument is dated March, then the realty is subject to the lien because it was owned by the debtor on the date stated in the note of indebtedness. It is thus a fraud on the purchaser in June. The realty purchased by the debtor in February should really be free of the creditor's lien, and thus the third-party purchaser should have the realty without the lien of the creditor. Instead he has a lien on his realty. If the instrument states that it is postdated, then the realty purchased by the debtor in February is free of the lien. If, however, the note of indebtedness states that it also liens after-acquired realty, then the lien rightfully attaches to the realty purchased in February, and the third-party purchaser is not prejudiced by the postdating of the note of indebtedness.

16. It is invalid if the seller did not realize that it was postdated and then the seller repurchased the realty from the purchaser. The purchaser can then produce the old postdated deed and claim that he had repurchased the property a second time from the seller. If the deed states that it is postdated, then the seller is put on notice and will be alerted if he repurchases the property from the purchaser. Thus he is able to protect himself. Say for example, that a seller sold realty to a purchaser on January 1, 1990, and the date put into the deed was March 1, 1990. On February 1, 1990, the purchaser resells the realty to the seller. The purchaser still has a deed in his possession dated March 1, 1990, and could thus allege that he once again purchased the realty from the seller on March 1, 1990.

considered a postdated[17] instrument and is valid.[18] There is an opinion that if the debtor in a suit brought on the instrument demands that the creditor take an oath that the witnesses did not intentionally postdate the instrument, then the creditor must take such oath. The foregoing holds true only if the note of indebtedness has been authenticated. If it has not been authenticated, then the burden of proof is on the creditor to prove his instrument.[19]

If an instrument had been lost and then is later found, the creditor must prove that it was delivered to him on the date stated in the instrument, or the instrument bears the date on which a *kinyan* was made.[20] If the possibility that it was paid is raised, then the creditor must prove that it was not paid.

If an instrument was written at night and contains the date thereof, but such instrument was signed the next day, then it is neither postdated nor predated.[21]

---

17. It is considered as if it was written on the day before the Sabbath or the Holy Day and was postdated to the Sabbath or the Holy Day.

18. See Volume I, Chapter 5, and notes therein for a discussion of the Sabbath and the Holy Days. Writing is prohibited on those days. Therefore, the date on the instrument could not possibly be accurate. It is therefore assumed that the instrument is postdated, and it is therefore considered valid.

19. If the debtor does not raise the defense, then beth din shall question an instrument that is dated as of a Sabbath or Holy Day.

20. The fact that the instrument was lost puts its effectiveness into question. It is presumed that a creditor would ordinarily take good care of an instrument. The fact that it was lost puts beth din on notice that the creditor may have been careless with it because it was paid. The creditor must now prove that the date was either the actual date of delivery of the instrument to the creditor or the date of the *kinyan*. The aforementioned presumption that an instrument is presumed to have been delivered on the date stated therein or on the date of the *kinyan* does not hold true for a flawed instrument, such as one that has been lost.

21. See Volume I, Chapter 5, wherein it is discussed that the Hebrew date commences at sunset and continues until the following sunset. For example, Monday is the tenth day of Nissan. The tenth day of Nissan would commence at sunset on Sunday night and continue until sunset on Monday night. Prior to sunset on Sunday night it is still the ninth day of Nissan. At sunset on Monday night, the eleventh day of Nissan commences. If an instrument was written on Sunday night, then it was written on the tenth day of Nissan. If it was signed on Monday during the daylight hours, it would still be signed on the tenth day of Nissan. If, however, the note of indebtedness was written on Sunday during the daylight hours and was dated the ninth of Nissan, but it was not signed and delivered to the creditor until Sunday night,

If a note of indebtedness was written during daylight hours and contained the date thereof, and the note was signed and delivered after nightfall, then it is considered predated and invalid.[22] This holds true if there was no *kinyan* made during the daylight hours.

If a *kinyan* was made, then the instrument may be written at any time thereafter and dated with the date of the *kinyan;* it is not then deemed a predated instrument. The instrument will state that a *kinyan* was made by the debtor on that date but that the instrument was written, signed, and delivered on the later date written in the instrument. However, it is valid even if it states only the date of the *kinyan.*

If the witnesses when writing the instrument at some future time do not remember the date of the *kinyan,* then the date of the instrument is the date on which they write the instrument. The instrument will state that a *kinyan* was made by the debtor but that the instrument is dated, signed, and delivered on the date in the instrument. If the witnesses do not remember the date of the *kinyan* but do remember the month, there are differing opinions as to whether they may date the instrument with the first day of the next month. If the witnesses remember which part of the month, they may so state in the instrument.[23]

If a transaction commenced during the daylight hours and continued into the night, and the instrument bears the date of the daylight hours and was signed and delivered during the night, it is valid.

## Place of writing of the instrument

It is preferable, but not essential, that the place where the instrument was written be included in the instrument.[24]

---

then the delivery would be on the tenth day of Nissan. The instrument would therefore be considered predated and void.

22. See previous note.

23. The burden of proof still rests with the creditor, for he is the plaintiff in a lawsuit on the instrument.

24. The place of writing may determine the type of currency to be used to repay the debt. Thus a Canadian dollar is not worth as much as a United States dollar. If the note was written in Canada and was being sued upon in the United States, there would be a difference in favor of the creditor.

If a *kinyan* was made in one city and the writing was thereafter in another city, the following rules apply:

1. If the date of the *kinyan* is contained in the instrument, then that city is mentioned as the place of the instrument, but the place of the writing is also mentioned. If the place of the writing is omitted, the instrument is nevertheless valid.

2. If the date of the writing is contained in the instrument, then the place of the writing is also to be included. If, however, the value of the money is different in both places, then the place of the *kinyan* is also inserted.

If the place of the *kinyan* or the place of writing is not included in the instrument, it is nevertheless valid.

## Rules of construction

If two instruments are produced by two creditors against the same debtor, and one instrument contains a specific date in a month while the other lists just the month, then the one with the specific date is given priority. For example, if one instrument is dated March 5, and the other states that it was written in March,[25] then the instrument dated March 5 has priority.[26] The two creditors may sign a joint power of attorney and then successfully proceed against the purchaser.

As noted in Volume I, Chapter 5, the Hebrew calendar during a leap year contains an additional month called *Second Adar*. Special rules of priority apply if one instrument states that it was signed in Adar in a leap year without specifying which Adar, and the other instrument states that it was signed in Second Adar. The rules are as follows: If one note states *Adar* and the other *Second Adar*, then the one that says *Adar* receives priority. It is assumed that the first *Adar* is meant, since the word *Second* was omitted. If both say only *Adar*, then the date is controlling as to priority. If one instrument says *First Adar* and another says just *Adar*, then both are presumed to be from the first Adar and the date will give the priority.

---

25. If there was no *kinyan*, then the date is also the date of signing and delivery to the creditor. If there was a *kinyan*, then the date is that of the *kinyan*.

26. If the debtor has assets sufficient to pay off only one of the notes, the priority is important.

If an instrument states that it will be paid "by Passover," it means before the first day of Passover.[27] If it states "after Passover," it is construed to mean not later than fifteen days after Passover. Some hold that it means not later than the midpoint between Passover and the next Holy Day, Shevu'oth. The same applies to all other terms of times of payment.

In cases in which the debtor defends on the basis of a receipt of full or partial payment, the presumption favors the debtor, since the creditor has the burden of proof that there is still money owed to him. Whenever the debtor produces a receipt, the presumption is that it is applied to the instrument held by the creditor, unless the receipt indicates otherwise. For example, if a note of indebtedness is for $500 and the receipt states that it is payment against a note of indebtedness of $300, the receipt will not be deemed to apply to the note. Or, if a receipt is silent on the matter of to which debt it is to be applied, it is presumed to be against the debt on which the suit is being brought. If the note of indebtedness was dated January, and the receipt states that it applied against an instrument dated January 15, the receipt is applied against the debt.

If the note of indebtedness stated January 15 and the receipt stated that it applied against a note of indebtedness dated January, the receipt is applied against the debt.

A receipt dated the same date as the note of indebtedness is applied against the note of indebtedness. A receipt dated prior to the note of indebtedness is not applied against the note of indebtedness.

A release is treated like a receipt. A release that relinquishes all claims until the date of the release is deemed to release all claims until the prior day. For example, if a note of indebtedness is dated January 10, and the release states that it releases all claims until January 10, then the release is not applied against the note of indebtedness.

If a release states that all claims are released until "this day," then the burden of proof falls on the holder of the release to include that date.

---

27. Passover is seven days long, and it should not be said that the intent was until the last day of Passover.

# Chapter 44

# THE FINAL LINES
# OF THE INSTRUMENT

## INTRODUCTION

When this author was practicing law in New York, it was standard procedure for the concluding paragraph of contracts and other documents to begin with the words "IN WITNESS WHEREOF the parties hereto have executed the foregoing agreement on the date and place first above mentioned." These words indicated that the document was at an end and that the parties now had only to sign in order to give effect to the document. Nothing else would be inserted after these words. Since agreements were generally typed on a typewriter or word processor, and since the agreements generally exceeded one page in length, some attorneys abided by the practice of having the parties initial each page and sign the last page. Many attorneys would also have penned-in changes initialed by the parties. All of these procedures were intended to help prevent fraud by one of the parties in substituting a page or inserting words in the agreement. Many bankers and persons in finance-related businesses have their instruments drawn on erasure-proof paper—that is, paper that will turn another color if there is an erasure.

The Talmud and the subsequent codes and commentaries and respondents also had to deal with the possibility that the holder of a note of indebtedness might attempt to forge some part of the note.

The usual note consisted of a single page and was signed by two witnesses. Several kinds of frauds could be perpetrated by the holder of the note. He could insert terms between the last line of the note and the witnesses' signatures. He could erase some of the terms and insert others. He could insert some terms between the lines as if they were additions made immediately prior to the execution of the note. The general method of dealing with these common attempts at fraud was to enact a decree that all instruments (notes of indebtedness, admission, and confession) had to have a summation of the operative terms of the instrument on the last line. If the instrument lacked this summary, then the last line was disregarded, as there existed the possibility that the holder had inserted some terms between the last words of the instrument and the signatures of the witnesses. This danger arose because not all witnesses signed immediately below the last line of the instrument, and thus there was often room for the holder to insert terms. Similarly, all emendations and erasures in the instrument had to be noted at the end of the instrument before the witnesses signed it. This procedure was followed even if the instrument was signed by the debtor, because he, too, might not have been careful to sign immediately after the terms of the instrument were stated.

## TEXT

### The instrument of indebtedness must be summarized in the last line

Every instrument must be summarized in the last line.[1-3] No new

---

1. If the instrument is not summarized in the last line, it is not necessarily considered invalid. However, there is a minority opinion that the instrument is void, since it does not conform to the rules established by the Rabbis.

2. The theory behind all of the rules herein stated is that if there was space between the last line of the instrument and the signature of the witnesses, then the holder might insert terms.

3. The summary evidences that the instrument was there completed and any operative terms that appear after the summary are a forgery inserted by the holder of the instrument after the instrument was delivered to the holder.

operative terms may be contained in the last line.[4] Any new operative terms that appear in the last line are disregarded.[5,6]

If the instrument is entirely in the handwriting of the debtor, then all of the terms included in the last line will also be deemed to be operative terms. If the instrument is in the handwriting of a scribe, then it is not deemed to be in the handwriting of the debtor, and the last line will not be given effect if it contains new operative terms. In such a case, even if the witnesses testify that they left no room for anything to be added to the instrument, the last line will not be given effect. A machine-produced document is obviously not a document in the handwriting of the debtor, even if he did the typing thereon.

If the instrument is not in the handwriting of the debtor, even if the instrument is signed by the debtor, the danger exists that he did not sign immediately at the end of the instrument.

If the instrument concludes with the words "firm and established" and is followed by the signatures of the witnesses,[7] then there is ample opinion that the instrument need not have the terms thereof summarized in the last line.[8] In such a case, the terms contained in the last line may be given effect as operative terms.

In modern times, most instruments are produced on machines. The beth din in each community should therefore establish certain terms that will show that the machine-produced instrument has terminated, and the witnesses should sign at the conclusion of such words or paragraph. If an instrument does not so conclude, beth din must pay

---

4. If the terms in the last line are not in contradiction to the terms of the instrument but may be in furtherance of the foregoing terms, then they may be deemed to be operative terms. There is also authority that questions this last statement.

5. If the terms contained in the last line are against the interests of the holder of the instrument, they will be given effect.

6. The practice has developed that the last line often states that the terms have been accepted by a *kinyan*, which is not a summary, since this had not theretofore appeared in the instrument. The prevailing view is that this is nevertheless an operative term that is binding on the debtor.

7. In Hebrew (as well as Aramaic) documents, the words are *sharir v'kayam*, which translate into English as "firm and established."

8. There is also opinion that the instrument must be summarized in the last line even if the concluding words before the signatures are "firm and established." This opinion would admit that if the last line summarized the instrument and thereafter contained the words "firm and established," then the words contained in the last line would also be part of the operative provisions of the instrument.

special attention to see whether it would have been possible to insert some terms between the legitimate last line of the instrument and the witnesses' signatures.

If beth din concludes that there was no such possibility, then all of the terms of the instrument, including the last line, will be given effect. There will also be no necessity for the last line to summarize the terms of the instrument.

## Corrections and erasures in an instrument

If there are corrections in handwritten, or even in machine-produced, instruments, then the corrections should be initialed by the witnesses and, where feasible, should be noted at the conclusion of the instrument before the witnesses sign it.[9] The foregoing refers to erasures and insertions and deletions of words or phrases or even sentences.

Special care should be given to names, places, and amounts, since these are usually short phrases and may lend themselves to forgeries.

The failure to adhere to the rules will not invalidate the instrument unless beth din feels that it cannot consider the instrument because the erasures, insertions, or deletions are questionable. The changes will then be disregarded, as if they were not present. If, however, these disregarded changes make it difficult to determine the nature of the original terms of the instrument before the changes were made, then beth din may invalidate the entire instrument.[10]

If the date of the instrument raises questions regarding any of the foregoing rules, it will not affect the validity of the instrument by itself; rather, the document will be deemed to be an instrument without a date.

If the witnesses signed the instrument and then referred to all of the

---

9. The better procedure would be for such references to be made before the final paragraph, which is the concluding paragraph. In typewritten instruments, however, the concluding paragraph is already typed in before the corrections, deletions, and additions are made. It is easier to cross out the lines for signatures and to make the references to the corrections, and then add new lines for the witnesses to sign.

10. A creditor should always insist on receiving an instrument upon which he can sue without any questions arising as to the validity of the instrument or any of its terms.

corrections, deletions, and additions, and then re-signed the instrument, it will ordinarily be considered valid.

Some communities have special procedures for writing the amount of indebtedness, such as having the amounts included in the margin or printed or written in such a way that they also appear on the reverse side of the instrument. In such communities, if the established procedure was not followed, some views hold that the instrument is not valid and others hold that it is valid. This author believes that it is a question for beth din to decide in each case.[11]

If the entire paragraph required or suggested by the beth din as the concluding paragraph is erased, then such erasure renders the entire instrument suspect.

---

11. The beth din should, of course, try to validate any instrument that meets the requisite proof of due execution, signing, and delivery. The failure of the instrument to conform to all of the rules raises a question of due execution but does not create a presumption in favor of its invalidity. On the contrary, there is a presumption of regularity if the signatures of the witnesses have been authenticated and the instrument is produced by the holder.

# Chapter 45

# THE SIGNING
# OF THE INSTRUMENT

## INTRODUCTION

Some of the previous chapters have focused on the writing of the instrument (Chapter 39), the date of execution of the instrument (Chapter 43), and the final line of the instrument (Chapter 44). This chapter concentrates on the signing of the instrument. As has been stated repeatedly, the signatures of the witnesses show that the instrument has ended, and no further statements may be given effect if they appear after the signatures of the witnesses.

By signing the instrument, the witnesses testify not only to the fact that they signed at the request of the debtor, but also to the facts stated in the instrument, which constitute the transaction. They must see that the instrument contains the agreed-upon terms and that it does not contain anything that has not been agreed upon. In addition, the instrument must be signed in such a manner that the witnesses are readily identifiable, so that they can be subpoenaed to appear in beth din if a question arises as to the genuineness of the instrument. They must sign so that there is no possibility that the instrument may afterward be altered to contain matters that were not contained in the instrument when they signed. There are also rules regarding the effect of erasures in the instrument. Paper or parchment was not always easy to come by. Sometimes the same paper, after it had served its

43

purpose, would be reused. Often, if a mistake was made in an instrument, the mistake would be erased, rather than having an entire new instrument drawn up and the one containing the mistake discarded. Apparently the beth din knew how to recognize an instrument that contained erasures. The rules by which they made this determination are also included in this chapter.

Chapter 39 discussed the presumption of regularity of the instrument as to its formal requirements. The present chapter concludes with the laws of the presumption of regularity of the signatures of the witnesses.

# TEXT

## The names of the witnesses

The witnesses are to sign in such a way that there is no doubt as to their identification. In Hebrew instruments, the witness signs in Hebrew, "Ruven the son of Shimon, witness." The signature thus has three component parts: (1) the name of the person signing, (2) his father's name, and (3) the word 'witness'. If the witness omits one of these three components, his signature is *de facto* valid. Thus, "Ruven the son of Shimon," or "Ruven, witness," or "the son of Shimon, witness" are all valid. However, "Ruven" alone or "son of Shimon" alone are not valid.[1] If the instrument commences with the words "Before us, the undersigned witnesses . . . ," then the instrument would be valid even in the first instance if a witness were to sign only his own name or "the son of . . ." without adding the word "witness," since this is already stated at the opening of the instrument.

If a witness were to sign in a language other than Hebrew, he would probably sign his given name and his family name.

In those communities where there are several people with the same name, then, regardless of the language, there should be some additional information to identify the witness, such as the name of his father or his address.

---

1. Such signatures would not be valid, since they could be misinterpreted to mean that they signed, without having fulfilled the requirements of a witness.

Titles, such as Rabbi, Sir, Doctor, or Professor, are generally not part of the signature.

## The witness must know the contents of the instrument

The witness must be familiar with every word of the instrument. The recommended procedure is for both witnesses to read the instrument word for word, either together or one after the other.[2]

There are exceptions to the requirement that both witnesses read the entire instrument. If there is no reason to fear that the person reading the instrument to the witness is going to read something other than appears in the instrument, then the instrument may be read to the witness. The example usually cited is that if the chief judge of the beth din was familiar with the contents of the instrument, and had confidence in the clerk of the beth din, then the clerk of the beth din may read the instrument to the chief judge. This is based on the assumption that the clerk would likely fear dismissal if the judge were to at some time ascertain that he did not accurately read that which appeared in the instrument.[3] There is also an opinion that if the instrument is read publicly, then it falls into the exception delineated in this paragraph. This exception is strictly construed and is not to be extended to apply to analogous situations, such as the clerk of one beth din reading to the chief judge of another beth din.

---

2. Some communities abide by the practice of having both witnesses read the instrument at the same time, with one reading aloud. Of course, the witnesses can take turns reading aloud, so long as both witnesses actually read the entire instrument word for word.

3. According to this opinion, the reading of the instrument to the witness is not considered hearsay, although it may appear that the witness only signs that which he heard and not that which he witnessed. Such a reading is not considered hearsay because the witness is familiar with the transaction: he witnessed the transaction and is now being called upon to memorialize that which he witnessed. He must know both the transaction and the contents of the instrument, not only the latter. Furthermore, if the reader did not read accurately, then the errors would be discovered when the instrument is read by another person. The other opinions do not make the aforementioned distinctions and apparently hold that such reading indeed constitutes hearsay.

According to one opinion, an exception also applies if two people read the instrument to the witness.[4]

If witnesses do not understand the language of the instrument, then the readers may translate for one or both witnesses, and the witnesses then sign the instrument.[5]

If the debtor signs an instrument written in a language that he does not understand, and if there are witnesses that the debtor signed without the instrument's having been read to him, then the debtor is nevertheless bound by what is written therein.[6] A similar result would obtain if an obligor signed a blank piece of paper and gave it to a third party or to the obligee; the obligor would be liable to all of the terms therein.

## A witness who does not know how to sign his name

If a witness does not know how to sign his name, and if it happened that a blank piece of paper was prepared for him in the nature of a stencil, and he signed using the stencil, then the instrument is void according to the opinion of R. Yosef Karo, and valid according to the opinion of Ramo.[7] Both agree that the witness is to be lashed for his conduct.[8] If, instead of a stencil, marks were engraved into the

---

4. The theory seems to be that each reader will see to it that the other reader is reading accurately.

5. There is opinion that this procedure should not be resorted to in the first instance, but if it was post facto done, then the instrument is valid.

6. The debtor on the instrument, who is also the signer, is deemed to have signed the instrument without reading it in reliance upon the person who wrote the instrument. And there is a general principle that if one individual relied upon the integrity of another, he makes a conscious decision to be bound by whatever the other put into the instrument. A similar situation arises when a husband has prepared a bill of divorce for his wife and entrusted it to a third party to hold. If the third party delivers the bill to the wife, alleging that this was the instruction of the husband, but the husband alleges that the third party was given the divorce for safekeeping and not for delivery, then it is held that the delivery of the divorce is valid, since the husband made the decision to rely upon the third party.

7. If the same procedure were followed in the case of a bill of divorce, it would be valid. (The reason being is that it might prevent a woman from remarrying if there were no other witnesses to sign the bill of divorce.)

8. There is also an opinion that the judge who permitted such conduct is the one to be lashed and not the witness, who obviously did not even know how to sign his name and certainly did not know the law.

instrument and the witness filled in the marks, then there is also a difference of opinion as to whether this is valid or is the equivalent of a stencil and is therefore void.[9]

A community may issue a decree that the scribe shall sign all instruments in the names and place of the witnesses. This procedure eliminates the possibility of embarrassing those who do not know how to sign their names. The scribe signs the name of the obligor and his own name as attorney-in-fact and states that he has done so on behalf of the witness whom he names, or at the behest of the witness.[10] If the scribe signs on behalf of the obligor, then he may do so even if there is no community decree to that effect. The obligor should hand the pen to the scribe to sign on his behalf.

## Where on the instrument the witnesses must sign

An instrument must be signed at the very end of the document. It may not be signed on the side nor in the margin, nor on the top nor on the reverse side, even if there is no danger of the instrument's being altered.[11]

When signing at the end of the instrument, the witness must make sure that there is no space between the end of the instrument and the first witness's signature. There must not be a space of two lines; if there is such a space, the instrument is void. This is the case because if such space were permitted, the holder of the instrument could conceivably cut the original instrument above the blank space above

---

9. The difference of opinion arises from a more basic dispute. Is filling in the mark considered writing on top of other writing (which voids any document, even a bill of divorce)? If it is *not* considered writing on top of writing, then it is valid.

10. If there is no community decree to permit such action and the scribe signed on behalf of the witness, then the instrument is not valid. But if the scribe signed on behalf of the debtor, the instrument is valid even if there was no such decree.

11. There is no danger that the instrument will be altered if one of the witnesses signed at the bottom. Even if the other witness signed in some other place, the signature of the witness who signed at the bottom would prohibit the addition of anything to the instrument after its completion. Alternatively, the instrument could be inscribed with the words "firm and established," which would show that nothing else had been added to the original instrument. Yet it is a decree of the Sages that notes of indebtedness, admission, and confession must be signed by both witnesses at the end.

the signature of the witnesses and insert a short instrument into the blank space. This rule holds even if the space was filled in with lines,[12] or even if the instrument contained the words "firm and established." If an instrument that contained a space of at least two blank lines was signed, then it is invalid not as against the debtor on the instrument, but only as against purchasers from the debtor.[13] In such a case the debtor still has all the defenses he would have had against an instrument that did not contain such spaces.[14] The two lines are measured according to the space of a line of the taller of the witnesses' signatures or that of the scribe, including the space between two lines. The space between the text and the space for the signatures of the witnesses, together with a space between the signatures of the two witnesses, should be approximated in order to determine whether there was a space of two signatures' length between the text and the actual signatures.

The beth din should examine each instrument that does not follow the usually accepted rules, and if there is a suspicion that an instrument could have been tampered with because the witnesses' signatures are too distant from the body of the instrument or too close to the middle of the signature line, or because the witnesses left blank spaces that could have been filled in, then the beth din should invalidate the instrument.[15]

The debtor can attack the validity of the instrument if the witnesses have left excessive space. However, he must do so before payment

---

12. The reason is that it may conceivably be thought that the witnesses are testifying with regard to the presence of the ink lines.

13. If the debtor borrows the money, and an instrument evidencing the debt has been properly executed, and the debtor thereafter sells some land, then the land in the hands of the purchaser stands as security for the debt, as if a written lien existed on the land.

14. The witnesses who read the instrument and know the details of the transaction may still testify to the transaction. If their signatures are confirmed, the debtor cannot deny that the transaction took place. He may still raise a defense such as payment.

15. Much of what has been said regarding the space left by the witnesses can often be obviated if the instrument has a concluding paragraph stating that that which follows is the signature clause, and if the witnesses sign thereafter. The final paragraph can commence with the words "IN WITNESS WHEREOF, the witnesses hereto have signed this instrument on the date first herein above written." The exact place for them to sign should also be typed in in the form of two lines, one beneath the other, so that the witnesses may sign on these lines.

has been made pursuant to a decision that has been rendered at a trial on the instrument.

If an instrument with such space before the signatures was purchased by a Jewish plaintiff from a non-Jew, and if the instrument would have been valid in the non-Jewish courts, then it will be held to be valid before the beth din.[16]

An instrument is void if it was written completely on one line and was signed by the witnesses on the next line or on the next two lines. This is so because the danger exists that the original instrument was larger and contained a space of one line between the end of the instrument and the signatures, and the holder of the instrument cut the document, leaving just the blank space and the signatures of the witnesses, and filled in the blank space to reflect a debt due to him.[17] However, if an instrument was written on one line together with the signatures of both witnesses on the same line, it is valid.[18]

## If one or more witnesses are ineligible to sign

An instrument may be introduced into beth din containing signatures of some ineligible witnesses as well as those of the requisite number of eligible witnesses. (See Chapters 33, 34, and 35 as to who is ineligible to witness an instrument.) If it can be shown by the testimony of the eligible witnesses, or in some other manner, that the witnesses did not all sign at one sitting with the intent that all would be witnesses to the instrument, then the instrument will stand on the strength of the signatures of the eligible witnesses. If it is shown by the testimony of witnesses, who may also be the eligible witnesses to the instrument, that it was the intent that all should act as witnesses, then the ineligible witnesses void the instrument, even though it contains

---

16. Even if the instrument was made by a Jewish debtor for a Jewish creditor, it could still be collected upon if the beth din determined that it had not been altered.

17. Similarly, if an instrument was written on a piece of paper consisting of a line and a half followed by two lines of signatures, then the instrument is void for the same reason. It is possible that the instrument had had one and a half lines of space between the text and the signatures and the instrument was cut off and the space was filled in before the signature lines to reflect a nonexistent debt.

18. This is true only if the witnesses' signatures are on the same line as the text of the instrument. If other witnesses' signatures also appear on the instrument, it is not valid.

the requisite number of eligible signatures. If two witnesses testify that the intent was for the ineligible witnesses to join with the eligible witnesses, and two witnesses testify that it was not the intent that the ineligible witnesses be among the signing witnesses, then the instrument leaves the parties as they were and may not be used to collect money from the obligor, since the money is in his hands and there is no valid instrument to deprive him of the money he holds. There is also an opinion, however, that if the requisite number of eligible witnesses signed first, then the signatures of the ineligible witnesses do not void the instrument. The eligible witnesses may have signed the instrument and then departed, and the ineligible witnesses may have thereafter signed without the knowledge of the eligible witnesses or without their signatures added to fill in the space. There is also a contrary opinion that if the last two witnesses were eligible, then the instrument is valid. If the witnesses are not available to be questioned, and if there is evidence that the intent was that all of them would be co-witnesses on the instrument, then it is void. If neither the eligible witnesses nor other witnesses are available to testify to the facts, then there is a presumption of validity and that the ineligible witnesses were not intended to join with the eligible witnesses, and the instrument is deemed valid. It is assumed that their signatures were used to fill in the space between the text of the instrument and the signatures of the eligible witnesses so that there would not be a space of two signatures to invalidate the instrument.

If the eligible witnesses recall the incident, even if they have to refresh their memories by viewing the void instrument, then their testimony is admissible to prove the facts contained in the instrument. The beth din will transcribe their testimony, and the new transcript will take the place of the void instrument and will carry the date of the sitting of beth din. However, if the obligor in the instrument authorized the witnesses to sign with a *kinyan*, then the beth din can date the instrument according to the date of the original instrument.[19] This can be done only by the beth din and not by the eligible witnesses.[20]

---

19. See Chapter 195 regarding rules of *kinyan*.

20. The witnesses cannot write a new instrument, since their agency to act as witnesses terminated when they signed the instrument together with the ineligible witnesses.

## Erasures of the signatures

An instrument that is written on erased paper, and that contains witnesses' signatures that are also on erased paper, is not invalid because of the erasure,[21] if the erased area seems to be similar in both parts.[22] Therefore, witnesses should not sign an instrument that contains erasures or that is written on erased paper unless the erasures were made in their presence.[23]

If the text of an instrument was written on an unerased part of the paper and the witnesses signed on an erased part of the paper, then the instrument is void. This is because there is the concern that the instrument could thereafter have been erased, so that now the entire instrument, including the text and signatures, is on erased paper. If the witnesses wrote between the first and second signatures on an erased part of the paper and the text was written on unerased paper, then the instrument is valid.

An instrument that was written on an erased part of the paper but has been signed on an unerased part of the paper is void. The written statement of the witnesses that the instrument was erased will not prevent the possibility of the erased part of the instrument's being further altered.

In those communities where the payment of the instrument is endorsed thereon, the aforesaid rules should be followed to the extent that beth din believes them necessary to the prevention of fraud by erasures. Of course, if the notation of payment is in the handwriting of the obligor, then there need be no concern about erasures.

---

21. In other words, the instrument is not void solely because of this. It must, of course, still comply with all other requirements of instruments.

22. The beth din should be convinced that the number of erasures are the same in both the text of the instrument and in the spaces where the witnesses signed, for example, if the instrument was on a section of paper that had not been erased even once, and the witnesses signed in a place that had been erased once. Then, if the lender erased the text of the instrument, both the text and the witnesses' signature would have each been erased once, and thus similar. This is what the beth din has to guard against.

23. There is also an opinion that all of the erasure of the paper should be done in one day, since erasures done on different days and then written over may not look the same, and the instrument might be suspect by the beth din.

## Presumption of regularity of the signatures

Any instrument introduced into beth din is considered valid if the witnesses testify that the signatures on the instrument are their signatures, or if other witnesses testify that they recognize the signatures in the instrument. This is based on the presumption that witnesses would not have signed an instrument unless they had first read it and knew how to sign. Even if other witnesses testify that the signing witnesses did not know how to read, if the signing witnesses testify that the instrument was read to them, then their testimony is relied upon. If the signing witnesses are not available, and if other witnesses testify that they know that the signing witnesses did not know how to read, then there is no presumption of regularity unless there is competent testimony that the instrument was read to the signing witnesses.

# Chapter 46

# AUTHENTICATION OF INSTRUMENTS

## INTRODUCTION

The best evidence of the occurrence of a transaction is the testimony of the witnesses as to what they saw and heard. This chapter discusses secondary evidence—a writing describing the events of a transaction, known as the written instrument that is discussed in Chapters 39 through 45 (the note of indebtedness, admission, or confession). These instruments describe the way in which indebtedness was incurred. The instrument is signed by two witnesses and delivered to the creditor in the presence of two witnesses. What effect does this instrument have?

According to Torah law, a written instrument signed by two witnesses may be admitted in beth din as proof of an event without any further testimony. The signing is the equivalent of authentication of the instrument in beth din, and beth din will assist the holder of the instrument to enforce payment thereof. There is no concern that the instrument might have been forged, since it is presumed that no person would be so arrogant as to forge an instrument. It is presumed that even a person who is somewhat dishonest will not attempt to forge a document, since his forgery will surely be exposed. An exception to this presumption would occur if the debtor were to produce the witnesses who the creditor alleges signed the instrument and they were to testify that they did not sign it. In such a case, even according to Torah law, the holder would have to prove its authenticity. Even if the debtor pleaded that the instrument was a forgery, the burden would be upon him to prove the forgery, and the holder would not be required to prove the authenticity thereof. There is also an opinion that if the debtor alleges the document to be a forgery, the holder even according to Torah law, would have to prove its authenticity. Torah law waives the requirement of authentication only if there are subscribing witnesses on the instrument. If there are not, then Torah law requires that the instrument be authenticated.

The Rabbis, however, required that even an instrument containing the signatures of two subscribing witnesses be authenticated. Unauthenticated instruments have no validity. The Rabbis also realized that if it became extremely difficult to prove the authenticity of the instrument, creditors would be loath to extend credit, whether in terms of loans, sales, or labor agreements, or in any other situation in which the need for credit would arise.

The law therefore has the task of weighing the conflicting interests, and beth din therefore has the task of weighing the conflicting claims: that of the holder of the instrument that it is valid, and that of the alleged debtor that the instrument is not valid.

This chapter of the *Shulhan Aruch* actually deals with several subjects in addition to that named in the chapter title assigned by this author. In addition to dealing with the authentication of instruments, it also deals with (1) witnesses who impugn the authenticity of an instrument by alleging that they were ineligible to act as witnesses on the instrument at the time that it was signed, and (2) the debtor's allegations that the instrument was really intended as one of trust and was not to be effective as an instrument of indebtedness until certain conditions occurred. The title of the chapter in *Shulhan Aruch, Hoshen haMishpat* is "Witnesses who now testify that they were minors or ineligible [when we signed the note of indebtedness] or that the note of indebtedness was a note of trust, and laws of authentication of instruments." Thus the allegations of the witnesses that they were not eligible also extends to the authenticity of the instrument, as does the allegation that it was a note of trust rather than a note of indebtedness.

The classes of persons about whom we will be speaking are as follows: (1) the "parties" to the transaction, usually the creditor and debtor, such as a lender and borrower; (2) the "subscribing witnesses," are the witnesses who sign the original instrument which is the subject of the authentication; (3) the "recognizing witnesses," who testify that they recognize the signatures of the subscribing witnesses; (4) the "authenticating judges," who will authenticate the signatures of the witnesses on the instrument; (5) the "sustaining witnesses," who sustain the signatures of the authenticating judges; and (6) the "enforcing judges," who will enforce payment of the instrument and who will render a judgment in the litigation between the creditor and debtor on the strength of the authenticated instrument.

# TEXT

## Instruments must be authenticated

By Rabbinic enactment, every instrument must be authenticated. Until the instrument has been authenticated, the debtor may allege that it is a forgery, or that he did not instruct anyone to write it.[1] He may also admit the authenticity, but may allege that it was paid, or that it was a note of trust,[2] or that it was written for the purpose of some future borrowing that never materialized.[3] He is believed in all of these instances "since" he could have denied the entire transaction or the

---

1. See Chapter 39, wherein it is stated that a note of indebtedness may not be written without the express instructions of the debtor. However, if there was a *kinyan* made, then it will take the place of the debtor's instructions.

2. A note of trust is on its face a note of indebtedness, but the debtor alleges that it was drawn up for the purpose of enabling the lender to lend money to the borrower without having to look for a scribe and/or witnesses later, when they might not be available. The debtor named therein now alleges that he gave the note of indebtedness to the lender to hold with a view toward the loan to take place, but that the loan never took place. The witnesses may not, however, state that the note of indebtedness was only a note of trust, since they may not sign on a note of indebtedness unless the loan is taking place. (See Chapter 37.) They may, however, state that the borrower requested their signatures and stated that he would keep the note of indebtedness until the loan took place.

3. The borrower alleges that the note of indebtedness was written for him to keep in his possession until the lender was ready to make the loan, but that the borrower lost the note of indebtedness and it is now wrongly in the hands of the lender.

authenticity of the instrument because it has not been authenticated.[4] The debtor is required to take a *hesseth* oath, in which case he will receive a verdict in his favor dismissing the complaint of the creditor.[5] If thereafter the instrument is authenticated in beth din, all of the laws that apply to authenticated instruments of indebtedness will apply to it.[6]

There is an opinion that his plea of "since" is not admitted if the instrument contained a credence clause—that is, if it stated that the mere allegation of the holder that he was not paid would be sufficient to enforce collection of the instrument. The holder of the instrument is therewith transferred into the category of two witnesses.[7] Of course, this skirts the entire question of the validity of the instrument. If the instrument is a forgery, the clause regarding the holder is also part of that forgery.[8]

## Who should authenticate the instrument

If there is a community-appointed beth din, this beth din should authenticate instruments. If there is no appointed beth din, the

---

4. This type of a plea is known as *migoo*, a loose translation of which is "since." It is a principle often used in pleadings. A party is believed in his allegation if he puts forward a plea that is less beneficial to him "since" he could have put forward a more beneficial plea that would have been believed. The theory is that if he had intended to tell a falsehood, he could have invented a more advantageous one. Thus the debtor is believed that he paid the unauthenticated instrument, "since" he could have denied that the instrument was authentic.

5. See Volume III, Chapter 87 regarding the different types of beth din oaths.

6. Even if the instrument is later authenticated in beth din, the allegations originally made by the borrower that it was for the purpose of a future loan may very well have been true, and the borrower is not deemed to be a perjurer as a result of his allegations.

7. According to this opinion, the credence of the holder of the instrument transforms him into the category of being believed like two witnesses. The entire concept of *migoo*, "since" in favor of the debtor may only be employed in the absence of testimony by witnesses as to the authenticity of the instrument. *Migoo* can never be used to refute witnesses. If the holder of the instrument is believed to the degree that two witnesses would be because of the credence clause contained in the instrument, and because he does have the instrument in his hands, the plea made by the debtor on the strength of *migoo* is not present.

8. There are some authorities who would adopt the principle of credence given to the holder only if the debtor admitted the genuiness of the instrument but raised some other defense, such as payment.

instrument must be authenticated before three persons, since it requires an act of beth din. Therefore, if it is authenticated before two persons or only one person, it is not a valid authentication. In those communities where the custom is to have one person, usually the rabbi or appointed judge of the community,[9] perform the functions of a beth din, he would by himself be authorized to authenticate instruments.[10] In Volume I, Chapter 5, it was stated that a beth din could not perform certain functions at night. This rule applies to the authentication of instruments.[11] However, if both parties agree that the instrument may be authenticated at night, beth din may do so.

The instrument may be authenticated even if the debtor is not present, or even if he is present and alleges that the instrument is a

---

9. The custom should not be enlarged to permit other synagogue or community functionaries to assume this duty of authenticating an instrument by themselves.

10. Ramo writes that the custom in the Ashkenazic countries (France, Germany, Eastern Europe) is to have one person perform the functions of a beth din. The reason that it may be done in authenticating instruments is that the requirement for authentication is of Rabbinic origin. The Rabbis by decree gave the expert individual the power of a beth din. Ramo continues by noting that although for the most part no individual is presently recognized as an expert, for the purpose of authenticating instruments we can rely on the individual so appointed. There are those who differ with the holding of Ramo regarding having the individual appointed to be the judge to authenticate the instrument, or if the debtor alleges that the instrument is a forgery, then the requirement for the authentication of the instrument is no longer just or Rabbinic origin, but is rather of Torah origin, and all would agree that Torah law requires three persons for authentication. However, this would be true only if the instrument came to beth din after the defendant's allegation of forgery. If it was presented by the holder of the instrument before the allegation of forgery was put forward by the defendant, then the authentication is only a Rabbinic requirement, for the question of forgery was not yet an issue when the instrument was first presented. If the creditor admits that he does not know who the witnesses were, then the requirement for the authentication of the instrument is also of Torah origin. Similarly, if the witnesses themselves testify that they did not sign, then, too, the requirement for authentication is of Torah origin. This is because the signatures on the instrument in such a case would be unknown to the beth din, and the Torah waiver of authentication applies only if the subscribing witnesses on the instrument are known.

11. In Volume I, Chapter 5, it was stated that although beth din is not permitted to commence proceedings during the nighttime hours, there was an opinion that if it nevertheless did do so, then the proceedings would be valid. This would also apply to authenticating instruments at night.

forgery.[12] If the instrument is a promissory note signed by the debtor, then it must be authenticated in his presence.[13]

## Methods of authentication

The witnesses' signatures on the instrument must be authenticated. There are five methods of authentication.

1. The judges may recognize the signatures of the two witnesses.
2. The witnesses may sign a blank piece of paper in the beth din, and the judges will then compare the signatures before them with the signatures on the instrument to see whether they are the same.[14] This may be done even at night, and the next day the judges will use the specimen writing to compare with the instrument that they are judging.[15]

---

12. There is an opinion that if the document is a promissory note signed by the debtor, rather than by witnesses, then the debtor's presence is required to authenticate the instrument. This is the case because the authentication of an instrument signed by the debtor without two witnesses is of Torah origin, and thus a full beth din of three persons is always required. However, even this opinion would permit the instrument to be authenticated in the absence of the debtor if that was the community's custom.

13. The difference between a note of indebtedness signed by two witnesses and a promissory note signed by the debtor is that authentication is required by Rabbinic enactment in the former case, and thus the Rabbis as part of the enactment relaxed the requirement that the debtor must be present. In the latter case, however, the requirement for authentication of the promissory note is of Torah origin, and the rule requiring the debtor's presence cannot be dispensed with. There is an opinion that even in the latter instance, if the custom in the community is to permit even promissory notes signed by the debtor himself to be authenticated in his absence, then the custom should be followed.

14. This method enables witnesses who do not remember the events regarding which they signed the instrument to testify rather than being disqualified from testifying according to the opinion that holds that the subscribing witnesses must remember the event when they testify as to their signatures.

15. The action of the authenticating judges to authenticate the next day that which they witnessed the night before is not in the class of permitting a witness to the matter to also be a judge in the matter. In this case the authenticating judge who witnessed the subscribing witness's testimony the night before is now sitting as an authenticating judge the next day. As was stated earlier, the authentication of

3. The witnesses who signed the instrument each testify that the signature on the instrument is his signature. According to one view recorded in *Shulhan Aruch*, the witness must also be able to testify as to the event.[16] If the witness has no recollection of the event, then he may not testify regarding his signature.[17] In such an event, one of the other methods of authentication may be used. According to a second view recorded in *Shulhan Aruch*, it is sufficient if each of the witnesses testifies as to his own signature and the signature of the other witness because each signature will then have been authenticated by two witnesses. However, if each witness recognizes and can testify to only his own signature, then some other person or persons will be required to join with each subscribing witness to testify to each signature.

4. Recognizing witnesses may come to beth din to identify each of the signatures on the instrument.[18] However, these witnesses need necessarily not come to beth din to testify as to the signatures, but may send a writing to beth din containing this information.[19,20] There is a difference of opinion as to whether the instrument is authenticated if the witnesses to the instrument identify the signatures as their own while other witnesses testify that the signatures are *not* theirs. A similar difference of opinion exists if the witnesses named in the

---

instruments is of Rabbinic origin, and in matters of Rabbinic origin, a witness may be a judge in the same case. (See Volume I, Chapter 7.)

16. This follows the view of Maimonides that the witness who testifies as to his own signature on the instrument must also testify as to the matter itself. The writing is merely a secondary way of proving the event. If the witnesses are present, their testimony provides the best reliable evidence. Maimonides writes that if a judge decides otherwise, then he does not know "his right from his left."

17. Even according to Maimonides' view he need not recollect all the details. He must recall only enough of the events to show that his signature was on an instrument that recorded that specific event.

18. The identity would be complete even if they recognize only part of the name. See Chapter 45 for the correct method of signing one's name as a witness.

19. A mute person is not permitted to send a writing. Only a person who could have orally testified may send the writing in this case. The writing must reach beth din while the recognizing witness who sent the writing is still alive.

20. In Volume I, Chapter 28, it was stated that the testimony of witnesses must be oral and that writing was not to be relied upon. However, in authenticating the signatures they are not testifying as to the event; rather, they are testifying as to the signatures of the subscribing witnesses. The Rabbis enacted the requirement to authenticate the signatures on the instrument, and they stated that in this situation authentication may be conferred by a writing.

instrument as subscribing witnesses state that the signatures are not theirs while other witnesses state that the signatures *are* theirs. If each of the recognizing witnesses identifies only one of the subscribing witnesses, then another recognizing witness must be added to each of the other recognizing witnesses so that there will be at least two recognizing witnesses for each subscribing witness.[21,22]

5. If the beth din has presented to it two other instruments that have been authenticated and on which the signatures of the two witnesses appear, then beth din will compare the signatures to determine whether they are the same. This is the case only if the two instruments that are used for comparison with the instrument before the beth din are deeds for two fields on which the time has elapsed for the prior owners of the fields to commence action to dispossess the grantees named in the deeds as trespassers on the realty and if the grantees in the deeds are occupying the real estate openly and notoriously.[23] These two deeds must be produced in beth din by someone other than the person who is proposing that the instrument be authenticated.[24] These deeds might have been contested at one time but were sustained by a beth din as being authentic. The signature can also be compared with those on two different *kethubah* instruments that the witness signed.[25] An instrument that was con-

---

21. If there are more than two subscribing witnesses on the instrument, then as long as there are at least two recognizing witnesses who can testify as to at least two of the subscribing witnesses, it is sufficient. The identity of the remaining subscribing witnesses is not essential.

22. In method 3, the two subscribing witnesses were sufficient, since in essence each testified as to the transaction. In method 4, the recognizing witnesses are not testifying as to the event, but rather as to the signatures of the subscribing witnesses.

23. It is necessary to produce two different deeds for two pieces of realty, since it may be just a coincidence that one owner permitted the occupier to remain on the realty for the entire three years despite the fact that the deed was a forgery. It would be more than just a coincidence if this happened on two separate pieces of realty and the witness just happened to sign both forged deeds.

24. If the alleged creditor presents all of the instruments to the beth din with similar signatures on them, he could have forged them all. But if they come from different sources, then it is not likely that he could have forged them all. This holds true even if the other instruments were already authenticated in beth din.

25. At a wedding ceremony, a *kethubah* is signed by two witnesses who state that the groom undertook certain obligations to the bride. This is usually done with a *kinyan* by the groom that he will abide by the terms of the *kethubah*. The *kethubah* may incorporate many obligations, but at the minimum it must state that in the event

tested and that was eventually authenticated by a beth din may also be used to compare signatures. There are those who hold that if the witness wrote a long manuscript, then his signature can also be compared with the handwriting in the manuscript, but not with the handwriting in a short letter. One can also introduce an instrument theretofore authenticated by a beth din for comparison of the signatures of the witnesses.[26] Any two instruments may be used, even if they are of different types.

If the signatures of the subscribing witnesses have been authenticated, then the beth din will cite on the instrument the method or combination of methods by which the determination of authenticity was made. In method 3, for example, the judges would endorse upon the instrument, "The three judges sat together and the two witnesses (whose names they also include) came before them to testify as to their signatures, and the beth din then certified the instrument and sustained it." The judges would then sign at the bottom. They would also specify any of the other methods they employed to authenticate the instrument. Even if they do not specify the method, however, the instrument is nevertheless authenticated. This author would suggest that if the instrument is authenticated by a beth din that is part of a unified beth din system (as advocated in Volume I, Chapter 1), then the clerk of the beth din should have a seal that can be placed on all authentications, and a record should be kept so that there is no danger of the seal's being forged. If the beth din that authenticated the instrument is the same beth din that is asked to enforce collection of the debt evidenced by the instrument, then the authentication procedure is over and the collection procedure commences. However, if for any reason the collection procedure is not about to commence, (perhaps the debtor is not present or has no assets on which to levy), then the enforcement procedure by enforcing judge will take place at a later time. If in such event there is no recognized

---

that the husband dies or divorces the wife, she will be entitled to a sum certain which is named in the kethubah. Two people sign the kethubah as witnesses to the husband's undertaking. In this case the kethubah does not have to be aged, as in the case of a deed.

26. Some hold that here, too, there must be two such instruments, but they would agree that one instrument is sufficient if it was authenticated as a result of adversary litigation.

beth din seal or other indication by which the later enforcing judges can recognize that the instrument has been authenticated, then the enforcing beth din will have to commence the procedure anew.

Thus, even after the instrument is authenticated in beth din, there may still be the requirement that the persons who will enforce collection of the instrument must recognize the signatures of the two witnesses or of at least two of the judges who signed the authentication. The earlier authentication made it easier for the later beth din that seeks to enforce the instrument to recognize two of the subscribing witnesses or two of the judges rather than just two of the subscribing witnesses.

If the requisite number of recognizing witnesses cannot be obtained, then the instrument will not be authenticated unless a combination of methods can be employed. It is not valid if one subscribing witness testified as to his signature and he and another person testified as to the signature of the other witness on the instrument.[27]

A similar situation would arise if one of the subscribing witnesses has died. It is not permitted for the surviving witness to testify as to his own signature and together with another recognizing witness testify as to the signature of the deceased witness. If two other witnesses who can testify to his signature or to the signature of the other subscribing witness are unavailable then the surviving subscribing witness together with another recognizing witness should testify as to the signature of the deceased witness, and the surviving witness should write his signature on another piece of paper outside of beth din, so that it may be used by beth din to compare to his signature on the instrument. The beth din may thus be able to authenticate the instrument by method 2, such that there is authentication by a combination of methods 2 and 4.[28] The signature of the dead subscribing witness should not be testified to by a strange recognizing witness or a recognizing witness who is related to the

---

27. The reason is that when the Torah required two witnesses to authenticate any matter, it divided each matter such that each witness testified, as it were, to one-half of the matter. In this case, the subscribing witness is testifying as to three-quarters of the result: one-half is his own signature, and one-quarter is the signature of the other subscribing witness's.

28. The suggested method is that he write it outside of beth din. If he were to write it in beth din, the danger of three-fourths of the instrument being authenticated on his testimony may still be present.

surviving subscribing witness who identifies his own signature because then three of the four witnesses are related, and that is prohibited.[29]

## Kinsmen, ineligible witnesses, and minors who have reached their majority as witnesses

Six classes of persons were listed in the Introduction to this chapter: the parties, the subscribing witnesses, the recognizing witnesses, the authenticating judges, the sustaining witnesses, and the enforcing judges. Relatives who may not testify to an occurrence are listed in Volume I, Chapter 33. It was stated in Chapter 35 that minors may not testify. What if some of the persons are related to one another? What if a person was a minor when he recognized a signature but has reached the age of majority by the time he is called to serve as a recognizing witness?

The recognizing witnesses may be related to the subscribing witnesses.[30] If a subscribing witness died when his son was a minor and the son now testifies that he recognizes the signature of his deceased father, his testimony is admissible.[31] A minor may also testify as a recognizing witness regarding his brother's or his teacher's signature that he learned to recognize while he was still a minor, providing that he testifies after having reached the age of majority.[32] These exceptions are strictly limited.

The recognizing witnesses may not be related to each other. If they are related to either party, they may not testify.[33] If the authenticating judges are related to the parties, their actions are void.

---

29. See Volume I, Chapter 33, as to which relatives may not testify together.

30. The recognizing witnesses testify only as to the signatures of the subscribing witnesses and not directly for the benefit of the parties.

31. Of course, there will still have to be another recognizing witness who can identify the signature of the deceased witness. The other witness must not have been a minor when he learned to recognize the signature of the decedent. The other recognizing witness may also be related, as set forth in this section of the text.

32. The underlying reason for permitting the testimony of relatives and persons who were minors when they learned to identify the signatures of the subscribing witnesses is that according to Torah law there is no necessity to authenticate the instrument. The Rabbis required such authentication, but also relaxed the rules regarding relatives.

33. There is also an opinion that they may so testify.

The recognizing witnesses may not be related to the authenticating judges.[34] The recognizing witnesses may be related to the sustaining witnesses. The enforcing judges may not be related to the subscribing witnesses. The enforcing judges may not be related to the authenticating judges.

Chapter 34 in Volume I enumerated persons who may not testify because they have transgressed. Thievery is one of those transgressions. If a person signed as a witness on an instrument before he became a thief, he may not testify as to his own signature.[35] But if *other* recognizing witnesses testify that they recognize his signature and that it was signed before he became a thief it is valid.[36] If there are witnesses to the fact that the thief signed before he became a thief but that there is no one to identify his signature, then the thief may, outside of beth din, write his signature on a piece of paper, which can be compared by the judges with the signature on the instrument.

If a person signed as a subscribing witness before he became the son-in-law of the creditor, but is the creditor's son-in-law when the instrument is presented for authentication, then he may not testify as to his own signature; however, others may so testify even if they did not learn to identify his signature until after he became the creditor's son-in-law. Or, another method may be employed.[37] If a person signed as a subscribing witness while he was law-abiding and is now a transgressor, then others can serve as recognizing witnesses if they saw the signature on the instrument before he became a transgressor.[38] If an insane person signed while he was still sane,

---

34. The reason is that the judges will not accept testimony that will impeach their relatives, the recognizing witnesses. There is also an opinion that would permit the recognizing witnesses to testify even if the authenticating judges are related to them, since the possibility of impeaching witnesses who appear in such situations is very remote.

35. The date on the instrument will show that he signed it before he became a thief.

36. If they cannot testify that it was signed by the thief before he became a thief, then the testimony of the recognizing witnesses is not admissible.

37. Another method might be for the subscribing witness, outside of beth din, to sign his name on a piece of paper and have his signature compared to the one on the instrument.

38. If they did not see his signature on the document before he became a transgressor, the danger exists that he may have forged the entire instrument. They may not authenticate the instrument even if it is dated prior to the time of his becoming a transgressor, since he may have forged the instrument and predated it.

others can serve as recognizing witnesses to his signature, even if they did not see his signature on the instrument before he became insane.

If the two subscribing witnesses whose signatures have not been authenticated died, and two other witnesses authenticate the signatures of the subscribing witnesses but simultaneously testify that the subscribing witnesses were minors or were otherwise ineligible when they signed the instrument, then the latter two witnesses are believed and the instrument is to be destroyed.[39] Even if the instrument can later be authenticated by one of the methods previously described, there will still be two witnesses on behalf of authenticating the instrument against two witnesses opposed to authenticating the instrument, and thus the instrument cannot be authenticated. There is a difference of opinion as to whether the result would be the same if the witnesses were alive and testified as to their signatures and two other witnesses came and testified that the subscribing witnesses were minors or were otherwise ineligible at the time they signed the instrument.

If an instrument cannot be authenticated by any of the methods except by the testimony of the subscribing witnesses, and they testify that they did indeed sign the instrument, but as part of simultaneous testimony state that they acted under compulsion,[40] or that they were minors and have now reached majority, or that they were kinsmen at the time of subscribing and are no longer related,[41] or that they were ineligible when they signed, or that the grantor in the deed protested against the deed, then they are believed and the instrument is void.[42]

---

39. The latter witnesses are believed with a *migoo*. If they had been silent, there would not have been two witnesses to recognize the signatures of the subscribing witnesses.

40. Only when they testify that they were coerced under the threat of death to sign as subscribing witnesses are they believed. If they testify that they were economically coerced, then they are not believed, on the theory that no one would subscribe a forged instrument under pressure of mere economic coercion.

41. An example would be two witnesses who were related by marriage; if the wife of one of the witnesses died, the two would no longer be related.

42. They are believed because in none of these cases have the witnesses incriminated themselves. If they acted under compulsion of death, they had no choice. If they were minors, they did not have the capacity to know right from wrong. If they were related, they can state that they relied on the fact that their relationship would become known and there could be no enforcement from the sold property of

However, the subscribing witnesses are not permitted to incriminate themselves, and thus they may not testify that although they signed the instrument they were bribed to do so, or that they were threatened with economic coercion, or that they were ineligible on account of religious transgressions,[43] or that the instrument was signed by them in trust.[44] Even if their signatures can be authenticated by another method, without their testimony, the subscribing witnesses may state that the deed was signed after the owner protested against the sale. In all of these cases where the witnesses are not believed to void the instrument, they are nevertheless obligated to make restitution to the debtor for the losses he sustained as a result of their subscribing the instrument. The general rule in any case in which the witnesses are given credence to invalidate an instrument because of any of the foregoing is that if their signatures are authenticated by some other method besides their own testimony, then the instrument remains valid. Some hold that except for the case in which the seller protested that he did not intend the deed to be valid, their testimony is believed.

If the witnesses testify that the deed of sale was made dependent upon a condition, and their signatures can be authenticated through another method, then no credence is given to their testimony as to the condition. If their signatures cannot be authenticated except by their own testimony, then they are believed as to the condition.[45] If

---

the debtor; thus nothing illegal would result. In the case of the seller's declaring that he did not intend that the deed would be valid, the declaration now by the witness shows that he signed not to transgress, but rather to aid the seller.

43. Even if they state that they afterwards repented, their testimony that they had been transgressors at the time when they signed is not believed.

44. The instrument was to be held in trust by the creditor until the credit or loan was actually extended and the witnesses did not see the loan. It was a transgression for the subscribing witnesses to state in the instrument that they saw the loan when in fact it did not take place.

45. If it is a condition that required action, then the person who was required to take that action must prove that the action was taken. If it was a condition that required that a certain action not be taken, then it is assumed that the action was not taken, until proof is offered that the action was taken and the condition was violated. This applies only to conditions yet to be performed. As for past conditions, whether they are of the nature of conditions that involved performance or refraining from performance, the witnesses should have ascertained the facts before they signed the instrument.

one of the subscribing witnesses testified that there was a condition that was not fulfilled, and the other says that there was no such condition, then the instrument is not authenticated because there is only one witness to testify that the instrument is now authentic. If the instrument stated that there were no other conditions that were not included in the instrument, then they cannot testify as to a condition not contained therein.[46,47]

If the subscribing witnesses verify their own signatures and testify that the borrower was a minor when they subscribed the instrument, then their testimony as to his being a minor is given no credence, even if their signatures cannot be authenticated by any other method.[48] They should have received permission from beth din or from the guardian of the minor before they signed.

## The act of authentication

Every instrument that has been authenticated in beth din requires an authentication clause signed by the judges of the authenticating beth din. The judges may sign even though they have not read the instrument. There is an opinion that they should at least have knowledge of the identities of the parties to the instrument.[49]

If two of the authenticating judges recognize the signatures of the subscribing witnesses and the third judge does not, and if they have not as yet signed the authentication clause, then the two judges who recognize the signatures may testify before the third judge. Once they have signed the authentication clause, they may not testify before the

---

46. They can testify, if they can explain that the clause in the instrument stating that no other conditions referred to the sale, but there might be other conditions, not contained therein, regarding payment and similar things.

47. Their subscribing the instrument after having read it and acknowledging that there is no condition therein, and now coming to beth din and stating that there was a condition, amounts to recantation of testimony, which is not admitted. (See Chapter 29.)

48. They are not believed because of the fact that they are incriminating themselves by stating that they signed an instrument that should not have been signed.

49. The judges will thus be able to see if any of the parties are related to them, or to the subscribing witnesses, which is prohibited.

third judge that they recognize the signatures of the subscribing witnesses.

The authenticating judges may write the authentication clause before the instrument has been authenticated, and according to the majority opinion, they may even sign as authenticating judges before actually receiving testimony to authenticate. There is no danger that the instrument will leave their possession until the actual authentication takes place. There is a minority view, however, that they may not sign the document until it has been authenticated.[50]

If it turns out that one of the authenticating judges was not eligible to sit on the panel of three judges in this case, then the authentication clause is cut off the instrument. If it is impossible to cut it off (if, for example, it was authenticated on the reverse side of the document), then the judges should draw lines in ink through the authentication clause. This does not affect the validity of the instrument.

If one of the judges who was on the authenticating panel died before he signed the document, then the authentication clause should read that the panel consisted of three judges, one of whom is no longer living, and the other two judges should sign.[51] Another opinion holds that if the authentication clause stated that the document was authenticated in a beth din, then it is not necessary to state that there were originally three judges on the panel, even if only two judges signed. Of course, if all three judges were alive and present during the signing and all three signed, then it is not necessary for the authentication clause to state that they were a beth din of three. Even if they signed by writing "we the witnesses have authenticated," and all three signed, it is also valid.[52]

The authentication clause must be written and signed close to the end of the instrument and the signatures of the witnesses, or in the margin, or on the back of the instrument.[53] If there is no room on the

---

50. The authentication clause is of no value without the signatures of the authenticating judges.

51. The reason for the addition of such a statement is that when a second beth din sees only two signatures, they will not know that there were three judges on the authenticating panel.

52. Some disagree, holding it to be invalid. They should not have written the term "witnesses" if they were judges. Writing that shows that they were not judges.

53. If the authenticating judges do not sign horizontally beneath the signatures of the subscribing witnesses, they should state how they are signing. For example, they

front or on the back of the instrument for the authentication clause and the signatures of the authenticating judges, a paper bearing the authentication clause and the signatures may be glued or attached by any other method that will not lend itself to fraud.[54] There should be no space for the insertion of extra clauses, terms, or forgeries into the instrument.[55] If more than the space of one written line and two blank spaces were left between the end of the signatures of the subscribing witnesses and the authentication clause, then the authenticating judges can fill in the space with inked lines.

## Allegations of authenticating judges or other witnesses to void the instrument

If two witnesses testify that all of the authenticating judges were not present at the time that the signatures of the subscribing witnesses were authenticated, then the authentication is void.[56] This applies only to the receiving of testimony to authenticate the instrument; it does not apply to the authenticating judges all signing the instrument at the same time. The authenticating judges cannot testify so as to incriminate themselves that they were not all present at the same time to authenticate the instrument.[57]

If, before all three authenticating judges signed the instrument, two witnesses presented themselves and testified that one of the authenticating judges who had not yet signed the authentication was ineligible because he had committed a transgression, and two other

---

should state that the subscribing witnesses signed horizontally and that they are signing vertically in the margin, or that there was no room in the front, so they signed on the back.

54. The appended authentication clause should make definite reference to the instrument to which it is attached, naming the parties, the date, and other terms. It should be attached in such a way that if it were removed, it could not likely be appended to another instrument.

55. See Chapter 45 regarding distances between the end of the text of the instrument and the signatures of the subscribing witnesses. There are similar requirements in the case of the signatures of the authenticating judges.

56. Only the authentication is affected; the instrument is not. The instrument can once again be authenticated.

57. This would amount to a confession of a transgression, and one is not permitted to testify against oneself.

witnesses testified that he had repented and was now eligible, the judge may sign the authentication clause.[58] If he had already signed before the second witnesses came to testify that he had mended his ways, then, if the other two judges testify that he mended his ways, the authentication is a nullity and the authentication process must be repeated.[59] Two other persons, however, may testify that he had mended his ways. If the allegation against the judge is regarding a statement of fact about his pedigree, such as that he is not Jewish, or that he is a bastard, the other judges as well as other persons may testify that it is not true, even if he had already signed, and his signature is valid, since in this case it had nothing to do with a changing status, but with his lifelong status.

## The benefit of having an authenticated instrument

As was stated previously, it is advantageous to the holder of an instrument to have it authenticated even if he is not planning to enforce it at the time of authentication. Even after the instrument has been authenticated, there may still be a contested litigation regarding performance of the instrument; or there may be an enforcement procedure regarding the instrument. In such a situation the enforcing judges can rely on the authentication of the authenticating judges. If the debtor contests the validity of either the instrument or the authentication proceeding, the enforcing judges must once again authenticate the validity of the instrument. They may recognize two of the signatures of the authenticating judges, or, of course, they may recognize the signatures of the original subscribing witnesses. If the enforcing beth din does not recognize the signatures of either the authenticating judges or the subscribing witnesses, then they must go

---

58. However, if two witnesses contradicted the first two witnesses and testified that the authenticating judge never committed the transgression, then the judge is not eligible to sign, since there are two witnesses against two witnesses as to the transgression's having been committed, and the burden of proof that the authentication is valid has not been met by the holder of the instrument. In the case in the text, the second witnesses do not contradict the first witnesses; they admit the truth of what they said, but they testify that there is now a change of facts.

59. If the ineligible judge had already signed, then the remaining two judges will feel compelled to testify that he had previously mended his ways, since they will be embarrassed to admit that they signed together with an ineligible person.

through a new authentication procedure. In this authenticating procedure, if one of the subscribing witnesses and one of the judges testifies as to their signatures, it is not valid, since the subscribing witness is testifying as to the transaction while the authenticating witness is testifying as to the authentication.[60] This lack of authentication affects only the validity of the instrument to enforce collection against the purchaser of the realty of the borrower. It would be valid as to the debtor himself. If each of two authenticating judges identifies his own signature, then the enforcing judges may treat it as authenticated. If two or more outside (or sustaining) witnesses recognize the signature of one of the subscribing witnesses and one of the signatures of the authenticating judges, then it is valid, since they are testifying on the signatures and not on the transaction.

If the previously suggested procedure whereby each beth din has a seal and a record of all instruments that have been sealed is followed, some of the problems herein stated would be alleviated.

If the instrument is written on an erased part of the paper and the authentication is written on the nonerased part of the paper, the enforcing beth din should examine the instrument to see whether it would have been possible to forge some of the terms or even the entire instrument.

---

60. The same result would follow if the signatures of one subscribing witness and one judge were authenticated by any of the other methods of authentication.

# Chapter 47

---

# THE CREDITOR IMPUGNS HIS OWN INSTRUMENT

## INTRODUCTION

This chapter begins with a discussion of the situation in which the holder of an instrument impugns that instrument after it has been authenticated. The holder might do this, for example, because he owes money and is afraid that his creditor will levy on the debt against the instrument, collect the instrument's amount, and keep the proceeds.

Say for example, that Shimon has lent $100 to Ruven, and Shimon holds a note of indebtedness against Ruven for the $100. Shimon, through another transaction, owes $100 to Levi, and Shimon has neither money nor assets to pay Levi, except for the $100 note that he holds against Ruven. Levi can demand the $100 note that Shimon holds against Ruven and then take the note and collect the $100 from Ruven. We can call Ruven the debtor, Shimon the holder of the note, and Levi the creditor. (Shimon, the holder, actually plays two roles: He is the creditor of Shimon and the debtor of Levi.)

As will be seen in Volume III, Chapter 86, Levi, the creditor, may levy on Ruven, the debtor, to collect his, Levi's, claim against Shimon the holder. But the holder, Shimon, perhaps in connivance with the debtor, Ruven, may wish to defraud the creditor, Levi. Thus Shimon may state that the note of indebtedness that he holds against the debtor, Ruven, is not valid, and thus the creditor, Levi, cannot levy against the debtor, Ruven. Perhaps some time in the future, when the debt from holder to creditor has been forgotten or perhaps paid, the holder will want to produce the note of indebtedness against the debtor.

The holder can allege that the note of indebtedness is not valid in several ways. He may state that although he still holds the note of indebtedness, it has been paid. Or he can allege that it was given to him as a note in trust—that is, to hold until he advanced money to debtor—but that the advance was never made. This chapter sets forth the laws that control these situations.

The chapter also deals with the situation in which the holder, instead of impugning the instrument in its entirety, states that the instrument is for an amount less than is stated therein. In so stating, does he void the note? In this part of the chapter, it is assumed that the holder has no creditors, so that the only party who will suffer if the instrument is impaired is the holder thereof.

## TEXT

### When the holder alleges that the note he holds is not enforceable

The holder is not permitted to state that the authenticated note of indebtedness that he holds is not enforceable if both of the following criteria are true: (1) He owes money to creditors and does not have the ability to pay except from the note of indebtedness[1]; and (2) the note of indebtedness is in the hands of an escrowee[2] or it was known to others that he was the holder of the note of indebtedness.[3] If these two criteria are met, then the holder may not allege that the note has been paid or that it is really a note in trust, or make any other

1. He may not impugn the note of indebtedness if it is in any other way detrimental to the creditors.
2. If the note of indebtedness is in the hands of an escrowee, it means that it is independently known that the holder owns the note.
3. If it was independently known to others that that holder holds the note, then beth din does not require the statement of the holder that he owns the note. Thus the holder could not have kept the note concealed.

allegation that will impede the collection of the note. He may not impugn the note even if the debtor joins the holder in stating that the note has been paid. Once the holder no longer has the ability to impugn the note of indebtedness, then his creditors may enforce collection of the note against the debtor.[4] It need not be known at the time that holder makes the statement about the note's unenforcea-bility that he is indebted to the creditor or others; he is not permitted to impugn the note even if it became known subsequently.

If the creditor had warned the debtor not to pay the note, and the debtor subsequently alleges that he paid the note after receiving the warning from the creditor, and the debtor produces a receipt of payment from the holder, then the receipt is disregarded.[5]

The holder may not impugn the note even if he will also lose thereby, such as would be the case if, for example, the note was for $200 and he owes the creditor only $100.

If any of the foregoing criteria is lacking, then the holder may impugn the instrument. Thus, if he has assets to pay his creditor then he may impugn the note, since no one would lose thereby except the holder himself.[6] If the note was not in the hands of an escrowee, and if no one knew of the note's existence, then the holder may impugn the note, since here, too, no one would lose thereby except the holder himself. Since no one, including the holder's creditors, knew of the note, the holder's producing the note and impugning it does not prejudice anyone except the holder himself, since the holder's creditors never knew of the note and thus could not levy on it in any event.[7]

---

4. If the holder has the ability to pay the creditor, then he will be believed, since the creditor could not in any event then proceed against the debtor, and only the holder would stand to lose if the note of indebtedness were to be declared void.

5. It is suspected in such a case that there is collusion between the debtor and the holder.

6. For example, Ruven owes Shimon $100 and gives Shimon a note for that amount. Shimon owes Levi $100, but Shimon has the $100 to pay Levi and pays it to him. Thus Shimon is no longer suspected of impugning the note to defraud Levi, and thus when Shimon now impugns the note, he is the only loser.

7. For example, Ruven owes Shimon $100 and gave Shimon a note of indebtedness for that amount. No one was aware of the note. Shimon owes Levi $100, and Shimon has no assets to pay Levi. As far as Levi is concerned, the $100 due to him from Shimon is uncollectable, since Levi does not know of the existence of the note from Ruven to Shimon. Thus when Shimon produces the note and declares it void, Levi's position has not changed, since even before Shimon produced the note Levi had no hope of recovering the $100 from Shimon.

If after impugning the note the holder pays his indebtedness to the creditor and now has no creditors, he may enforce collection of the note against the debtor if he can show that his desire to discredit the note arose from the claim that the creditor was making against him. But if the holder, without the creditor's pressing him for payment, declared the note to be a note in trust or declared that it was paid, then he can no longer enforce collection of the note against the debtor even if the holder now has no creditors.[8]

## When the holder alleges that the amount of the instrument is less than stated therein

If the holder of an instrument states that the debtor instructed the scribe and witnesses to prepare and sign a note for $1,000 even though the loan was for only $500 because the debtor trusted the holder and was confident that the holder would not collect more than $500, then the instrument is enforceable for $500. If, however, the holder states that the witnesses made an error and wrote "$1,000" instead of "$500," which they were told to write and sign, then the instrument is void. This is true even if the instrument contained a credence clause. Since the instrument is void, the loan is considered an oral loan.[9] Thus, if the debtor denies liability, the debtor may take an *hesseth* oath and be freed from liability. If the debtor admits part of the amount, he may be compelled to take a Torah oath to free himself from liability.[10]

---

8. In such a case, the holder may not even ask beth din to impose a *hesseth* oath on the debtor.

9. See the Glossary regarding the difference between an oral loan and loans evidenced by writings.

10. See Volume III, Chapter 87, regarding oaths.

# Chapter 48

## PRE-PREPARATION
## OF LEGAL FORMS

### INTRODUCTION

Scribes often want to have the opportunity to prepare legal forms before the requesting parties appear before them. It may be that the parties themselves are in a hurry, as would be the case if the lender was about to depart the city and the borrower wished to borrow money from him first. Or, a seller or buyer of realty might be about to depart the city. Or perhaps the witnesses are about to leave and the parties want the instrument prepared in a hurry.

An instrument, whether a deed, or a note of indebtedness, admission, or confession, or a receipt, or a *kethubah*,[1] generally consists of two parts: the *formal* part, which appears in all instruments of the same type, and the *operative* part, which consists of the names of the parties, the date, monetary terms, and any other operative clauses that the parties wish to have in the instrument. This chapter deals with the pre-preparation of the instruments.

The chapter also deals with a note of indebtedness that has been

---

1. A *kethubah* is a document the groom gives to the bride at the wedding ceremony. It contains certain obligations of the husband to the wife, including certain sums of money to be paid to her in the case of divorce or his death.

fully or partially paid. If fully paid, may it be reused? For example, on the morning of January 1, 1991, the lender loaned $100 to the borrower, and a note of indebtedness was written and subscribed by two witnesses and delivered to lender in the presence of two witnesses. In the afternoon of that day, the borrower repaid the $100 and received back the note. Later that day the borrower was once again loaned $100 from the lender. May they use the same note that they used that morning?[2] If the note was partially paid, may the amount repaid be reloaned and the note will now be effective for the full amount? Say, for example, that on the morning of January 1, 1991, the lender loaned $100 to the borrower and a note on indebtedness was written and subscribed by two witnesses and delivered to the lender in the presence of two witnesses. In the afternoon of that date, the borrower repaid the $30 and still owed $70. Later on that date, the borrower borrowed $30 from the lender, so that the total outstanding loan debt from the borrower to the lender is again $100. May the note now be effective for the same $100? In each instance when the note was written and subscribed by the two witnesses and delivered to the lender in the presence of two witnesses, there was a lien effected on the realty of the borrower. Did the repayment or partial repayment deprive the note of its efficacy to re-create a lien on the real estate of the borrower?

## TEXT

### The scribe may pre-prepare the forms of instruments

A scribe may pre-prepare forms of instuments. According to some opinions he may also pre-prepare the operative parts, such as the names of the parties, the monetary amounts, the parcel being

---

2. The same day is given in the example, for if the second loan was on another date, there may be the prohibition of using the old note since it would then be predated, and a predated note may not be used.

conveyed in the case of a deed, and any other operative terms that the parties would like to see contained in the instrument.[3] He need leave only the date blank.[4] Others hold that the scribe may not pre-prepare any of the operative information.[5] The custom of the community should be followed regarding the writing of the operative provisions.

## Reusing an instrument of indebtedness

If an instrument of indebtedness (a note of indebtedness, admission, or confession) was used for one loan and the loan was repaid, it may not be used for another loan even if the parties, amount, and date are the same. The reason is that as soon as the loan was repaid, the lien on the real estate of the borrower originally established by the instrument of indebtedness is released.[6]

If part of the loan has been repaid, the instrument of indebtedness may not be used to reloan the amount that has been repaid.

There are those who hold that if a new *kinyan* was made on the same day as the original loan, then the same note may be used, since the new *kinyan* reestablishes the liens that were released by payment.[7]

---

3. The pre-preparing of the instruments does not appear to the onlooker as a possible fraud, since they are not signed by witnesses.

4. If the scribe predates the instrument, it may void the entire instrument, since a predated note of indebtedness is void. (See Chapter 43.)

5. Those who hold that the scribe may not pre-prepare the operative information fear that he may also pre-prepare in the case of a divorce document (*get*), which is forbidden.

6. Some say that not only does it release the originally established lien, but it does not even permit the lender to employ it to levy on the unsold assets of the borrower, since the instrument is now worthless.

7. The same result would follow if the borrower delivered the note of indebtedness to the lender in the presence of the two subscribing witnesses on the note. If there were no subscribing witnesses on the note, then delivery may be made before any two witnesses to establish the lien on the realty of the borrower.

An instrument in the handwriting of the borrower without any subscribing witnesses may be reused.[8] So may one reuse an instrument that does not contain the name of the lender or payee, but is made payable to the bearer.[9]

---

8. If the instrument was in the handwriting of the debtor and did not have any witnesses thereto, it stands in the same position as an oral loan and creates no lien on the borrower's property. In such a case, the instrument may be refused by the parties, since it subjects only the unsold assets of the debtor to the levy of the lender. But even in this case it may not be delivered by the borrower to the lender in the presence of at least two witnesses, since their presence may establish a lien on the realty of the borrower as against purchasers of the realty, and this reused instrument cannot be used to establish such lien, since its lien was once released. Similarly, if the instrument contains a clause that it establishes no liens on the realty of the borrower, it, too, may be reused.

9. If there were witnesses present when the loan was made, although it is payable to bearer, if the date is prior to the date of the advance by the current holder of the instrument of indebtedness, then it is not valid, since the holder might use it to levy on assets of the borrower with a priority to which he is not entitled. (See Chapter 104 in Volume IV regarding priorities of levies to be made on the unsold assets of the borrower.)

# Chapter 49

---

# WITNESSES MUST RECOGNIZE THE PARTIES

## INTRODUCTION

This chapter deals with the witnesses' recognition of the parties to an instrument. Chapter 46 delineates the laws governing how the names of the witnesses are to be written and how they should sign. This chapter also discusses the names to be inscribed on an instrument.

The name of the person in an instrument must be the exact name of the person intended as the obligor or grantor. Otherwise, there is a risk of fraud. For example, a person may state that he is Ruven, the son of Shimon, and that he is conveying a certain parcel of land to a Levi, the son of Yehuda. He may ask the scribe to draw a deed and then ask persons present in the scribe's office to act as witnesses on the deed. The grantor, in stating that he is Ruven, the son of Shimon, is not telling the truth. Nevertheless, he takes the deed prepared by the scribe and duly witnessed by two witnesses and gives it to Levi, the son of Yehuda, the grantee named in the deed in the presence of two witnesses. Levi commences an action to evict the real Ruven from the land on the strength of the duly witnessed and delivered deed. It may be that Levi knows that Ruven is not the real Ruven, but the beth din judging the eviction has no way of knowing that. Beth din recognizes the signatures of the witnesses and will evict Ruven from the land. To avoid such fraud, the witnesses who sign the instrument must know that the person who is named in the instrument as grantor, donor, or obligor be the person who stands before them and asks them to sign.

A similar situation may arise in the case of a receipt of payment. A person may represent himself as the lender, who now wishes to release the borrower. The scribe and witnesses might then prepare and sign the receipt. It will then be presented to the borrower, who will use it to defend against the claim of the true lender, who was not the person who asked the scribe to write and the witnesses to sign the receipt.

There are occasions on which a person may adopt a name other than the one he was born with, or other than the one people have called him for many years. Or, a person may move to another town where the citizens do not know whether the name he calls himself is really his name. When can they rely on the name he calls himself?

There are many discussions in the Talmud and in the Codes regarding two people in the same community who share the same name. Sometimes the names of the father and/or the family names are the same. How can beth din know which person is the defendant when the defendant alleges that it must be some other person with the same name? Or, the defendant may admit his indebtedness but alleges that it is to the other person in the community who has the same name as the creditor to whom the defendant owes the money. This author suggests that the addresses of the parties be included on the instrument as a way of obviating some of these problems. The discussion of several persons sharing the same name has been included here because it has traditionally been discussed and because confusion can still arise even in our technologically advanced times.

# TEXT

## Knowing the names of the parties

The instrument must name the parties, such as the lender and borrower, the grantor and grantee, or the donor and donee. Before the witnesses sign the instrument, they must be able to identify the parties named in the instrument. They must know the names of the parties so that when a person is sued on the basis of the instrument, the beth din will be able to identify him as the proper obligor, or grantor, or fulfiller of any role that he has under the instrument.

If a person's name is not known independently, and if he has been known in his community by a certain name for at least 30 days, then that is the name that can be put into the instrument.[1] Similarly, if he responds when his name is called out, then it is assumed that this is his correct name.[2]

## Writing the names of the parties in the instrument

If any of the parties has more than one name, one of which he uses more frequently than the other, then it is sufficient if the instrument contains the more frequently used name. Of course, the better practice would be to include both names.[3] The most important thing is to determine whether the party is adequately identified as the obligor or grantor. If there are several persons with the same name, then the father's name, or, nowadays, the family name, could be used.[4] The additional identity of address can also be used, even if there is more than one person of the same name in the community.

## The witnesses must recognize parties named in the instrument

The subscribing witnesses must recognize that the persons standing before them are the persons named in the instrument—in the case of an instrument of indebtedness, that they are the borrower and lender;

---

1. The beth din does not suspect that he intentionally changed his name to confuse the witnesses and beth din and thereby perpetrate a fraud. After 30 days it is assumed that this is the name of the person.

2. This is true even if he has not been in the community for at least 30 days.

3. See Chapter 45 regarding names as contemplated in halachah.

4. Instruments are not similar to bills of divorce, which have their own rules to protect a divorced wife. (See *Shulhan Aruch, Eben haEzer,* Chapter 129.)

in the case of a deed, that they are the grantor and grantee; in the case of a gift, that they are the donor and donee; and in the case of a receipt of payment, that they are the lender and borrower.

The most reliable identification is obtained when the witnesses know the persons standing before them to be the persons who are named in the instrument.

If the subscribing witnesses do not know the identity of the parties to the instrument, then the witnesses may ask others to identify the parties. Two possibilities exist:

1. If the identifiers are two eligible persons, then the subscribing witnesses may rely upon them as correctly identifying the parties and the subscribing witnesses may sign the instrument. If one of the parties thereafter alleges that he was not present when the witnesses signed, and that it was someone else who was erroneously identified by the identifier, he is not believed on his mere word. Neither are the subscribing witnesses believed if they now state that the person alleging not to be the party who was present when they signed was actually not the party who was then present and that they were misled by the identifiers. However, the party named in the instrument who now denies that he was present when the witnesses signed can still prove his allegation, but the burden of proof is on him.[5]

2. If the witnesses do not know the identity of the parties and there are not two eligible witnesses to identify the parties, then the witnesses may rely on one identifier,[6] even if such identifier would have been ineligible to be a witness,[7] unless the ineligibility stems from the fact that the identifier is a transgressor of the law.[8] (a) If the witnesses signed on the basis of one identifier, then the instrument should state that the witnesses did not know the identity of the parties and they were identified by one person. If the instrument so states, then the witnesses can recant and state that the person now in beth

---

5. There is a presumption of regularity that the witnesses would not have signed the instrument unless they had investigated the identity of the parties.

6. The reason that the ineligible witness or one witness only is believed is that the identity of the party can later be verified, and if they were not truthful, this will eventually become known.

7. The ineligible person might be a relative or a woman, neither of whom would be eligible to testify at a trial.

8. The transgressor does not care that his lie will later be discovered.

din who states that he was not present when the witnesses signed is not the person who was identified as the party. (b) If the instrument does not so state, then the witnesses may not now state that they did not properly know the person named in the instrument. However, in this latter situation, if one of the witnesses was a scholar who was so engrossed in his thoughts that he really did not pay attention to the party's identity, then the scholar may recant and state that the person who is now alleging that he was not the same person identified as the party in the instrument is telling the truth; the scholar's statement will then be given effect, even if the other witness contradicts him. Some authorities would limit the circumstances under which a scholar can recant to a situation in which the party was a woman, and thus the scholar would not have paid attention to her. Similarly, if the scribe made an obvious mistake in the instrument, it may be corrected.

## Allegation by defendant regarding authenticity of the instrument

If an instrument is produced in beth din and the defendant alleges that he is not the person named in the instrument and that he owes no debt to anyone, suggesting that perhaps some other person borrowed money and used his name and identification, then his defense is dismissed. Similarly, if he states that he is the person named in the instrument, but that the plaintiff is not the lender named in the instrument, then his defense is dismissed. These rules are based on the presumption that the witnesses would not have signed unless they knew the identity of the parties. It is also presumed that they knew that the parties were adults of sound mind.

## Correcting mistakes in instruments

In Chapter 41 it was stated that if an instrument was lost or destroyed, then the beth din cannot proceed to write another instrument even if the same witnesses appeared and wanted to write the instrument and sign it. However, if there is a mistake in the naming of a party (if, for example the scribe put in the nickname of a party and he was actually known by another nickname), then this error may be corrected by writing another instrument.[9] Similarly, if there was a mistake in the amount of the indebtedness, or if there was a mistake in the writing of the name of a party, then a new instrument may be executed.[10] The new instrument may be executed without even notifying the debtor. There is also an opinion that holds that the lender may sue on the error-containing instrument without going to the trouble of having a corrected instrument written and signed.[11]

## Two persons in the community who share the same name

It has been suggested that an obligation-containing instrument should include the addresses of the parties and, if that is insufficent, an identifying number, such as a passport number. What follows in this section occurs if there is no such definitive identification in the instrument. If there are two persons in the same community with the same name, such as Yosef, the son of Shimon, then neither one can sue the other on an instrument that contains the name Yosef, the son of Shimon, as the debtor and Yosef, the son of Shimon, as the lender.[12] The reason is that the defendant, who is being sued on the instrument, can allege that he was the lender in the instrument and that the Yosef, the son of Shimon, who is now the plaintiff, was actually the borrower in the instrument; thereafter, when the other Yosef repaid the loan, he,

---

9. The new instrument may be executed by the witnesses, and it is not said that they exceeded their authority to sign, since they had already signed and thus their authority to sign had terminated. Their authority lasted until they had correctly completed their task; thus, it terminates only when the instrument is correct.

10. The doubt is not as to the identity of the parties. There was a mistake in not inscribing the name correctly.

11. There will be no likelihood that the plaintiff will be able to obtain a judgment on the incorrect instrument if it is obvious that it contains an error.

12. Ramo states that the reason is that a borrower can ask the scribe and the witnesses to execute a note of indebtedness even if the lender is not present. Thus a person named Yosef, the son of Shimon, will tell the scribe that he is going to borrow money from someone who is also named Yosef, the son of Shimon. In this case the note will name the borrower as Yosef, the son of Shimon, but it will also name the lender as Yosef, the son of Shimon. Thus the person whom the scribe thought was the borrower can attempt to sue the other Yosef on the note, alleging that he is the lender therein.

who is now the defendant, returned the instrument to Yosef, who is now the plaintiff.[13]

If there are two men with the name Yosef, the son of Shimon, in the city, even another lender cannot sue either of the two men, since each can allege that he is not the debtor named in the note. However, if the subscribing witnesses testify that they signed the instrument and that the borrower therein is the defendant, then the defense that the other Yosef was meant will be dismissed. If other witnesses testify that they witnessed the event, then the loan is sustained as an oral loan.[14]

If there are two men with the name Yosef, son of Shimon, in the community, each holding a note naming the defendant whose name is not Yosef as the borrower, and each note naming a Yosef as the lender, each Yosef may sue on his note, and the defendant may not defend against either one on the grounds that the other Yosef is the true lender and the proper party plaintiff.[15] However, if another person sues on the note as the assignee of Yosef, the son of Shimon, the defendant may allege that he is not the proper party, since the assignee did not receive the note from the right Yosef, son of Shimon. If the plaintiff has a power of attorney from a Yosef named as the lender in the instrument, the defendant cannot defend on the basis that the wrong Yosef gave the power of attorney.[16]

If the defendant has a receipt of payment from Yosef, son of Shimon, neither can sue on a note naming Yosef as the lender, since the defendant may plead that the plaintiff who is now suing is the Yosef who executed the receipt. The two Yosefs may then give each other cross powers of attorney, and then the receipt cannot be raised as a defense against both who are suing at the same time under

---

13. The defendant alleges that he was the lender in the instrument and when the borrower by the same name repaid the loan, the defendant returned the instrument to the borrower, who is now the plaintiff, little thinking that the borrower would proceed to sue on the paid note. That was the reason that he did not tear up the note when it was paid. The party who is now the plaintiff alleges that the note never left his hands, since he was the lender.

14. See Chapter 39 for obligations of the debtor under oral loans.

15. There is a presumption that the person who produces the instrument in beth din is the lender or other obligee named therein.

16. In the situation of an assignment, the assignee sues in his own name and thus the borrower can plead that the wrong party made the assignment to the assignee. In the case of a power of attorney, the lawsuit is brought by the attorney-in-fact in the name of the assignor, who is Yosef, son of Shimon.

powers of attorney, since the defendant admitted that he paid only one of them. Even in such a situation, however, the defendant can plead a valid defense by claiming that he insisted on only one receipt of payment because he knew that he could produce the receipt as a complete defense. If the notes were escrowed with a third party, then the defendant must prove the defense of payment beyond the production of the receipt of payment.[17]

---

17. If payment was made on both notes, the borrower should have had the notes released from escrow.

# Chapter 50

## AN INSTRUMENT THAT DOES NOT CARRY THE NAME OF THE OBLIGEE

### INTRODUCTION

Some of the instruments that we have discussed thus far dealt either with notes of indebtedness, notes of admission, or notes of confession. They were subscribed by two witnesses and contained the names of the parties. In an instrument of indebtedness, the names of the lender and the borrower would be included. Also discussed was the promissory note, which is signed by the obligor and does not bear the signatures of two witnesses. The obligor is the person who is obligated to make the payment provided for in the instrument. In the case of a loan, the borrower is the obligor.

This chapter will deal with the situation in which the name of the obligee is not included in the instrument of indebtedness or the promissory note. The obligee is the person to whom the debt is owed. In the case of a loan, the lender is the obligee.

The instrument of indebtedness can state that "I, Ruven, owe money to you" without naming the payee (obligee); it is then signed by two witnesses. Alternatively, the debtor can write "I, Ruven, owe money to you" without having the signatures of two witnesses. Or else the instrument can state "I, Ruven, will pay to you or to bearer." These instruments may be presented for payment by either the original obligee or an assignee of the obligee.[1] If there is a receipt held by the obligor, does that constitute a defense against an instrument that is payable to a bearer thereof? These are the topics discussed in this chapter.

## TEXT

## An instrument of indebtedness that does not name the obligee

Whoever produces an instrument of indebtedness that has been signed by two witnesses and that states "I, Ruven, borrowed from you $100" may collect on the note.[2,3] The holder of the instrument must plead that he is the original holder of the note, and the debtor, Ruven, is precluded from pleading payment.[4,5]

However, since the promissory note does not contain witnesses but is in the handwriting of the obligor, the obligor can defend on the grounds that the plaintiff who produced the note is not the lender named in the note.[6]

---

1. The assignee need not be the original one designated by the obligor. He may be one of many assignees in the chain of ownership of the instrument or promissory note, since many such assignments can be issued. (See Chapter 66.)

2. The production of the instrument by the plaintiff raises a presumption that he is the original obligee; it is not suspected that he merely found the instrument.

3. This type of instrument has the same legal status as a note that recites all of the facts of the loan and was then signed by two witnesses.

4. If the holder of the instrument does not allege that he is the original holder, then he must also produce a written assignment and delivery of the assignment. In an instrument that is marked payable to the bearer, it is not necessary to produce a written assignment with proof of delivery.

5. The two witnesses on the instrument have witnessed the entire transaction, not only the signing of the instrument by the debtor. It is therefore a note of indebtedness in the full sense of the word.

6. The obligor may plead that the plaintiff is not the obligee and that he probably found the promissory note after it was lost by the original obligee. The obligor is believed "since" [migoo] he could have pleaded payment, which would have been a complete defense without having to prove payment. A note of indebtedness that is not signed by witnesses is the equivalent of an oral loan. (See Chapter 39.) The obligor

## A beth din decision that does not name the plaintiff

The result is similar if a person holds a judgment of the beth din that states "Judgment requiring Shimon to pay to the plaintiff the sum of $100." The holder of the judgment can collect on the judgment even though his name does not appear therein.[7]

## An instrument of indebtedness that is payable to lender or to bearer

If an instrument of indebtedness has been signed by two witnesses and states "I, Ruven, borrowed and I am obligated to pay to Shimon or to the bearer hereof the sum of $100," whoever produces it may collect on the instrument. The holder of the note need not plead that he is the original holder of the note and the creditor therein, but he must trace how the note came to him from Shimon.[8] If the note states that the holder need not trace its route into the hands of the bearer, the bearer need not do so.[9] If the note contains a credence clause waiving defenses, then the waiver will be given effect.[10]

---

can plead payment of an oral loan. (See Chapter 69.) He cannot plead that the note was prepared in jest, or that it was prepared as a memorandum rather than as a genuine promissory note. The defense of payment would not be available if the note contained a credence clause that included a waiver of defenses.

7. The defendant in the judgment of the beth din is not permitted to raise a defense of payment. He is also not permitted to plead that the person producing the judgment is not the person meant by the beth din to be the judgment creditor.

8. The holder of the note must plead in general terms how the instrument came into his hands. He may be a holder in due course, or he may be an agent for the original obligee or an assignee thereof. He need not produce a power of attorney to sue on the note in the case described in the text.

9. In order to make his note more transferable, a lender may insist that it contain a credence clause (which may also include a waiver of defenses) stating that the bearer need only produce the note and may sue on it without showing its route into his hands. The person producing the instrument may be a holder or an agent of a holder. This clause or any other clause may be added to instruments, since the parties may agree on any stipulations that are not contrary to law. For example, they may not provide for a loan with payments of interest thereon, since that is illegal.

10. The holder of the instrument need not prove that the loan was actually made,

If any person in the chain of holders of the instrument delivered a receipt of payment to the obligor, then it is not a defense against any person who presents the bearer instrument for payment.[11] If the receipt appears on the note itself, however, it is a complete defense.

---

such as by producing the subscribing witnesses. In fact, the obligor will be liable even if no loan was made to induce the instrument's preparation and delivery.

11. The person who acquired the note can assume that if it had been paid, the obligor would not have left it in the hands of the person to whom he made payment. If the obligor actually paid the bearer note and did not ask for the note to be returned to him, he is permitting a fraud to be perpetrated by the holder on an innocent third-party purchaser and the obligor must pay the third party the amount he paid for the note. The third party will take an oath attesting to the amount he paid for the note, and the obligor will have to pay the third party that amount. If it is well known that the note had been paid, then the person presenting the note may not allege that he is an innocent purchaser for value and require the obligor to pay a second time.

# Chapter 51

## NOTES WITH ONLY ONE SUBSCRIBING WITNESS[1]

### INTRODUCTION

As was stated in many of the previous chapters, an instrument of indebtedness must contain the signatures of at least two eligible witnesses if it is to create a lien on the realty of the obligor. Such an instrument is self-enforcing; the witnesses need not testify as to the event in beth din if there are others, such as the judges or other witnesses, who can recognize the signatures of the subscribing witnesses on the instrument. If an instrument does not contain the signatures of two witnesses, then it does not rise to the level of an instrument of indebtedness that creates a lien on the debtor's realty. It will, however, permit the lender to levy on the unsold property of the debtor.

An instrument that contains the signatures of two witnesses cannot be defended against by stating that the loan did not occur. The law states that if an instrument is delivered to the lender in the presence of at least two eligible witnesses, then it creates a lien on the realty of the borrower.[2]

What if the instrument contains the signature of only one witness?

---

1. An instrument of indebtedness that contains only one subscribing witness or if one of its witnesses is ineligible.
2. There are two opinions in the Talmud on the issue of which witnesses create the

Or, what if there were two witnesses and one of them was ineligible, leaving only one eligible witness?

As will be shown in Volume III, Chapter 87, if the plaintiff, not having an instrument of indebtedness, produces one witness to testify in his favor, then the defendant, upon taking a Torah oath of denial of the claim, will be awarded judgment dismissing the plaintiff's complaint. The same will apply if the plaintiff produces an instrument that contains the signature of one witness: the obligor named therein may take a Torah oath and have the complaint dismissed, because in any case in which two witnesses will cause a judgment to be entered in favor of the plaintiff, one witness will permit the defendant to take a Torah oath and obtain a judgment dismissing the complaint.

# TEXT

## One subscribing witness signs the instrument and another witness testifies orally

If the plaintiff produces in beth din an instrument of indebtedness that contains the signature of one witness, and he also produces another witness who orally testifies that he witnessed the event,[3] then their testimony is combined to be the equivalent of that of two witnesses, and the plaintiff will win the case. There is an opinion, however, that although the defendant cannot deny the loan, he can nevertheless successfully defend on the grounds of payment by taking a hesseth oath.[4,5]

---

lien, the subscribing witnesses on the instrument or the witnesses to the delivery. Very often the subscribing witnesses are also the witnesses to the delivery of the instrument to the holder. It can be assumed that both create the lien, although there is authority that the witnesses to the delivery do not create a lien.

3. There was no kinyan when the witness who testifies orally was appointed. If there was a kinyan made when he was appointed as a witness, then he may act as a subscribing witness at any time and thus the instrument will now have two subscribing witnesses.

4. The reason is that according to this opinion, the loan remains an oral loan and therefore could have been paid without the need for witnesses to be present. (See Chapter 69.)

5. Oaths are discussed in Volume III, Chapter 87.

If there was a *kinyan* made with the second witness,[6] then he can be included as a witness on the instrument, which then becomes similar to an instrument with two signatures in that the defendant cannot plead payment.[7] The lender could have chosen to ask the nonsigning witness to sign because a *kinyan* had been made with the debtor, and the instrument would then have risen to the level of an instrument of indebtedness. Since the lender did not make this demand on the nonsigning witness, the loan still consists of one witness on the instrument and one witness by way of *kinyan*. If the *kinyan* was made in the presence of the witness who signed the instrument, it is equivalent to an instrument containing the signatures of two witnesses and rises to the level of an instrument of indebtedness; it can thus be enforced against purchasers of the debtor's realty. If the witness who did not sign the instrument testified that he was also present when the instrument was delivered to the plaintiff, then the note acquires the power of an instrument of indebtedness that has been signed by two witnesses.[8]

If two witnesses signed the instrument but each signed in the absence of the other, and if the lender did not notify the first witness

---

6. If there was a *kinyan* made with the debtor at the time the loan was made, and if there were witnesses present when the loan was made, then the lender has the authority to demand that the witnesses who were present write a note of indebtedness and then sign it. In this case, since one witness had already signed the instrument, the witness who did not sign the instrument but with whom the debtor made a *kinyan* may now also sign the instrument on the plaintiff's demand. There are thus two witnesses on the note. *Kinyan* is discussed in Chapter 195.

7. Since the second witness is still not a subscribing witness, it is not altogether similar to an instrument of indebtedness in that it cannot be enforced against purchasers of the debtor's realty.

8. It then serves as a lien on the realty of the debtor. The reason is that if there are two witnesses to the delivery of the instrument to the lender, the instrument causes a lien on the debtor's realty. The assumption is that if the witness who did not sign the instrument witnessed the delivery, then the witness who did sign the instrument was also present when the instrument was delivered, and thus there are two witnesses to the delivery of the instrument and a lien is effected on the realty of the debtor. The witness who signed the instrument may state that he did not witness the delivery; in that case, the instrument is not the same as an instrument of indebtedness that permits a lien on the debtor's realty, but it may be used to enforce collection against the debtor.

that the other would sign,[9] then the instrument does not permit the lender to enforce collection from purchasers of the debtor's realty. The same would be true if each of the witnesses made the *kinyan* with the debtor in the absence of the other and without the knowledge that the *kinyan* was made with the other. The reason for this is that the report of the *kinyan* did not become public knowledge. But if each witness notified the other that he was going to sign, or that the debtor would make a *kinyan* with the other witness, then the note rises to the level of an instrument of indebtedness, and the lender may enforce collection from the purchasers of the debtor's realty because the report of the loan will become public knowledge. In any of these cases the debtor may not allege payment, since he knew that there were two witnesses, and he should not have paid until the instrument was returned to him or until he had a receipt of payment.[10]

## An instrument of indebtedness with only one witness's signature

If the plaintiff produces an instrument of indebtedness that is inscribed with the signature of only one witness, and if the defendant denies having made the loan, then the defendant may swear a Torah oath and be acquitted of liability. This would apply even if the instrument of indebtedness contained a credence clause stating that the debtor had waived his rights to contest the instrument.[11] However, if in response to the production of the instrument containing the signature of only one witness the defendant admits having made the loan but his defense is payment, then the defendant may take a *hesseth* oath and

9. When the second witness signed, he would, of course, see the signature of the first witness.

10. In the case of the two witnesses making a *kinyan* with the debtor, he knows that the possibility exists that the lender may ask them to execute a note of indebtedness and sign the note as witnesses. He thus should have protected himself and requested a receipt of payment if the note was not yet written; if the note was written, then he should have either had the note returned or obtained a receipt of payment—this in spite of the fact that neither of the witnesses knew that the other witness had also made a *kinyan* with the debtor.

11. Since the debtor contests the validity of the note of indebtedness, then the credence clause is also part of the instrument that is being contested.

win the case. If a witness testifies that he knows that the loan was not paid, then the defendant may take a Torah oath and win the case.[12] There is another opinion that the defense will be dismissed,[13] but that the defendant may demand that the plaintiff take an oath that he has not been paid.[14]

## An instrument containing the signature of one ineligible witness

If one of the witnesses on an instrument containing only two witnesses is found to be ineligible, one opinion holds that the instrument is worthless, even if it was delivered to the lender in the

---

12. The reason for the Torah oath is that the defendant directly contradicts the testimony of the one witness. (See Chapter 87.) When the defendant directly contradicts the testimony of one witness, whether he is a subscribing witness or a witness who testifies orally that he witnessed the loan, if the defendant denies making the loan, he takes a Torah oath of denial. Thus if one witness says that the loan was made, and the defendant says that no loan was made, the defendant may take a Torah oath of denial to win the case dismissing the plaintiff's complaint. However, if the defendant does not deny making the loan, and thus does not contradict the witness, but rather raises a defense of payment, then the defendant need not take a Torah oath. He may take a *hesseth* oath and win the case. If the plaintiff produces one witness who testifies that the defendant did not repay the loan, and if the defendant pleads payment, then the defendant is directly contradicting the witness, and the defendant may take a Torah oath of denial to win the case.

13. The debtor should have taken an oath to contradict the instrument that contained the signature of one witness. However, in the case discussed in the text, the witness testifies that the loan was made. The debtor does not deny taking the loan and pleads payment. A defendant's oath against one witness applies only if the defendant is going to contradict the witness. If the defendant cannot contradict the witness, he does not swear. Since he cannot swear, he has to prove this statement. This statement of the law follows the opinion of Rambam, who holds that if the instrument of indebtedness was paid, the debtor should have received it back from the lender. However, Rambam also holds that in the case of a promissory note signed only by the debtor and with no other witnesses' signatures, the debtor may defend on the grounds of payment, for here the debtor is less careful about having his promissory note returned by the lender.

14. The defendant can demand that the plaintiff take the oath even if the instrument of indebtedness contained a waiver clause stating that the plaintiff could proceed to judgment upon production of the instrument by stating that it was not paid.

presence of two witnesses. This opinion holds that the defendant need not even take an oath to bolster his plea that the instrument is void.[15] The other opinion holds that if the two witnesses did not intend to be joined as witnesses at the time they signed, the instrument still has the validity af an instrument subscribed with one valid signature. The foregoing is true unless it can be proven that the lender wanted the ineligible person to be a witness. According to this latter opinion, the instrument has the effectiveness of any instrument with only one subscribing witness (in other words, that of an oral loan), and the defendant may take a *hesseth* oath and obtain judgment dismissing the complaint. If another person who witnessed the loan joins with the eligible witness to testify as to the loan, then, based on the oral testimony of both, it will become a valid oral loan with two oral witnesses.[16]

If an instrument was inscribed with the signatures of more than two witnesses, and one of them was ineligible, and neither is available to be questioned, then the instrument is void as long as there is conclusive testimony that all of the witnesses intended to be joined as witnesses. If there is no convincing proof that they intended to be joined as witnesses, then the instrument will be authenticated on the strength of the signatures of the eligible witnesses on the instrument, as it can be said that only the eligible persons signed as witnesses, while ineligible persons signed to fill in the space between the text of the instrument and the signatures of the eligible witnesses.[17]

On any instrument, including a will, on which one of the witnesses was ineligible, if the eligible witness remembers the event, then he can

---

15. The eligible witness on the instrument gives less effect to the instrument than would be the case had he been the only witness on the instrument. The ineligible witness reduces the effectiveness of the eligible witness.

16. See Chapter 39, wherein it states that there are circumstances under which the witnesses need not be specifically designated to be witnesses.

17. See Chapter 45, which discusses the laws governing situations in which there is more than one witness on an instrument and some of them are ineligible. If all of them intended to be witnesses, then they are all bound together in their testimony and become sort of joint witnesses. See also Volume I, Chapter 36, where it is shown that if the testimony of one witness is void, then the testimonies of all other persons who participated with him as witnesses are also void. Thus, if the eligible witness signed before the ineligible witness, then the note is void because the theory of leaving space does not apply.

testify as to what occurred, and if there is another eligible person who was also present but was not designated to be a witness,[18] then their testimony can be combined.

If a person, by will or any other instrument, leaves or disposes of all his possessions to Ruven and Shimon, and if one or more of the witnesses on the will was related to either Ruven or Shimon, then the will is not valid.[19] There is an opinion, however, that if the beneficiary to whom the witness was related renounces his inheritance, then the will is valid.[20] If the will was not reduced to writing, then the witnesses can testify on behalf of the beneficiary who is not related to the witnesses. If the testator in a written will made specific bequests to Ruven and Shimon, and if one of the witnesses was related to either beneficiary, then the bequest to the remaining beneficiary will stand.[21] The result would be similar if part of a will was not enforceable; the balance would be given effect.

## Witnesses to the delivery of an instrument

If an instrument of indebtedness was delivered to the lender in the presence of two witnesses, then the instrument acts as a lien on the realty owned by the debtor at the time the instrument was delivered,[22] even if the instrument does not bear the signatures of any subscribing witnesses. However, if there were witnesses on the instrument of indebtedness and one or more were ineligible, then the instrument is void, even if it was delivered in the presence of two eligible witnesses, since the instrument contains an inherent defect.[23]

---

18. If he too was designated, then he may be disqualified on the grounds that he is a joint witness with an ineligible witness.

19. The witnesses are considered to have testified to a single event, the elements of which cannot be separated.

20. There is an opinion that the renunciation had to take place before the writing of the will. See Volume I, Chapter 37, regarding renunciation of beneficiaries.

21. Since there are specific bequests, each bequest is treated as a separate will even though they are all in the same instrument.

22. Some authorities hold that even if there are witnesses to the delivery of the instrument of indebtedness, this fact does not raise the note to one that effects a lien on the realty of the debtor.

23. The witnesses to the delivery of the instrument may still testify as to the event.

# Chapter 52

# INSTRUMENTS WITH INTEREST PROVISIONS TORN INSTRUMENTS

## INTRODUCTION

It is prohibited by Torah law for one Jew to charge interest to another Jew.[1] This is so axiomatic that the laws of the prohibition against taking interest do not even appear in the code of jurisprudence, *Shulhan Aruch, Hoshen haMishpat*. Instead, the laws of interest appear in *Shulhan Aruch, Yoreh De' ah*, which concerns itself with ritually prohibited actions and things. Therefore, if an instrument of indebtedness contains a clause stating interest, the loan is considered tainted.

This chapter discusses the extent to which the loan is tainted. Does it void only the interest, or does it void the entire loan including the interest? If it voids the entire loan, then the borrower would be left unjustly enriched by the transaction. It should be noted that every person who participates in a usurious loan is a transgressor. This includes the lender, the borrower, the guarantor, the loan broker, the scribe, and the witnesses. The amount of the interest is not important: any amount is prohibited.

An interest-containing transaction is void insofar as it relates to the interest and valid insofar as it relates to the principal. The sole question relating to the principal is whether the instrument is valid.

---

1. See Leviticus 25:37 and Deuteronomy 23:20.

Since the witnesses to a usurious transaction are transgressors, the instrument is subscribed by transgressors and is thus void.

Also discussed in this chapter is the subject of the instrument that is partially or completely torn or blurred. Chapter 41 contained a discussion of instruments that are decayed or obliterated. Many of the laws are similar. The concern when an instrument is partially torn is that it may have been torn because it has been paid and the lender therefore neglected to take care of it. If the validity of such an instrument is reinstated, it may subject the borrower to paying the same indebtedness twice.

## TEXT

### Instruments of indebtedness that contain interest provisions

If an instrument of indebtedness contains a provision for a specific amount of interest, then the interest may not be collected but the principal may be collected, even from purchasers of realty of the borrower.[2] There are some who hold that the entire instrument is void and even the principal may not be collected with this instrument.[3]

If the interest is not separately designated but is lumped together as one amount, including principal and interest, and the entire sum is labeled as principal, then the witnesses, if they are aware of this, become ineligible and the entire instrument is void. This holds even

---

2. The instrument is not automatically voided because the witnesses have transgressed by signing an instrument that contains an interest provision. The witnesses may not have realized that they have transgressed, since most people believe that only the lender, and perhaps the borrower, has transgressed. Furthermore, the witnesses may assume that the beth din will not enforce the interest provisions of the instrument because it is specifically designated as interest, but that beth din will enforce the repayment of principal.

3. This opinion holds that the entire instrument is void. The witnesses' transgression renders them ineligible, and their signatures must be disregarded; thus there is no longer an instrument. It seems to this author that if there are other witnesses who observed the transaction, or if the borrower admitted the transaction to others and designated them to be witnesses of admission, then the lender should be able to enforce collection of the principal as an oral loan.

according to the first view in the preceding paragraph.[4] If the witnesses were not aware that the lump sum in the instrument included interest as well as principal,[5] and the lender amended the instrument before the instrument was presented to beth din to provide that he will not collect that part of the instrument that represents interest, then the lender will be permitted to collect the principal of the instrument even from purchasers of the realty of the borrower. If the instrument was presented to beth din without the lender so writing, then the instrument is void and the loan is relegated to the status of an oral loan, enforceable if the borrower admits the loan or if the witnesses on the instrument or different witnesses testify as to the event.[6] There is an opinion that the entire loan is void and the lender may not recover anything.[7] The first opinion seems to be the more widely followed. According to all opinions, if it was the lender's agent who carried out the usurious transaction, then the principal must be repaid, since an agent is assumed to do things that are beneficial for the lender.[8]

## A torn instrument of indebtedness

If a torn instrument was produced in beth din and the lender pleads that it became torn by itself, and if it appears to the judges that it was

---

4. Since the interest is not separately labeled as such, it is possible that the instrument will be enforced in its entirety, including the interest. If the interest was separately labeled, the assumption is that the beth din will not permit it to be collected.

5. The witnesses would not be aware of the interest in the loan if the lender and borrower both conspired to deceive the witnesses by telling them that the amount stated in the loan was all principal.

6. Since the witnesses were unaware that the loan was usurious, then the instrument is not void for failure to have eligible witnesses. It may be void because the interest and principal are lumped together and designated as principal. If the lender remedies this before presenting the instrument to beth din, then the instrument no longer contains any flaws. If the lender fails to remedy this flaw before presenting the instrument to beth din, then he has presented a flawed instrument.

7. This opinion permits the borrower, who is equally guilty of transgressing the injunction against interest, to be unjustly enriched. The justification given is that it will prevent the lender from doing the same thing again because there are many hard-pressed borrowers who will borrow on interest if there are unscrupulous lenders who will not make a loan without interest.

8. This would apply even if the lender had instructed the agent to lend the money on interest, since the lender could claim that he intended that the interest should be separately stated and thus the principal of the loan could be collected.

torn along the creases or because it was in storage for a long time or because it was roughly handled, then the instrument will be admitted as valid. This is the case even if the crease was along one of the lines containing the operative clauses of the instrument, such as the names of the parties, or the amount of the instrument, or the date, or the signatures of the witnessess. It is up to beth din to decide whether the instrument just happened to be torn in any of these areas or was torn there deliberately because it had been paid and a prior beth din had intentionally torn the instruments in these areas. If the tear was intentional, then it does not matter what part of the instrument was torn, because the assumption is that it was torn because it had been paid. Many of the laws relating to obliterated instruments described in Chapter 41 apply to torn instruments. If the tear was in the form part of the instrument, then it is not void. Upon application from the lender, beth din may rewrite the torn instrument if beth din believes that it is still valid.

If an instrument is partially obliterated or blotted out, but the letters are still recognizable, then the instrument is valid. If the letters are not recognizable, then the instrument is void unless the lender produces witnesses who satisfactorily explain why the instrument is obliterated or blurred. If beth din can discern the letters but fears that after some time it will become impossible to do so, then beth din may write a new instrument according to the laws stated in Chapter 41.

An instrument that has rotted or is riddled with holes is still valid. Similarly, if the instrument has been partially destroyed by fire or insects or rodents but the operative parts of the instrument can be discerned, then the instrument is valid. However, it should be well examined by the judges of the beth din, as should a very old instrument.[9]

---

9. The question arises of why a lender should permit an instrument to remain unpaid for a protracted period. The length of time and/or the physical condition of the instrument testify to the fact that the lender did not take proper care of the instrument because it was paid.

# Chapter 53

# PROHIBITION AGAINST EXCHANGING INSTRUMENTS OF INDEBTEDNESS

## INTRODUCTION

This chapter discusses the situation in which, for whatever reason, the lender or the borrower wishes to exchange the instrument of indebtedness for another note or for two or more other notes. Perhaps, for example, the lender holds one note for $100 and will find it easier to sell two $50 notes than one $100 note. Or, perhaps the borrower wishes to repay $20 of a $100 note and wishes to cancel the $100 note and have an $80 written note in its place.

## TEXT

### Prohibition against exchanging instruments of indebtedness

If a lender holds a note for $100, the lender may not request that the note be exchanged for two $50 notes; conversely, if the lender holds two $50 notes, he may not request that they be exchanged for one

$100 note without the permission of the borrower.[1, 2] This applies even if it is known that the original notes were not paid.[3] This would also apply even if $50 of the $100 is unpaid and the lender surrenders his $100 note and authorizes that it be torn and one note for $50 be issued in its place. In cases of partial payment, the better practice would be for the note to reflect in its margin that part has been paid. The date of payment should be included.

## Substituting an instrument of indebtedness collectible in Gentile courts

If the lender demands that the beth din compel the borrower to execute the type of note that can be enforced in the Gentile courts, then beth din should determine whether the borrower is likely to

---

1. There are times when the lender may need money and will be satisfied to collect only $50 or to sue for only $50 if he holds two $50 notes instead of having to sue on one note that he holds in the sum of $100. The lender will not want to collect part of a note because when he comes to beth din to sue on the note and he admits that part has been paid, he may be compelled to take an oath if the borrower so demands.

2. If the borrower agrees, then the notes may be exchanged. The new note should be dated with the date on the original note, and beth din should authenticate the new note. Beth din need not fear that there is a conspiracy between the lender and borrower to defraud purchasers of the borrower's realty. They need not fear that the loan has been repaid and that the parties fraudulently want to revive the instrument to perpetrate a fraud on purchasers from the borrower. If the note is written by the original witnesses rather than by the beth din, then the date should be that of the substitute note or notes.

3. The reason for not exchanging two $50 notes for one $100 note is that each exchange adversely affects the borrower. If the lender is holding two notes for $50 each and the borrower wishes to pay off $50, he will receive one of the two notes in return. If the notes were combined to make a note of $100, then when the borrower paid $50 he would not get a note in return but only a receipt, which he would be obligated to keep safely in case the lender sued for the full $100 on the note. If the lender could exchange the $100 note for two $50 notes, the borrower again might be adversely affected. For example, if the lender should have been paid $50 on the $100 note, and the lender should have given a $50 receipt to the borrower and retained the note in his own hands, there would be nothing to prevent the lender from suing on a $50 note and claiming that the borrower's receipt refers only to payment against a $100 note, and not to either of the $50 notes.

disregard the decision of the beth din compelling him to pay.[4] If beth din has no such fears, then it will not comply with the lender's request in this respect.

There are times when such a note may be written even if the borrower intends to heed the decision of the beth din. Such would be the case if, for example, the borrower has many creditors and they will all sue in the Gentile courts except for one who would prefer to sue in beth din. He may be at a disadvantage if all of the other creditors obtain judgments in the Gentile courts and levy on such judgments so that by the time the lender wants to collect on his beth din judgment there is nothing left in the hands of the borrower on which to levy. The beth din must judge each case on its merits.

---

4. Beth din must write the notes in such a way as to protect the borrower against the possibility that the lender may attempt to collect on both notes, one before beth din and the other in the Gentile courts. The first note should state that a second note was also drawn, in the event that the lender wishes to sue in a Gentile court if the borrower will not heed the decision of the beth din.

# Chapter 54

# WRITING RECEIPTS OF PAYMENT

## INTRODUCTION

Until now we have been discussing instruments of indebtedness evidencing the loans (notes of indebtedness, admission, and the note of confession). This chapter deals with the receipt to be given to the borrower who has made payment or partial payment. As was noted in Chapter 53, there are cogent reasons that it is not the policy of the beth din to provide for exchange instruments to reflect partial payment. Instruments may be fully or partially paid on, before, or even after the due date. The time of payment may affect the type of receipt of payment to be given. Will the receipt be endorsed on the original instrument, or will there be a separate receipt? Who has the option to ask for a separate receipt, the debtor or the creditor? Can the debtor ask to have the original instrument returned to him in lieu of a receipt, or, conversely, can the creditor insist upon giving a receipt and retaining the original instrument? Can beth din write a new instrument? What are the powers of beth din in this matter?

## TEXT

### Option to give a receipt or write a new instrument

If the time for payment of the loan has arrived and the debtor has repaid only part of it, then the lender has the option of asking beth din to write a new instrument of indebtedness for the balance of the debt as of the date of the original instrument and to destroy the original instrument of indebtedness, or the lender may write a receipt on a separate piece of paper. The debtor has no option to choose which of these methods he desires, nor to insist that the receipt be endorsed on the original instrument.[1,2]

If the instrument of indebtedness provided for partial payments, then if the borrower made timely partial payments, he may insist that the payments be endorsed on the instrument of indebtedness or that the instrument be exchanged.[3]

In those cases in which either the lender or the debtor may insist that a new instrument of indebtedness be written, only beth din may write a new instrument as of the date of the original instrument; or, beth din may instruct the original witnesses to write such an instrument. The witnesses may not on their own write a new instrument as of the date of the original instrument, even if both the lender and the borrower agree.[4] However, if both parties agree and if a *kinyan* was made in the writing of the original instrument, the witnesses may write a new instrument dated with the date on which a partial payment was made. If both parties do not agree, then the witnesses may not write a new instrument, since their authority to do so terminated when they wrote the first instrument.

There is a difference of opinion as to whether the responsibility for paying the scribe to draw the receipt rests with the lender or the borrower.[5] If the lender does not have the instrument of indebtedness

---

1. The debtor has no option, although he may legitimately fear that if the instrument of indebtedness remains intact and the receipt given to him by the lender is misplaced, the lender may be able to collect a second time on the same instrument of indebtedness.

2. The debtor's lack of option will accelerate his desire to repay the past-due loan.

3. Timely payments should not prejudice the borrower and put him in danger of having to pay the debt a second time if the receipt is lost.

4. Since part of the loan has been repaid, if the witnesses were to write another instrument dated as of the original date, it would appear to be a predated loan, which might invalidate the note. See Chapter 43.

5. The opinion that holds that it is the lender's responsibility states that it is to the benefit of the lender not to have to mark up his instrument; thus he benefits by the receipt. The other opinion holds that if the debtor paid the entire debt, then there would be no need for a receipt, since he could receive the instrument in return for the payment.

to return and thus a receipt has to be written, he would have to pay the scribe. On the other hand, if the loan was an oral one and the borrower wants a receipt of payment, he would have to pay the cost of the scribe. In such a case, if the lender says he does not want to have a receipt written, then none is written, unless the situation calls for a receipt. For example, a receipt should be written if at the time the oral loan was made the lender instructed the borrower not to repay the loan unless there were witnesses present and the lender is now accepting payment without requiring the presence of witnesses.

## The writing of the receipt

The receipt should refer to the original loan, including the date in the instrument of indebtedness if it is remembered, the name of the lender who is receiving the payment, the amount he received, and the amount of the balance of the loan, if any. If any of these items are not remembered and the original instrument of indebtedness is not available, then, in situations in which the loan was made with an instrument, the receipt may just state that the lender received from the borrower a certain sum on a certain date.[6] Even if the dates of the original instrument are known, the receipt may not be predated or postdated.[7] If the witnesses are instructed to write a general release to

---

6. If the loan was accompanied by the writing of an instrument and the date of the instrument is not remembered when the receipt is being written, then the receipt should not refer to the date of the loan, since the date in the instrument might have been a later one. Thus, if the borrower defends on the basis of the receipt and the date thereon does not match the date on the instrument, the lender can allege that the receipt refers to another loan. In cases in which the time of the loan or of the instrument of indebtedness is not known, no date should be inserted into the receipt, since conceivably the witnesses may have delayed in writing the instrument of indebtedness until some time after the loan was paid and there was a receipt in the hands of the borrower. In such cases, since the date of the receipt will predate that of the instrument, the lender can allege that the receipt does not refer to the loan mentioned in the instrument. If the receipt does not contain a date because of the reasons stated here, then the lender should not lend money to the borrower in that same sum because there is the danger that the receipt might be presented as a defense against such later loan.

7. This may not be done without the authorization of the lender. The reason is that unbeknownst to the witnesses to payment, who will witness the receipt, the lender

the borrower, it must not be postdated because new obligations could arise between the date on which the release is given and the date in the postdated release. A predated general release may, however, be given.[8]

## Receipts acting as general releases

A receipt that simply states that "borrower paid lender" acts as a release of all debts due from borrower to debtor as of the date of the receipt.

If the borrower produces witnesses to testify that the lender has an instrument of indebtedness in his possession that has been paid, and for some reason the instrument was left in the possession of the lender, and it is this instrument that is the basis of the lawsuit by the lender, and the lender alleges that another debt is the one that was paid, then judgment will be rendered in favor of the borrower unless the lender can prove that the debt that was paid was another debt. If the lender sues on two separate instruments and the facts are the same as just stated, then the defense will be permitted to be applied to the greater of the two instruments.[9]

If the receipt notes *dollars* and does not state how many, then it acts as a general release of all moneys due from the borrower to the lender.[10] However, if there was a sum written in the receipt but it was

---

had made another loan to the borrower and the date of the other loan happened to be the date of the misdated receipt.

8. In such a case, it is the borrower who must protect himself because he may have borrowed money after the date of the predated release and before the date on which repayment was actually made.

9. It will be assumed that the larger instrument was paid, since the holder of the instrument under these circumstances stands in an inferior position.

10. This is not similar to the situation in which an instrument that says "dollars" will be construed to be the smallest amount in the plural, and would thus be held to be for only $2. The reason is that the instrument that is to be used to take money from another person, in this case the borrower, is construed against the holder who had it drafted. (See Chapter 42.) In the case of the receipt, however, where it is not to be used as a method of obtaining money in litigation, but rather as a defense, it can be said that perhaps the witnesses who drew the receipt did not know the exact amount of the debt and thus wanted to combine all outstanding indebtedness because they were not told that some debt still existed.

erased, then the sum will be construed as being the least possible sum in which the receipt can be construed.[11]

## Receipts in cases in which the instrument of indebtedness is lost

If the lender alleges that he lost the instrument of indebtedness, the borrower cannot insist that he will not pay until the instrument is produced. At the lender's request, a receipt will be prepared and the loan repaid.[12]

If the lender alleges that the instrument is not readily available but that he will furnish it, and the beth din verifies that the lender needs the proceeds of the repayment, then they will order the borrower to make repayment, ruling that he should accept a receipt and that the lender should post some sort of guarantee that he will return the instrument to the borrower by a specified time. But if beth din suspects that the instrument is in fact accessible and the lender just does not want to return it to the borrower but prefers to have a receipt given to the borrower, then the borrower need not repay the loan until the instrument has been returned to him. This applies even if the borrower took an oath to repay the loan by the date when he demands the receipt.[13]

## The return of the instrument precedes repayment

If the lender demands that he be repaid before he will return the instrument to the borrower, and the borrower demands that the

---

11. Whenever a party produces a writing that contains erasures, it will be construed against him.

12. The borrower can invoke a ban on all those who claim that the instruments that they hold on him are misplaced. However, the borrower cannot insist that the lender take an oath that the instrument is lost, since the borrower does not know for sure that the instrument is not misplaced and can allege only that he believes that the lender is not telling the truth. But if the borrower alleges that he is certain that the lender has the instrument in his possession and is suppressing it, then the lender will have to take a *hesseth* oath that it was lost. If the lender is not able to take the oath immediately, then the loan must nevertheless be repaid. The borrower will receive a receipt, and the oath can be taken at some later date.

13. Beth din will release the borrower from his oath, since it is certain that he assumed that when he made the oath he would be given the instrument in return for repayment.

instrument be returned first and then the repayment will be made, beth din will heed the request of the borrower. He can refuse to pay even if the lender agrees to place the instrument in escrow until payment is made. If beth din finds that the lender is justified in wanting to have the instrument escrowed until repayment is made, they will order this procedure to be followed.[14]

## Request for receipt when making partial payment and contesting the balance of the claim

Say, for example, that the lender holds an instrument for $100. The borrower admits that he owes $60, which he wants to pay, and he claims that he has a defense to the remaining $40. The lender demands that borrower pay the uncontested $60 and states that he will provide a receipt for that $60; as for the remaining $40, the lender states that he will produce evidence after some time. The borrower replies that he will not pay until the instrument is returned to him, or until the lender produces his evidence for the remaining $40. It is up to beth din to determine whether the lender is in a position to produce his evidence at once. If he can, then the borrower's demands will be followed. But if beth din ascertains that the lender is not able to produce such evidence at once, or if beth din has to take the case regarding the remaining $40 under advisement to deliberate, then the borrower is ordered to pay the $60 that he admits owing and to obtain a receipt from the lender. Upon the borrower's demand, the receipt will be endorsed on the original instrument.

## An instrument of indebtedness that states it is effective until the beth din tears it

Even if an instrument of indebtedness states thereon that it will be effective until it is torn by the beth din or until a receipt is endorsed thereon, if the borrower produces a receipt it will cancel the instrument.[15] But if the instrument states that it can be cancelled only

---

14. The borrower is not prejudiced by this procedure.

15. Although an instrument states that it must be cancelled only if torn by the beth din or by having the receipt endorsed thereon, the intent includes that the instrument can be cancelled by a receipt even separate from the note.

by endorsing the receipt on the instrument, then it will not be deemed cancelled until the receipt is endorsed on the instrument itself.[16]

## A receipt given in error

If the lender delivered a receipt to the borrower, and it was later found that a mistake had been made in calculating the amount due on the instrument, or in the amount paid, or in any similar provision, then the receipt is void even if a *kinyan* was made, since a *kinyan* made in error is not binding.[17]

---

16. This follows the general principle that the parties may stipulate any conditions that they agree to in monetary matters.

17. See Chapter 195 for types of *kinyan*.

# Chapter 55

## PARTIAL PAYMENT AND ESCROWING INSTRUMENTS

### INTRODUCTION

A person may make certain promises or commitments in the hope that he will never have to keep them. As will be seen in Chapter 207, halachah will ordinarily not enforce such promises or commitments. This unenforceable promise or commitment is known as *asmachta*. There are certain exceptions. For example, even if a surety or guarantor hopes that he will not be called upon to keep his commitment, it is nevertheless binding. The basic difference seems to be that in the case of *asmachta*, the promisor does not believe that the time can possibly come where he will have to keep his commitment. He is certain that the conditions of his commitment will never be fulfilled. The guarantor, on the other hand, would prefer to avoid keeping his commitment by having the debtor pay his own debt, but he realizes that it is possible that he may be called upon to perform.

The commitment discussed in this chapter is of the type that the promisor does not imagine he will ever have to keep. However, if he realizes that he may someday have to keep the commitment, then the commitment is binding on the promisor.

Say, for example, that the borrower has an instrument of indebtedness that is due, and he does not have enough money to repay the loan in full. He wishes to persuade the lender not to commence a lawsuit against him by offering the lender a proposal. He will make a partial repayment of the debt; he will repay $20 on a $100 loan. He authorizes the lender to escrow the instrument of indebtedness with a third-party escrowee, with the agreement that if the $80 balance is not paid by a date certain, then the escrowee will return the instrument to the lender, who will then be able to sue for the face of the instrument, which is $100. Under the rules of *asmachta*, such a promise should not be binding, since the borrower would not make such a proposal unless he was sure that he would pay the $80 balance on time; thus he does not have the requisite intent to bind himself to this promise.

The question of interest will also arise, since if the lender reacquires the instrument from the escrowee, he will sue for $100 and thereby obtain a gain of $20.

# TEXT

## The escrowing of the instrument of indebtedness

A borrower has made partial payment of an instrument of indebtedness. He then authorizes the lender to deposit the instrument with an escrowee, with the agreement that if the borrower fails to pay the balance due by a certain date, then the escrowee will return the instrument intact to the lender. However, if the instrument is paid by the agreed-upon date, then the escrowee will return the instrument to the borrower. If the instrument is not paid by the established date, then the escrowee may not return the instrument to the lender, since this is an *asmachta*.[1]

However, if it can be proved that the borrower really intended to be bound by this arrangement, then he may be bound. Such would be the case, for example, if the borrower made the arrangement in a special beth din composed of experts in the law who explained to him all of the ramifications of what his actions and the losses he might

---

1. It is assumed that the borrower would not have permitted the lender to obtain a windfall of the moneys already paid on the instrument unless he was absolutely sure that the situation would never come to pass wherein he would have to pay the entire amount of the instrument and would thus also lose the monies he had already repaid.

incur, and he consented and manifested the assent by a *kinyan*, and he also escrowed whatever rights he might have in the instrument of indebtedness. The beth din experts must explain to him that the money that he theretofore paid to the lender is considered a gift as of the time of the escrowing of the instrument if the balance is not paid.[2] If the borrower still consents and if all of these conditions have been met, then the escrow arrangement is binding on the borrower.

If the borrower fails to make the balance of the payment at the time indicated, then the escrowee will turn the instrument over to the lender. If the borrower or the lender had deposited with the escrowee a receipt for the amount that had been paid, then the escrowee will also return the receipt to the lender.[3]

If the borrower was prevented from making a timely payment by an unforeseeable act of God, then his nonperformance will be excused.[4]

The additional money that the lender may collect if he is able to collect the full amount of the instrument in addition to that which he collected as partial payment is not considered interest. The reason is that if the borrower were to pay on the promised date, he would pay

---

2. The amount paid must be considered a gift from the time the partial repayment was made; otherwise it would impair the instrument that the lender is holding to the extent to which repayment was made. The lender would not be able to levy on the purchasers of the borrower's realty except to the extent of the unpaid amount—that is, the entire amount of the loan less the part that was repaid. Most opinions permit the lender to collect the unpaid balance even from the purchasers of the realty of the borrower and permit the lender to collect the full balance from the borrower. There is even an opinion that if the money paid is not a gift, then the entire instrument may not be used to levy against the purchasers of realty from the borrower, and that he may collect from the borrower only the unpaid balance.

3. If the receipt was treated separately from the instrument and the borrower held on to the receipt and did not deposit it with the escrowee, and if the borrower did not pay the balance by the date certain, then the lender would receive the instrument from the escrowee. However, the borrower would still have the receipt, and thus the entire procedure would be in vain as far as the lender is concerned.

4. If it is a situation that might be anticipated, then a stipulation providing for such a contingency should have been attached to the escrow agreement. Failure to provide for such contingency will not excuse the borrower of such from performance. For example, if the place of performance is in a flood area, then the borrower should provide that if he cannot appear because of floods, his performance may be delayed. However, if the borrower were to become ill, or if there were a flood in a nonflood area preventing travel to the place where payment should be made, then these events would excuse performance because they could not be anticipated.

only the balance of the instrument because he would also get credit for the amount of the partial payment. Once the new promised date passes, even if by only one day, the instrument must be paid in full plus the amount of partial payment theretofore made, and the result would be the same if the borrower made payment a long time after the new due date.[5]

## The delivery of the escrowed instruments

Many of the duties, obligations, and rights of the escrowee are discussed in Chapter 56.

In the situation just discussed, if the escrowee returned the instrument to the lender contrary to the escrow agreement, then the lender must either return the instruments if he is available to do so, or write a receipt for the partial payment that he had already received. If the lender is not available to return the instruments, then the escrowee must guarantee that he will be liable for any losses incurred by the borrower because of wrongful delivery of the instruments to the lender.[6]

If beth din is aware that the instrument on which the lender is suing was returned to him by the escrowee in error, then it should remedy the situation.[7] If the beth din is not aware of the error and permits the lender to enforce collection on the instrument, then the escrowee is free of any monetary liability to the borrower, but he is still liable to

---

5. Interest is often defined as the amount that the lender exacts for having to wait for the return of his money. In this case the loan is past due, and there is no extra payment for the extension of time until the new date if the borrower pays on the new due date. By paying on time, the borrower can avoid any extra payment. It is only if the borrower fails to pay on the new due date that he will end up paying more than he borrowed. The extra sum remains the same no matter how late the payment.

6. The escrowee is put under a ban until he agrees to so indemnify the borrower. The escrowee is so obligated although he is only the indirect cause of the loss that the borrower may incur. There is a general principle that the person who is the indirect cause is free of monetary obligation, but this applies when the damage was already caused. In the situation of the escrowee, the loss will not arise until the lender sues on the instrument.

7. In addition to dismissing the lender's lawsuit, they may also order him to write a receipt for the partial payment that he received, or they may so endorse on the instrument.

the judgments of heaven until he makes restitution to the borrower for the loss that he occasioned.

If the escrowee erred and returned the instrument to the borrower before it was paid, then he is not an indirect cause of loss to a party, but is rather a direct cause.[8]

## Rights during the escrow period

A lender loans $100 to a borrower, to be repaid 1 year from date. To secure the loan, the borrower executes a currently dated deed to the borrower's land, and the deed is placed in escrow with the instructions to the escrowee that if the borrower does not make the repayment on the due date, the escrowee should deliver the deed to the lender. The borrower should have the use of the land during the escrow period so that there is no question of interest being paid.[9] During the year, and thus before the lender has a deed, the lender sells the land to a third-party buyer. At the end of the year the borrower does not repay the loan. The escrowee delivers the deed to the lender, and the buyer takes possession of the land. The borrower now wants to evict the buyer from the land on the grounds that when the buyer bought the land, the lender still did not have rights to the deed and thus could not sell it to the lender. On these facts the beth din rejected the pleas of the borrower and held that the buyer had good title from the lender. When the lender received the deed from the escrowee, he obtained title retroactively to the date of the writing of the deed, since the deed was given without conditions. If the borrower makes the payment due to the lender within the specified time, the lender would be required to reconvey the land to the borrower.[10]

---

8. In the case in which he returns the instrument to the lender, it is possible that the lender may sue for only the unpaid portion, or that when the lender moves to collect on the instrument, the borrower or others could testify that the instrument was partially paid. In the situation in which the instrument was given to the borrower, and thus is no longer in the lender's possession, the lender has no way to enforce the instrument. See Chapter 386 regarding direct and indirect causes of loss.

9. See *Shulhan Aruch, Yoreh De'ah,* Chapter 174.

10. This is not *asmachta,* since the sale is final on condition that the borrower does not repay the loan within the specified time.

# Chapter 56

## LAWS OF ESCROW

### INTRODUCTION

Chapter 55 covered some laws relating to escrows. This chapter is the one that deals with the subject at length. An escrow agreement usually provides that two parties, whether in litigation or in an agreement outside of litigation, place something in escrow, to be released from escrow after a certain event has occurred or a certain time has elapsed. The party or parties who place the deposit in escrow are the escrowers, and the party holding the deposit is the escrowee. The deposit may consist of money and/or instruments and/or personal property. For example, one party may deposit the price of a piece of land, and the other party may deposit the deed. The escrowee shall release the money to the seller of the land and the deed to the purchaser upon the occurrence of a certain event, such as the purchaser's obtaining permission from the city by a certain date to build a certain size building on the land. Should the purchaser fail to obtain such permission within the stipulated time, the money will be returned to the purchaser, the deed will be returned to the seller, and the parties will no longer be liable to each other. There are certain facts that the escrowee must ascertain before the parties are entitled to a return of the thing deposited or to obtain what the other party has deposited.

The halachah considers the escrowee to occupy a special place in the relationship between himself and the escrowers. The escrowers apparently had special trust in the escrowee, which made them willing to escrow the deposit with him. The trust was in both his integrity and his ability to carry out their intent.

This chapter also deals with what happens in the event of a difference of opinion between the escrowee and the escrower or both escrowers regarding the terms of the agreement.

What if the escrowee failed to abide by the terms of the escrow agreement? What are the rights of the escrowee? May he testify as to the facts and contradict the version of either or both of the parties?


# TEXT


## Credence given to the statements of the escrowee regarding terms of the escrow

During the time that the escrowee is acting in that stead, his statements regarding the terms of the escrow are given the same credence as the testimony of two witnesses. His statements are believed without his having to take an oath, even after he has given up the opportunity to do with the escrow deposit that which the escrowers desired him to do.[1] He is given the same credence even if he is ineligible to testify regarding the matter. His credence remains in effect even after the agreed-upon time for the escrow has expired, so long as he is still the escrowee.[2]

He may thus state that an instrument in his care has been paid even

---

1. This special credence accorded the escrowee arises from the fact that the parties obviously had trusted him since they named him the escrowee. For example, if the escrow was an instrument of indebtedness, the escrowee was able to release the escrow deposit to the lender and thus allow him to enforce the instrument, or he could have released the instrument to the borrower, thus preventing the lender from collecting the debt. The fact that he no longer can do with the escrow deposit what he wants to do does not diminish the fact that the parties had had faith in him.

2. However, if a judge or arbitrator is given security to hold by the parties pending his decision by a certain date, and if that date passes before he renders a decision, then his authority expires and he must return the deposited security.

if the creditor contradicts him, or he may state that no part of the instrument has been paid, even if the borrower alleges that he has made partial payment.[3]

If the escrowee discloses the terms of the escrow in the presence of witnesses, he may not later state that the terms are different (unless he can explain the variance). Thus, if the terms of the escrow are known to others (for example, if they were shown to beth din or were reduced to writing and copies signed by the escrowee were given to the parties, or if there were witnesses present when the escrow was set up), then he cannot state that there are other terms.[4] However, if signed copies of the writings are not given to the parties, then the escrowee has the same credence as any other escrowee whose writing has not been known to others.

If the statements of the escrow are contradicted by two witnesses, then the escrowee's special credence is void.[5] As against one contradictory witness, however, his special credence is not impaired.

If the escrowee dies, then any memoranda that he may leave will be given credence.[6] All items that were escrowed with him should be handled by the beth din. If a decedent's affairs are being taken care of

---

3. Even in those situations in which one of the parties, if contradicted, would have to take an oath, the escrowee is relieved of this requirement.

4. The fact that the escrowers do not rely solely on the escrowee but have various safeguards shows that they have a certain reluctance to give the escrowee all of the credence that is usually reserved for escrowees. The escrowee no longer has the credence to state that certain terms were agreed upon. Since he did not have it within his power to do whatever he pleased, he is not given the credence of two witnesses to contradict the escrowers.

5. Thus if the two witnesses contradict the terms of the escrow as stated by the escrowee, then the witnesses's statements will be given credence. However, if the testimony of the witnesses does not necessarily contradict that of the escrowee, then his statements will be given credence. For example, if the witnesses testify that on a certain date the escrow was established with certain conditions, and the escrowee states that the escrow terms are different without stating the date on which they were established, then his version will be accepted, since he does not state that the escrow terms were established on the date stated by the witnesses. The possibility exists that the terms were later modified as stated by the escrowee. There would have to be a direct conflict between the escrowee's statements and the witnesses' testimony for the escrowee to lose his special credence.

6. For example, if there was a memorandum that a certain instrument that he was holding in escrow was paid, it will be deemed that it was paid.

by a wife or manager or some other trustee, and if it is known that the decedent had items belonging to others among his own possessions, and if the owners can be identified, then the trustee must return these items to the rightful owners. In stating to whom the items belong, these persons have the same credibility as would be accorded the escrowee.

Once the escrowee returns the escrow deposit, his credibility is equal to that of any one witness.[7]

## Credence accorded the escrowee regarding the escrow deposit

The escrowee is given no more credence regarding the escrow deposit than is the escrower.[8] For example, the borrower alleges that the instrument of indebtedness delivered to the escrow is a forgery, or was paid.[9] The fact that the escrowee states he was told by both parties that the instrument was valid when deposited and had a certain balance outstanding would not give special credence to his statement; the instrument would still have to be authenticated, as would any other instrument.[10]

## Conflict regarding the appointment of the escrowee

That which has been said about the credence accorded the escrowee applies if both parties admit that he is the escrowee. If either or both

---

7. If he is related to one of the parties or is otherwise ineligible, then he will not be able to testify.

8. The escrowee is given more credence only as regards his relationship between himself and the escrowers. He is relieved of an oath in situations in which parties may have been required to take an oath. Also, the escrowee may deliver the escrow deposit to whomever he desires as part of the escrow agreement.

9. This holds true if the payment is past due. However, if the date of payment has not yet arrived, then the defense of payment will not be accepted so long as the escrowee still has the instrument.

10. In those situations in which the borrower can insist that the lender take an oath, the same will still apply, even if the escrowee states that the facts sustain the lender.

parties deny that he was appointed as escrowee and claim that the deposit that he holds is not an escrow deposit at all,[11] then there is a difference of opinion regarding his status. Some authorities hold that if he maintains that he is an escrowee, then he is believed even if both parties allege that he is not an escrowee. Dissenting authorities hold that if both parties, or even one, allege that he is not an escrowee, then he is not to be deemed an escrowee.[12] The latter authorities have worked out a sort of compromise solution. If the escrowed item is of a type that the escrowee could claim to have purchased, then he will be believed if he states that he is the escrowee so long as he takes an oath to that effect.[13,14]

If there is a conflict between the lender and a person who, when transmitting the article to the escrowee, informs the escrowee that he is the agent of the lender in arranging for the escrowee to so act and to take possession of the escrow deposit, then the alleged agent will be believed, since he could have alleged that he was the escrowee because he had the escrow deposit belonging to the lender in his hands.

## The escrowee as an interested party

In the event of a dispute between the escrowee and the parties as to the escrow deposit, the escrowee is not given special credence as to

---

11. The allegation is that he is holding a bailment, or else that he stole or found it. Of course, if the allegation is that he is holding the item as a bailment, it certainly is closer to being an escrow than if it is alleged that he stole or found the thing he is holding.

12. These authorities are fearful that the situation may result in fraud. For example, if Shimon is holding an item that belongs to Ruven, Shimon can then allege that he is holding the item in escrow under an agreement between Ruven and Levi that provides that the item should be turned over to Levi on a certain date. On that date, Shimon will turn the item over to Levi, and Shimon and Levi will then divide the proceeds. Shimon will not even have to take an oath, since escrowees do not take oaths; this exemption would also apply to Levi. Thus Ruven will illegally be deprived of his property.

13. Depending on the type of item, the holder's claim that he purchased it may or may not be believed. Chapter 133 will distinguish one type of item from the other.

14. Since the escrowee would be liable to an oath, the party who agrees that he is the escrowee would also have to take an oath. Thus, in the example given in note 12, Levi would also be subject to an oath.

the disputed part of the deposit. Say, for example, that the parties allege that the escrowee is holding $500, but the escrowee maintains that he is holding only $300. The escrowee's statement regarding which of the parties is entitled to receive the $300 is given special credence; as to the remaining $200, the escrowee must take an oath that he is not holding the money.[15] This limitation to the escrowee's special credence applies only if he has lost his ability to act as he wishes under the escrow agreement; however, if discretion still rests with him, then his special credence is not limited.

## Duties of the escrowee

The escrowers may at any time dismiss the escrowee and demand that he return all that he is holding to the parties or to whomever they designate as the new escrowee. All that he performed pursuant to his escrow agreement will remain, and he will not be required to undo it.

The escrowee may at any time resign his assignment, and if the parties refuse to accept his resignation, he may apply to the beth din to take custody of the escrow deposit and relieve him of any further liability. However, if the escrowee has received compensation for acting as escrowee, then he cannot resign until he has fulfilled his duties.

Either one of the escrowers may apply to beth din to remove the escrowee for cause.

If there is litigation pending between the plaintiff and the defendant, and if one of the litigants deposited his evidence with an individual, then he may at any time demand the return of his evidence without

---

15. Say, for example, that the escrowee is holding a note for $100 deposited by the lender and $60 deposited by the borrower. The agreement provides that if the borrower pays the balance of $40 by a certain date, then the escrowee will turn the $100 note over to the borrower and the $100 to the lender. If the borrower does not pay the $40 by that date, then the escrowee will turn the $100 note together with the $60 over to the lender. (See Chapter 55.) The borrower alleges that he paid the remaining $40 to the escrowee on or before the due date, and the escrowee and lender allege that the borrower did not pay the $40, but instead paid a smaller sum or no sum at all. The escrowee is not accorded special credence in this case, since he could have received the entire amount due and kept some of it for himself.

applying to the beth din or receiving permission from the opposing litigant.[16]

The escrowee may not deviate from the duties delegated to him.[17] If he has any question as to how to proceed, he may seek guidance from the parties; and failing that, he may apply to beth din for advice.

When the escrowee has completed his duties pursuant to the escrow agreement, he should receive from the parties a receipt so stating. If the parties refuse to give him such a receipt, then he may apply to beth din for a hearing to determine whether he has satisfactorily completed his duties.

If the escrowee has forgotten the names of the escrowers, he may insist that individuals who state that they are the escrowers produce validating witnesses. If they do not do so, then he or the escrowers should apply to beth din for an order regarding the escrow deposit. Similarly, if he remembers the persons involved in the escrow agreement but does not know which of them is entitled to the return of which part of the escrow deposit, he may apply to beth din for guidance.

If the borrower alleges that he paid the instrument directly to the lender and demands that the escrowee return the instrument to him, the escrowee should not believe the borrower and should return the instrument to the lender according to the terms of the escrow agreement as if the instrument had not been paid.[18]

The escrow agreement may provide for the compensation of the escrowee. If the escrow agreement is silent as to compensation, and if there is a custom to compensate the escrowee in the community where the escrowee resides or does business, then both parties should pay the escrowee equally according to the custom of the community.

---

16. If the opposing litigant can show to beth din that justice will be prejudiced if the deposited evidence is returned to the other litigant, then beth din may investigate the matter and make such holding as will enable the parties to properly proceed with their cases.

17. He must not attempt to be a judge in the matter unless this is designated as one of his duties.

18. The borrower may demand that the lender take an oath that he was not paid. But if the instrument contains a credence clause including a waiver of proof and permits the lender's allegation of nonpayment to suffice to enforce payment, then the lender need not take an oath of nonpayment.

# Chapter 57

# THE PROHIBITION AGAINST RETAINING PAID INSTRUMENTS OF INDEBTEDNESS

## INTRODUCTION

The admonition in Job 11:14, "And let not unrighteousness dwell in thy tents," teaches us that a person must not retain an instrument that has been paid, for he may be tempted to sue on it.

## TEXT

### The prohibition against retaining paid instruments of indebtedness

A creditor may not retain an instrument of indebtedness or a promissory note that has been paid or forgiven, even if the borrower consents thereto.[1,2] If the creditor refuses to return the instrument,

---

1. This admonition applies regardless of whether the instrument contains the signatures of witnesses or is a promissory note signed by the borrower.

2. The consent of the borrower may be misplaced. The lender in time of distress may be tempted to try to collect on the instrument. The danger also exists that if the instrument is not returned to the borrower, the lender and borrower may enter into some conspiracy to use the instrument to levy on purchasers of the borrower's realty.

beth din may compel him either to do so or to destroy the instrument in the presence of witnesses.[3] The lender may not retain the instrument even if the borrower has failed to pay the fee for having the instrument drawn.

The lender may, however, in the presence of witnesses or in the presence of the borrower, mark the word *paid* on the instrument and retain the instrument. The lender may also retain in his possession an instrument that has been only partially paid so long as he gives the borrower a receipt for the amount paid or endorses such payment on the instrument.

## The prohibition against reusing a paid instrument

If an instrument was paid and then reused for another loan,[4] the lender has no lien against the realty of the borrower to levy against purchasers of the realty purchased after the date of the loan.[5] However, the instrument may be enforced against the borrower if the borrower admits the second loan. If the lender does not admit that the instrument now secures a second loan, but claims that it secures the original loan and that the payment made by the borrower to repay the instrument was not completed, then the instrument remains in effect as it was before the borrower made this partial payment.[6]

---

3. This assumes that the borrower has no use for the instrument.

4. See Chapter 48 regarding the laws of reusing instruments of indebtedness that have been fully or partially repaid.

5. This is the case because when the loan was paid, all of the liens established by the instrument were discharged. (See Chapter 48.)

6. Say, for example, that the borrower gave the lender a check in payment, and the check was returned because the borrower did not have sufficient funds in the bank to pay the instrument. In this case, the loan remains the same; it does not now secure a new loan.

# Chapter 58

# APPLICATION OF PAYMENT TO ONE OF MANY DEBTS

## INTRODUCTION

If a lender makes more than one loan to a borrower, and the borrower repays an amount, to which of the outstanding debts should the repayment be applied? Who has the option to decide? What if the lender can prove only one loan? What if the borrower cannot prove payment of even one loan? What if the borrower sent the repayment with an agent? What are his obligations and responsibilities? This chapter discusses these questions.

## TEXT

### When there are two provable loans outstanding

If the borrower has more than one due or past due loan outstanding to the same lender and makes a payment on one of them, the lender may apply the payment to either loan. This is the case even if the borrower states at the time he makes the payment that he wants it applied to a certain loan and the lender does not object to the borrower's request. But if one of the loans is due or past due and the other loan is not yet due, the lender must apply the repayment to the loan that is due or past due. If at the time he accepts payment the lender states that he is applying the payment to a certain loan, he may not later apply the repayment to a different loan.

## When the second loan is not provable

Consider the case in which a lender has an authenticated written instrument of indebtedness (or an instrument that can be authenticated) with two subscribing witnesses thereon evidencing a debt from the borrower, and the borrower pleads payment.[1] The lender admits payment by the borrower but alleges that the payment was for a different loan that is not evidenced by a writing—an oral loan.[2] If the borrower admits the other oral loan, then the lender may apply the repayment to such loan as previously stated.

If the borrower does not admit the oral loan, then there are two possibilities: (1) the borrower made payment in the presence of witnesses or (2) there were no witnesses present when he made payment. If the payment was made in the presence of witnesses, then it will be applied against the written instrument.[3] If the borrower

---

1. If the instrument is not authenticated and the lender has no proof with which to authenticate it, then the borrower is believed if he states that the repayment was for the unauthenticated instrument. He is believed with a *migoo,* since he could have said that the unauthenticated instrument was a forgery or had been paid.

2. The law would be the same if the lender alleges that the other loan to which he applied the repayment was a written loan but that he returned the writing to the borrower when he made payment.

3. The lender cannot prove another loan, and the borrower can prove payment. The payment will be applied to the written instrument if the witnesses testify that the money was given in payment of a debt, regardless of whether they state that the borrower made the payment to apply to the instrument or that he made it without any particular statement as to its application. However, if they did not know why the borrower gave the money to the lender, then it could have been given as a gift or as a bailment, in which event the lender, if he takes an oath that the authenticated instrument is still unpaid, may allege that the money was given for a different loan, since he could have denied that it was a payment at all. There are those who hold that even if the witnesses did not know what the money was being given for, it would be applied to the authenticated instrument. There is a difference of opinion as to whether or not the foregoing laws would apply if there was only one witness instead of two when the borrower gave the money to the lender. All of the foregoing would apply whether or not the instrument contained a credence clause.

requests time to produce witnesses, then the beth din will determine whether to grant his application. If it is granted, the borrower must produce his witnesses within the time allocated. If the borrower fails to produce the witnesses before the end of the trial, then judgment will be granted to the lender on the authenticated instrument even though the borrower has already given money to the lender for repayment of a loan.[4] If, after judgment is granted to the lender and he has been paid, the borrower produces witnesses to the initial payment, and if they testify that the payment was to be applied to the authenticated instrument, then the lender must return the second payment to the borrower.[5] If the witnesses testify that they saw the transfer of money but do not know the reason for the transfer, then the lender need not make the second repayment.

If the payment was not made in the presence of witnesses, then the lender may apply the first payment to the other loan, which he claims was outstanding when the payment was made.[6] Where the lender can apply the payment to the oral loan, the written loan remains intact; if it contains a credence clause, then the lender can collect on the written instrument without having to take an oath.[7,8] The borrower can still insist that the lender take a *hesseth* oath that the money was due on the oral loan. If the written instrument does not contain a credence clause, then the lender will have to take an oath before he can collect on the instrument because he admitted receiving payment from the borrower.

## The lender may apply to his loans moneys given to him by the borrower for other purposes

If the borrower gives the lender money to deliver to a third party, the lender may retain the money and apply it to the money due to him from the borrower if the loan was due.

---

4. Judgment will be granted to the lender if he takes an oath that the instrument was not paid.

5. The repayment is made despite the fact that the lender had taken an oath that he had not been paid on the instrument.

6. The lender is believed because he could have stated that he never received any payment from the borrower.

7. The credence clause provides that the holder of the instrument may enforce collection in beth din without having to prove his case beyond the presentation of the instrument and without having to take an oath.

8. The borrower may still thereafter bring a lawsuit to recover the second payment.

## A receipt in the hands of the borrower

If the borrower has a receipt stating that the lender received payment from the borrower, then even if it does not refer to the instrument that the lender holds, it will be applied to cancel that instrument, which will be taken by the beth din and destroyed. This applies if the date of the receipt is the same as or subsequent to the due date of the instrument or if the instrument does not contain a date. But if the date of the receipt precedes the due date of payment of the instrument, then neither the lender nor the borrower has rights against the other.[9]

## Borrower alleges that the instrument
## is not for a loan

A borrower may plead that an instrument produced by the lender is not for a loan, but rather represents the amount of an item that was sold to the borrower for resale, and that the lender was repaid out of the proceeds of the resale. The lender admits all of these facts but states that the proceeds of the resale were used to pay another debt that the borrower owed the lender and that the instrument is still outstanding.[10] According to one opinion, the instrument is to be deemed paid.[11] Another opinion states that if there are no witnesses

---

9. The lender cannot collect, since the borrower has a receipt; yet the borrower cannot demand that the instrument be delivered to him, since the receipt precedes the due date of the instrument.

10. The defendant named in the instrument as a borrower pleads as follows: He is not a borrower, but is rather a purchaser (hereafter, "the purchaser"). The lender is not really a lender, but actually a seller (hereafter "the seller"). The seller sold an article to the purchaser. The seller knew that the purchaser was going to resell the article to a third party. The purchaser did not make any payment to the seller but gave the seller a note of indebtedness to hold until the purchaser obtained money from the third party. The purchaser contends that he did indeed sell the article to the third party and that the third party paid for the article, with part of the proceeds going to pay the seller. Therefore, the instrument that the seller is holding should be returned to the purchaser. To this the seller pleads that the story of the purchaser is true up to a point. He states that the money he received from the third party was applied to another loan that the buyer owed to the seller, and therefore the instrument is still outstanding.

11. This opinion holds that since the lender admitted that the instrument represented the credit for merchandise and that he was repaid out of the resale of the

that the borrower paid the proceeds of the resale to the lender, then the lender is believed when he states that he applied the proceeds to another outstanding indebtedness.

## Payments made by an agent of the borrower

A borrower may send an agent to repay his debt. The agent may pay the lender and request the return of the borrower's instrument. The lender may then inform the agent that the borrower is still indebted to him and that he is applying the payment to the other debt. If the borrower did not instruct the agent not to pay the debt unless the instrument is returned to him, then the agent is not liable to the borrower for the loss that may be sustained if the lender collects again on the instrument.[12] If the borrower *did* instruct the agent not to pay the debt unless the lender returned the instrument to him, and the borrower is subsequently required to pay the same instrument twice, then the agent is liable to the borrower for the amount that the borrower sent with the agent.[13]

---

merchandise, the instrument is cancelled if the borrower takes a *hesseth* oath that the loan was paid, and the borrower has no liability.

12. The agent can plead that since the borrower did not instruct the agent to obtain the instrument, the borrower trusted the lender, and thus the borrower put himself into the position of having to pay twice.

13. It would not matter if the borrower told the agent to pay the debt and obtain the instrument or if he told him to obtain the instrument and then pay the debt. The agent is liable in either case, since he should have known that the borrower did not trust the lender when he instructed him to retrieve the instrument. The agent should not have made the payment until the instrument was returned or at the very least escrowed pending payment by the agent. Alternatively, the agent should have made the payment in the presence of witnesses in order to ensure that the lender could not claim application of the payment against another loan.

# Chapter 59

# BORROWER ALLEGES PAYMENT, BUT LENDER UNCERTAIN

## INTRODUCTION

The lender (plaintiff) holds an authenticated instrument evidencing the indebtedness of the borrower (defendant), and he commences a lawsuit on the instrument. The borrower pleads payment, and the lender, in response to the borrower's defense, pleads that he does not remember whether the instrument was paid. If both parties plead with certainty, then it is presumed that the instrument was not paid, for if it had been paid, the borrower should have had the instrument returned to him when he made the repayment, or he should have obtained a receipt. The difference in the case presented in this chapter is that the borrower pleads with certainty that he has paid the instrument, while the lender pleads that he does not recall whether he was paid. There is a general principle that when one party pleads with certainty and the other party pleads that he is uncertain, the party who pleads with certainty will prevail.[1]

If the instrument held by the lender is not authenticated, then the borrower will win the lawsuit if he pleads payment, since he could

---

1. In Hebrew, the maxim is *bari v'shema, bari adif.* That is, if there is *bari,* a plea of certainty, and *shema,* a plea of uncertainty, *bari adif,* the plea of certainty will prevail.

have alleged that the instrument was not authentic and the lender cannot prove its authenticity.

## TEXT

### Plaintiff pleads that he does not know whether the instrument was paid

If the lender/plaintiff sues on an authenticated instrument, and the borrower/defendant raises a plea of payment, the plaintiff must plead with certainty that the instrument was not paid.[2,3] If the plaintiff cannot so plead, the defendant can move to dismiss the complaint.[4] This would hold true even if the instrument contained a credence clause stating that the holder's allegation that the instrument has not been paid will permit him to obtain a judgment, for in this case the holder does not plea with certainty that the instrument was not paid.

If the lender is holding collateral for the payment of the instrument, he must return the collateral upon the borrower's application, since the underlying debt for the collateral is now of no effect.[5]

If the borrower dies, then the lender must plead with certainty against the heirs that the instrument was not paid, even if the heirs do

---

2. The same would hold true if the instrument had not yet been authenticated, but the lender has witnesses available to authenticate it. If the instrument is not authenticated, then it remains the equivalent of an oral loan alleged by the plaintiff, which can be defeated by the defendant's pleading payment or denying the loan.

3. In a situation where the lender without any proof pleads with certainty that a loan was not repaid and the borrower pleads that he is unsure, the certainty cannot be said to prevail over the plea of uncertainty. In this situation the concept would be used to extract money on the strength of the concept, which cannot be, since the plaintiff must prove his case by evidence and witnesses. The concept cannot be used to change the status quo of the defendant holding his money, which the plaintiff seeks to obtain. But in the case described in the text, the concept prevails to the extent of defeating an attempt to make someone pay money, which is a change in the status quo.

4. See note 1, that a plea of certainty can defeat a defense based on uncertainty.

5. This is not an example of the concept of the borrower's pleading of certainty prevailing over the plaintiff's pleading of uncertainty resulting in a change of the status quo. The giving up of collateral is certainly not the giving up of the lender's property being held for security for a loan no longer considered extant.

not raise the defense of payment.[6] There may be situations in which the lender is not expected to know whether the instrument was paid. Such would be the case if, for example, he appointed an agent to collect the debt but did not give the instrument to the agent. Until the agent returns, the lender does not know whether the borrower has repaid the loan. In such an instance, the failure of the lender to plead with certainty about nonrepayment cannot be held to place him in the category of an uncertain pleader as against the heirs.

If the lender pleads uncertainty in response to the borrower's plea that he is certain that the instrument was paid, the borrower may insist that the instrument be returned to him.[7] But if the borrower has died, the heirs cannot insist that the instrument be returned to them.[8]

## Both parties' pleas based on uncertainty

If both the lender and the borrower plead that they are uncertain as to whether the instrument has been paid, the lender will prevail without even having to take an oath.[9] If, however, the borrower pleads that he is uncertain as to whether the loan was ever made, then he may take a *hesseth* oath and will not have to pay the loan.

6. The heirs cannot raise a defense of payment, since it would not be usual for them to be familiar with the financial affairs of the decedent. There may be situations in which they do know whether the decedent has paid, either by personal knowledge or because they have found a receipt among his records, but the case does not depend upon this. The lender must plead with certainty that the instrument was not paid.

7. The borrower may plead that he is afraid that in case the lender dies, his heirs will not have to plead with certainty that the loan was not repaid, since they would not be expected to have such knowledge. The authenticated instrument is presumptive proof that it was not paid.

8. The borrower's heirs may ask the beth din to escrow the instrument in order to prevent the lender's heirs from collecting on it in case of the lender's death. The lender cannot collect on the instrument because he does not plead with certainty that the instrument was not paid. Once the instrument has been so impugned, there is no reason to put the lender's heirs in a better position than that of the lender.

9. The authentic instrument will speak for itself, and the borrower has no defense, since he is not certain of whether he paid it. The borrower's plea of possible payment already authenticates the instrument, since he pleads that he may have repaid that instrument. Without the plea of certainty of payment, the lender does not have to plead that he is certain that the instrument was not paid. The presumption is that it was not paid, for if it had been paid, the instrument should have been returned to the borrower, or else the borrower should have insisted on a receipt when he made payment.

If the borrower admits that the instrument was not paid, but pleads that he has a counterclaim against the lender for an amount equal to the amount of the instrument, and the lender denies the borrower's plea or does not remember whether he owes such a sum to the borrower, then the lender will collect on the instrument upon taking an oath that he does not remember.[10]

## The lender changes his plea
## from uncertainty to certainty

If the lender first pleads that he is uncertain as to whether the debt had been paid, and later states that he has examined his records and is now pleading with certainty that the debt has not been paid, he may now collect on the instrument. The reinstatement of the instrument is for all purposes; it even permits the lender to enforce the claim against purchasers from the borrower who purchased before the lender pleaded that he was not certain and against those who purchased after he repleaded that he now knows with certainty that the instrument has not been repaid.[11] If anyone purchased the realty between the times that he pleaded that he was not certain and the time that he repleaded that he was certain, the purchased realty cannot be levied upon.[12]

---

10. The reason is that the debtor has admitted that the loan is unpaid. As for his counterclaim, it is the equivalent to an oral loan, which can be defeated by the lender's taking a *hesseth* oath of denial as a defendant can do to defeat any oral loan.

11. Say for example, that the loan took place on January 1, and the instrument was then and there written and witnessed by two witnesses and delivered to the lender in the presence of two witnesses. Thus the instrument acted to place a lien on all of the realty that the borrower owned on January 1. On February 1, the borrower sold his realty to a third party. On March 1, the lender sued the borrower; the borrower pleaded with certainty that he had repaid the loan, and the lender pleaded that he did not remember. On April 1, the lender repleads that he has examined his records and has realized conclusively that the loan was not repaid. The lender thus on April 1 obtains a judgment against the borrower. The borrower has no money or other assets with which to pay the lender. The lender may thus proceed to levy on the realty that the third party purchased on February 1.

12. If in the example in the preceding note the real property was sold by the borrower on March 15, the property purchased would not be subject to the lien, since on that date there was no plea of certainty by the lender regarding the repayment of the loan.

The lender may change his plea even if the instrument is not in his possession but the contents thereof can be proved or the loan can be proved independently by witnesses. But if the instrument is not in his possession because it was taken from the lender by the beth din after he had pleaded uncertainty as just described, then he can no longer plead that, having examined his records, he is now certain that the instrument was not paid. His new plea of certainty has the status of pleading an oral loan, and the borrower may take a *hesseth* oath and defeat the plaintiff's claim.

# Chapter 60

## LIENS ON PERSONAL PROPERTY
## CONTRACTS
## PROPER PARTY NOT NAMED

### INTRODUCTION

This chapter has been divided into three parts. In the *Shulhan Aruch*, the title is "Laws of liens on personal property along with real estate and laws of liens on things not yet in existence." However, the *Shulhan Aruch* actually discusses the three topics named in this chapter. The first topic is the same in both. *Shulhan Aruch*, in discussing liens arising out of obligations, also discusses the obligations arising out of contracts. Both the *Shulhan Aruch* and this chapter discuss the last topic, which arises when the obligee is not the person named in the instrument of indebtedness.

### PART I
### LIENS ON PERSONAL PROPERTY

### INTRODUCTION

According to Talmudic law, if the debtor fails to pay his debt, the creditor must first attempt to collect the debt from the debtor's assets. If the debtor does not have sufficient assets (whether real estate, personal property,[1] or money), the creditor may trace and collect from real estate owned by the debtor at the time the debt was incurred and subsequently transferred by him to third parties. It does not matter whether the realty was transferred by sale or by gift. It also does not matter whether or not the instrument of indebtedness states that the realty of the debtor is liened to pay the debt, since it is assumed that the omission of such a lien was an error on the part of the draftsman.[2]

Absent a special provision to the contrary, realty acquired by the debtor after the debt is incurred is not liened to the debt. If there are insufficient assets in the debtor's hands to pay the debt, then the creditor cannot levy on such after-acquired realty if it was sold by the debtor prior to the levy.[3] However, if the instrument of indebtedness states that the lien thereby created also covers after-acquired realty, then such realty is included in the lien of the instrument and can be traced by the creditor if the debtor does not have sufficient assets to pay the debt.[4] This is by mandated special Rabbinic enactment, the theory of which is that the repayment of the debt is a personal obligation, and the assets (when specifically agreed) may stand as security for the repayment; thus the enactment did not create a new right, but merely enlarged the scope of the security available to the creditor.

If the instrument of indebtedness is silent as to personalty, then the creditor cannot trace any of the personalty that the debtor shall have

---

1. Everything not designated as real estate (or realty) will be designated as personal property (or personalty).

2. In order to prevent the instrument of indebtedness from placing a lien on the debtor's realty, the instrument of indebtedness would specifically have to exclude such intent.

3. This is because only such real estate as is owned by the debtor when the loan is made is relied upon by a creditor as security when he makes the loan.

4. Although a lien cannot take effect on property not owned by the debtor when the lien was given (see Chapter 111 in Volume IV), the Rabbis enacted a special decree so that the lien would be effective if the parties so agree and if it was so stated in the instrument of indebtedness. This enactment was made to prevent creditors from denying credit to debtors. (See Chapter 112 in Volume IV regarding instruments that state that the creditor may collect out of after-acquired realty but that do not specifically state that after-acquired realty is also liened to the payment of the debt.)

sold prior to the levy, whether or not it was owned by the debtor when the debt was incurred.[5]

According to Talmudic law, if the instrument of indebtedness states that the personalty of the debtor is liened "along with" the real estate, then the lien also attaches to the personalty owned by the debtor at the time of the making of the loan, and may be traced.[6] The instrument must state that "it is not merely an aleatory contract nor a draft form." If the instrument states that there is also a lien on after-acquired personalty "along with" the lien on the realty, then it will also attach to such after-acquired personalty. As will be seen in the "Text" section, the foregoing laws regarding personalty no longer apply.

# TEXT

## Collection of debts from real estate sold by the debtor

When a creditor lends money to a debtor and a written instrument of indebtedness is executed with at least two subscribing witnesses, the making and delivery of the instrument in the presence of at least two witnesses acts to place a lien on the real estate owned by the debtor to secure repayment of the loan. The fact that the instrument does not state that the real estate of the debtor is liened does not affect the foregoing, since (absent a specific clause negating a lien) it is assumed that the draftsman of the instrument inadvertently neglected to insert the lien clause.

The creditor who would enforce his rights under a written instrument[7] must first enforce collection from the property owned by the debtor at the time the collection is made, whether real estate or

---

5. The reason that personalty was not automatically liened to pay the debt was that the creditor realizes that personalty can be easily secreted or sold or otherwise disposed of, and thus the credit is not extended to the debtor on the strength of the debtor's personal assets.

6. See Chapter 113 in Volume IV regarding nonenforcement of collection from disposed-of personalty.

7. See the Glossary for definition of *instrument*.

personalty, according to the law as set forth in Chapter 101 in Volume III. If the debtor's assets are insufficient to pay the debt, then the creditor may trace the real estate owned by the debtor at the time the loan was made to the current holder of the real estate and make his levy against the real estate. The real estate may be traced regardless of whether the debtor had sold it or had given it away as a gift. Unless there is a specific provision covering after-acquired property, the tracing of the debtor's real estate does not apply to any real estate not owned by the debtor when the loan was made.[8] If the instrument of indebtedness states that the creditor's lien will extend to after-acquired realty, then the creditor may trace real estate that the debtor acquired after the loan was made and disposed of by the debtor before the creditor comes to collect the loan.

## The creditor's lien does not attach to personalty

The personal property that the debtor sells prior to the time when the creditor comes to collect the debt is not traceable by the creditor. This applies even if the personalty is owned by the debtor when the loan is made, and even if the instrument of indebtedness states that the personalty is subject to the lien of the creditor "along with" the lien of the real estate.[9] This is to protect innocent purchasers of personal property. All commerce would suffer if customers had to examine the source of all the merchandise in the stores and hands of vendors. However, this policy intended to protect commerce does not pre-clude tracing instrument of indebtedness; if the debtor sells an instrument of indebtedness from some other debtor that he owned when he borrowed the money from the creditor, then his creditor may trace the instrument to the hands of the purchaser of the instrument.[10]

If a debtor transfers all of his assets and retains nothing for himself,

---

8. This is because it is only real estate owned by the debtor when the loan is made that is relied upon by the lender as security when he makes the loan.

9. Personalty may not be traced to the current holders even if they are holding it only for a specific time.

10. The sale of instruments of indebtedness is rare, and thus commerce will not be thwarted by the fact that a creditor can trace the instrument in the hands of a purchaser.

then it is assumed that this was done with the intention of defrauding his creditors and all of the assets may be traced, since the enactment to protect commerce does not apply to this situation.

# PART II
# LAWS OF CONTRACT FORMATION

## INTRODUCTION

Contracts form obligations between the parties to the contract. A contract may be a unilateral contract whereby X agrees to pay Y, if Y will perform some task for X. For example, X says to Y that he will pay Y $100 if Y will paint X's fence. X is under no obligation to pay Y until Y performs the act, and Y is under no obligation to perform the act. The aforesaid contract is for personal services. A contract may also be made for the sale of goods. X agrees to sell goods to Y, and Y agrees to buy the goods and pay to X the agreed-upon price. Title will pass when the buyer performs an act of acquisition, as stated in Chapters 189 through 226. A contract of sale differs from a sale in that the contract contemplates that the title will pass in the future, while a sale passes title at the time it occurs. As noted in Chapter 209, a person cannot sell a thing that is not yet in existence or not in his possession. A person, may, however, *contract* to sell a thing that is not yet in existence or is not then in his possession. Sales will be discussed in Chapters 189 through 226. The author deals here with contracts, including contracts of sale.

In order for a contract to be binding, there must be an act by the party who must perform under the contract, which will bind him to perform. In a bilateral contract, each party performs an act that binds him to the terms of the contract.

Usually the act that binds the party or parties is a *kinyan*.[11] In its simplest terms, a *kinyan* consists of the taking of an object by the party who accepts an obligation from the person for whose benefit the obligation is undertaken. The person obligating himself is the *obligor,* and the person for whose benefit the obligor has undertaken

---

11. The laws of *kinyan* are discussed in Chapter 195.

the obligation is the *obligee*. Thus, in the case of X undertaking to pay Y if Y paints X's fence, X is the obligor and Y is the obligee. The usual method of *kinyan* will be for Y to hand his handerkerchief over to X. When X takes hold of Y's handkerchief, X is bound to pay if Y paints the fence. If the agreement between the parties is that Y undertakes to paint the fence and X undertakes to pay Y for the painting, each party will give his own handkerchief to the other and thus both will simultaneously be bound. (The foregoing is an oversimplification of the process; details are described in Chapter 195.)

Ordinarily, without an act of *kinyan*, the obligor is not bound under the contract. There are several exceptions, in which the psychological benefit flowing to the obligor may bind him to perform even though no formal act of *kinyan* has been made.

This part of this chapter will discuss contracts entered into by way of *kinyan*, and then contracts entered into without a formal *kinyan*.

## TEXT

### The formation of the contract

All contracts (except those discussed in the section entitled "Cases in which mere words can effectuate a contract") must be entered into by the obligor's performing an a act of *kinyan*. If both parties have undertaken obligations, then both parties must perform an act of *kinyan*.

It is not necessary to the validity of a contract that it be in writing or that there be witnesses to the *kinyan*. But the better practice, from the point of view of proof in the event of misunderstanding or dispute, is that the contract be witnessed and be reduced to writing and signed by the witnesses to the agreement.

### Contracts for things not yet in existence

As is noted in Chapter 209 there cannot be a "sale" of things not yet in existence. There may, however, be a contract for the delivery of things not yet in existence. For example, wheat that has not yet been planted cannot be sold, as when X says to Y that X sells to Y the wheat that X will grow the next year.[12] There can, however, be a contract whereby X obligates himself to deliver or sell to Y the wheat that X will grow the next year. In the case of a sale, the object that is sold is the subject of the transaction (e.g., wheat to be grown is sold to Y), while in the case of a contract, the person who is obligated to perform is the subject of the transaction (e.g., X obligates himself to sell to Y the wheat that he will grow next year).

That which has been said regarding things not yet in existence also applies to things that are not in the possession of the obligor. There is a difference of opinion as to whether a person can obligate himself to a person not yet in existence.[13] There is also a difference of opinion as to whether a person may obligate himself *not* to perform an act.

The obligor becomes bound if he expresses his obligation in terms of "I hereby obligate myself to deliver." Since the person who makes the promise by *kinyan* is in existence, the obligation to perform is binding upon him.[14] The obligation is binding immediately and may not be withdrawn by the obligor even if the thing to be delivered is not yet in existence when he wants to withdraw.

According to the majority view, partnership agreements are also entered into by the method of *kinyan*, whereby each party obligates himself to perform certain acts on behalf of the partnership and to turn over to the partnership the income earned on behalf of the partnership, which income is then to be divided according to the terms of the partnership agreement.[15]

There are certain exceptions to a person's ability to obligate himself to deliver an object not yet in existence or not in his possession. For example, if a person wants to obligate himself to sell a house or any

---

12. The obligor is not bound to deliver the wheat even if he left collateral security with the obligee in case the wheat was not delivered when grown. Since there is no obligation to perform, the collateral does not support a binding transaction. There is, however, an opinion that the obligee can continue to hold the collateral until the obligor does perform.

13. Can Ruven say that he obligates himself to give a gift to the first child to be born to his oldest daughter?

14. This is similar to the undertaking by a guarantor of obligations that may never come into existence.

15. But see Chapter 176, where Maimonides notes that this method of *kinyan* may not be adequate to commence a partnership.

unique item that he does not own, but that belongs to a third party, then his undertaking to deliver is of no legal consequence, even if made with a *kinyan* and using the words of obligation, since the possibility exists that the third party will not sell the house or item to him.[16] There are those who hold that if the obligor obtains the house, then he is obligated to sell it to the obligee.[17] But if the thing that he undertakes to deliver or sell is readily available in the marketplace, then the obligation is binding upon the obligor. Even in the former case, although the obligation to sell or deliver is not binding on the obligor, if the obligor inserted a penalty into the contract for nondelivery, then the penalty must be paid.[18] If the obligor who obligates himself to deliver a thing not yet in existence dies before it comes into existence, then his heirs are not obligated to deliver the thing after it comes into existence, since the obligation was only upon the obligor and is not passed on to heirs.

## Acceptance of a lien without acceptance of an obligation

Shimon promised to pay money to Ruven or to deliver personal property or real property to Ruven, and Shimon stated that his property is liened to ensure delivery or payment. Thereafter Shimon pleads that when he made the promise, the realty was not owned by him or the personal property was not yet in existence, and the money was not yet in his possession. He further pleads that he is therefore not obligated, since he did not undertake the delivery of the property or the delivery of the money using words of obligation, and since there was no liability on his part, the lien on his property was of no legal consequence.

There is one opinion that the burden of proof is on Ruven to prove

---

16. My friend Marvin Klitsner points out that the result might be different if the proposed seller had entered into a contract with the house's owner for the house to be sold to the proposed seller.

17. There are those who hold that if the obligation was to deliver the house or the item as a gift and the owner will not sell the house to the obligor, then the obligor must give the obligee/donee the money equivalent of the gift.

18. This assumes that the obligor has complied with all the laws to make a penalty binding upon himself, rather than being an *asmachta*. The law assumes that most penalty clauses are not binding. (See Chapter 207.)

that the property was in the hands of Shimon when the promise was made and was thus binding on Shimon. The majority opinion, however, is that since Shimon stated that he gave the property to Ruven, and all that was lacking was delivery, it is assumed that the property was in the hands of Shimon when he made the promise. Regarding the money, it is assumed that it was acquired by Ruven through delivery to a third party on his behalf, since Shimon's intent was obviously to make a gift that would be effective.

## Obligations that are not specific

According to Maimonides, if someone obligates himself to perform or deliver a thing that is not specific, the obligor is not liable under the contract.[19] For example, if the obligor obligates himself with a *kinyan* to feed or clothe Ruven for five years, his promise is illusory and therefore not binding. Although the time is specified, the amount of the food or clothing is not specified, and this is all the more true if the number of years was not specified. There are commentators who hold that even according to Maimonides' view, if the nonspecific obligation was undertaken in return for consideration given to the obligor, then the obligation would be binding. All the other authorities hold that the obligation is binding on the obligor, and this is the accepted law.[20] The examples that follow are typical and can be applied to all situations in which one person has obligated himself, by *kinyan* and with words of obligation, to perform an act for another person. The obligation may even arise from a bilateral contract, as when Shimon pays Ruven a certain sum to obtain the obligation from Ruven.

If Ruven obligates himself to feed Shimon, and Ruven insists that Shimon eat with him or that Ruven will supply Shimon with food to eat by himself, and Shimon says that he wants Ruven to give him the money and he will buy the food for himself, the beth din will find in

---

19. A person is not apt to obligate himself to an open-ended amount. This comes under the heading of *asmachta* and is discussed in Chapter 207.

20. The law is so widely accepted by all other authorities that one may not state that he desires to follow the opinion of Maimonides. In some disputes, a litigant may state that he wants the beth din to follow the opinion that is favorable to him, but in this case the authorities are so overwhelmingly on one side that one may not request that the opinion of Maimonides be followed.

favor of Shimon.[21] The undertaking of the obligation to feed Shimon means that the recipient of the obligation may decide how he wants to be fed, and Ruven must supply Shimon with money to buy food according to the standard of Ruven's household. In all such cases, the beth din shall try to ascertain the true intent of the obligor when he made the promise. If Ruven states that his obligation is to feed Shimon only in Ruven's home, then the obligation ceases if Shimon refuses to eat in Ruven's home. If Ruven or members of his household make it uncomfortable for Shimon to eat with them, then Ruven will have to supply Shimon with money to buy food to eat elsewhere. If Shimon became ill, the obligation to provide food does not include the requirement to provide medication or medical care.[22] If, however, Ruven obligates himself to provide for all of Shimon's needs, then medical services and clothing are also included.

If Ruven obligates himself to feed or to provide for all of the needs of Shimon according to his position, then beth din will appraise the manner to which Shimon was accustomed to eating and living.

If Ruven obligates himself to feed Shimon, then it is inferred that he meant to do so for all of the days of Shimon's life, or for at least such time as is necessary. There is an opinion that if Ruven obligates himself to feed Shimon without specifying a time, or if he states that he will provide Shimon with $100 a year, then if he provides Shimon with food for a year, or gives him $100 the first year, then Ruven is free of his obligation. There are those who differ in the last case, holding that he must supply him with $100 all the years of his life.

If Ruven obligates himself to feed Shimon or to give him $100, and he does feed him for a while and then stops, he need not pay Shimon the $100, but need only give him the $100 less the amount of the food that he had already supplied.[23]

In another case, Ruven obligates himself to feed Shimon and Shimon's wife, and after he commences feeding them, Shimon's wife dies. Ruven is not obligated to pay to Shimon, who is his wife's heir,

---

21. A typical example would be for the father of the bride to obligate himself to support his future son-in-law while he pursues his studies.

22. See, however, *Shulhan Aruch, Eben haEzer,* Chapter 79, that part of of the husband's obligation to feed his wife includes providing her with medical care and medication.

23. The intent was to pay to Shimon $100 if Ruven did not feed him at all.

the money that Ruven would have used to feed the wife had she not died.[24]

If Ruven obligates himself to feed Shimon at his table, and after some time Ruven dies, the heirs of Ruven must continue to feed Shimon out of the estate.[25]

If Ruven and Levi both obligate themselves, as partners, to feed Shimon, then each is jointly and severally liable to Shimon. If Ruven ceases to pay for half of the food, then Levi must pay the entire amount and seek contribution from Ruven.[26] If each undertakes to meet half of Shimon's food bills, then neither one is responsible for the half that the other does not supply.

## Cases in which mere words can effectuate a contract

Ordinarily, mere words, without a kinyan, cannot make binding an agreement between parties. There are certain exceptions to this rule, however, such as those cases in which the person who takes on performance by mere words binds himself because of the psychological benefit that he derives from entering into the contract. There seem to be ten cases in Rabbinic literature in which such an agreement was held to be binding without the necessity for a kinyan.

**1. Bailee case.** There is a Baraitha cited in Baba Mezia 94a that teaches that a paid bailee may orally stipulate that he will accept the liabilities of a borrower, which are much greater than those of a paid bailee.[27] The Talmud asks how the paid bailee can accept this added liability with mere words. The Talmud records two answers: (1) that of Samuel, who held that there was a formal kinyan, and one may

---

24. There is an opinion that if Ruven specified a certain sum to be used for the feeding of Shimon's wife and then she died, then Shimon, as her heir, can collect the balance from Ruven.

25. The heirs may insist that Shimon eat at their table.

26. Ruven and Levi stand as guarantors one for the other, and thus there is joint and several liability toward Shimon.

27. A paid bailee is liable if the article placed under his watch was negligently cared for and was was lost as a result. He is also liable if the item was lost or stolen even without negligence on his part. However, he is free of liability if the item was lost through an act of God. The borrower is responsible in all cases in which the paid bailee is liable, and he is also liable if the item was lost through an act of God.

undertake liability upon himself by a formal *kinyan;* and (2) that of R. Yohanan, who stated that even if there was no formal *kinyan,* the undertaking is binding in return for the benefit that the bailee receives in that he achieves a reputation for being trustworthy. This consideration makes him liable for the higher standard of care. In Talmudic language this is known as the *hanahah* (benefit) that he receives. *Hanahah* can be translated to refer to psychological benefit.[28]

**2. Marriage case.** In *Kiddushin* 9b, Rav Gidal, in the name of Rav, taught that if the parents of the prospective bride and groom agree to bestow certain gifts on the newlywed couple, their promises are binding. As explained by Rashi, no formal *kinyan* need be made, since the *hanahah* that the parents derive from the marriage is sufficient motivation to bind them to their promises.[29]

**3. Surety case.** In *Baba Bathra* 173b, the question of the liability of the surety is discussed. In concluding the aforementioned discussion, the Talmud states that the assumption of the obligation by the surety does not require a *kinyan.* After the question of how he became liable is discussed, Rav Ashi concludes that his obligation is binding upon him because of the *hanahah* he receives in being trusted by the creditor. As explained by Rashi, the *hanahah* that the surety derives in that he is trusted obviates the necessity of a *kinyan,* and the mere words bind him.

**4. Case of transferring an obligation (*Ma'amad shloshtan*).** In *Gittin* 13b, the Talmud states that if the creditor and debtor and a third person are present together, the creditor may direct the debtor to pay the debt to the third party, and the obligation is effectively transferred. When the question was raised as to how the debt could be transferred without a *kinyan,* Rav Ashi, after some discussion, answers that the *hanahah* that flows to the debtor in that he can now face the new creditor with the same dilatory tactics is sufficient to bind the debtor. (The Talmud eventually gives another answer— namely, that the Rabbis arbitrarily made this rule of law. This reason

---

28. To make an agreement binding, there must be some act to show that the parties intend to be bound. In the case of *kinyan,* the drawing of the handkerchief shows that the parties are at that moment ready to be bound by the terms of the agreement. Without the formal act, actual agreement cannot be shown. The psychological benefit, *hanahah,* that the obligor derives from the agreement is determined by society to be sufficient consent to make the act binding on the party.

29. *Rashi* stands for *Rabbi Shlomo Itzhaki,* commentator par excellence on the Bible and Talmud. He lived in France from 1040 until 1104.

had to be given in response to a question raised in the Talmud, but not to question the basic assumption of Rav Ashi.)

**5. Case of the partners dividing property.** In *Baba Bathra* 106b, it is stated that if brothers (or partners) wish to divide property by lot, then as soon as the first brother draws his lot, he acquires that piece of property and the other brothers can no longer renege on their agreement. Since no *kinyan* had been made, what binds the brothers? Once again Rav Ashi states that they are bound by the mutual *hanahah* that each of the brothers obeys the others. (It seems significant that Rav Ashi is the Rabbi cited in so many of the of these cases in showing that mere words can sometimes create an obligation. Rav Ashi lived toward the end of the Talmudic period and could thus include all the prior thinking of the Talmudic sages in permitting agreement between parties to stand.)

**6. Forgiveness of a debt.** In *Kiddushin* 16a, in discussing the right of a slave to redeem himself by paying to his master a proportionate share of the purchase price according to the years still remaining to work, the Talmud states that the case of the slave is unique, since he cannot be freed on the mere declaration of the master that he is remitting the balance of the purchase price. Tosafoth there comments that the inference is that if the person owing the money is not a slave, then a mere declaration by the creditor can remit the obligation.[30] While Tosafoth here questions their own conclusion, in *Baba Mezia* 112a, they cite this Talmudic passage and hold that forgiveness of a debt does not require a *kinyan;* mere words are sufficient. Although it is not stated, this author assumes that the *hanahah* that the creditor derives is the pleasure that he has in being magnanimous enough to extinguish the debt.

The foregoing six cases demonstrate that there are situations in which the mere declaration together with the *hanahah* will be sufficient consideration to bind the person making the declaration. In the next four cases, the declaration is binding without even the necessity of *hanahah.* This is so because of the nature of the declarant.

**7. Case in which the declarant is bound without any *hanahah* to him.** This case in Chapter 40 deals with the situation in which the declarant states that he is obligated to someone.

---

30. Tosafoth were Rabbinic scholars residing in France and Germany from the twelfth through the fourteenth centuries. Their commentaries are included on the printed pages of the Talmud.

**8. Case in which one of the parties is a community.**
Mordechai[31] was asked whether a community that had engaged a
teacher could back out of the agreement prior to the teacher's having
commenced his work.[32] He answered that the community, or any
large group, or representatives thereof, if they are acting on behalf of
the group, may not rescind their oral agreement even if no *kinyan* was
made. In the case of individuals, however, the agreement would not
be binding until the teacher had actually commenced work.[33]

**9. Case of the Holy Temple as a party.** The Talmud, in the first
chapter of *Kiddushin*, describes the various methods for transferring
property, real or personal. In a *Mishnah* on page 28b, it is stated that
the (oral) dedication of property to the Holy Temple is the equivalent
of the delivery of the property in the case of an individual, which
would, of course, in his case have completed the transaction.

**10. Case of gifts *causa mortis*.** A gift *causa mortis* is a gift made
by a dying person in contemplation of death. In *Gittin* 13b, the Talmud
teaches that the words of the dying person are to be given effect as
if his words had been written down and the writing delivered to the
donee, even if no *kinyan* was made. The reason is that the dying man
should not have the anguish of not knowing whether his wishes for
the disposition of his property will be followed after his death.

(Other topics dealing with contracts will be treated in their own
chapters.)

---

31. Mordechai ben Hillel, who lived in Germany from 1240 until 1298, was the
author of a code of halachah that was greatly relied upon by subsequent codifiers and
respondents. His codes appear toward the back of the printed editions of the Talmud.

32. This appears in the *Baba Mezia*, secondary glosses to Chapter 6, sections 457
and 458.

33. It would seem that Mordechai's reasoning could be extended so that the
teacher also could not rescind the agreement. Mordechai was a student of Rabbi Meir
of Rottenberg, as was Asheri, who lived in Germany and then Spain (1250–1327).
Asheri was asked (*Responsa*, Chapter 6, Responsum 19) about a taxpayer who had
entered into an oral agreement with the city authorities to absolve him from paying
some local taxes, since he also paid taxes in another community. Could the
community rescind the tax exemption granted to him? Asheri answered that all
agreements entered into by a community or its representatives were binding on the
community, even if its members had not entered into a formal *kinyan*. Agreements
made by the community are equivalent to their having been written and transmitted
to the other side.

# PART III
# PROPER PARTY NOT NAMED IN THE
# INSTRUMENT OF INDEBTEDNESS

## INTRODUCTION

There may be times, for any number of reasons, when a lender will lend money through an agent and will have the agent named in the instrument of indebtedness. There may also be times when a creditor will want to name another person as the creditor in the instrument of indebtedness. This section discusses situations in which the lender is not the person named in the instrument, the debtor has not paid, and the lender now wants to sue the debtor. What rights does the lender have in the instrument, and what rights does he have against the debtor?

## TEXT

### Agent named as creditor in the instrument of indebtedness

The instrument of indebtedness produced by Ruven in beth din names Levi as the creditor and Shimon as the debtor. Ruven pleads that Levi, when he made the loan to Shimon, was acting as an agent of Ruven. Since Ruven was not decisive as to who was named as the creditor, the instrument named Levi as the creditor. Shimon, in defense against Ruven, pleads that Ruven has no legal connection with Shimon and thus Shimon cannot sue; furthermore, if he wants to have standing to sue, he should bring a power of attorney from Levi, or an assignment of the instrument from Levi to Ruven. If Levi admits in the presence of witnesses that the money that was loaned was Ruven's and that he, Levi, acted as Ruven's agent, then the beth din will permit Ruven standing to sue Shimon. This can be done if the recognition of Ruven, rather than Levi, as the true holder of the instrument will not prejudice any persons, such as creditors of Levi.[34] Beth din will compel Shimon to recognize Ruven as the true holder of the instrument, although he has no assignment from Levi.[35] However, if the instrument was originally delivered to Ruven, then Shimon will be compelled to pay Ruven because Levi's creditors could not have enforced collection from Levi's debtors, since they did not have the instrument in their possession.

If there are witnesses who can testify that they saw Ruven give the money to Levi to lend to Shimon and that Levi was instructed to do so as the agent of Ruven, then there is no necessity for Levi's admission, and the instrument will be transferred to Ruven even if it prejudices Levi's creditors, since the witnesses prove that Levi had no interest in the instrument.

## Lender instructs that the instrument be written in someone else's name

Ruven loans money to Shimon and instructs the draftsman to name Levi as the creditor.[36] The instrument is so written and, pursuant to Ruven's instructions, delivered to Ruven. When Ruven presents the instrument to Shimon for payment, Shimon asserts that Ruven is not the proper party to make a claim against Shimon, but rather that Levi is the proper party, since Levi is named as the obligee in the instrument. Shimon's plea is rejected, since it is Ruven who produces the instrument. Levi may, but is not under any obligation to, write an assignment of the instrument to Ruven. Shimon cannot allege that

---

34. If the instrument is taken from Levi and acknowledged to be Ruven's, then if Levi has any creditors, they will be deprived of an asset on which to levy if Levi does not pay their debt. Thus Levi's admission that the money was Ruven's and that Levi was acting as Ruven's agent will not be recognized by the beth din.

35. An assignment of an instrument from the assignor to the assignee is necessary only if the assignor was the true owner of the instrument and now wishes to transfer his ownership in the instrument to the assignee. An assignment is not necessary from the agent of the assignor who made the loan for the assignor as his agent. This type of recognition also differs from an assignment in that the assignor may retain the right to forgive the debt even after he has assigned the instrument to the assignee. In the case discussed here, Levi cannot forgive Shimon the debt, since Levi had no actual interest in the debt. (See Chapter 66.)

36. Ruven's motivation is not critical in this section.

Levi has the true interest in the instrument, since Ruven is the one who produces the instrument, and it is he who at the time of the writing of the instrument gave the instruction to insert Levi's name as the obligee.

Shimon owes $100 to Ruven. The parties agree that a note of indebtedness in the sum of $20 will be written naming Levi as the obligee. Thereafter, Ruven forgives all of Shimon's indebtedness. Levi comes to enforce collection of the $20 note, which names Levi as the obligee. Shimon defends on the grounds that the true party in interest in the note is Ruven, and Ruven has forgiven Shimon all of his debts. If the note, after it was written, was first delivered to Ruven and then given by Ruven to Levi, then the plea of Shimon will be accepted and the $20 will be deemed forgiven. If, on the other hand, the note was delivered directly to Levi, then Shimon will have to pay Levi when he presents the note.

Ruven loans money to Shimon and takes a mortgage on land owned by Shimon as security for the loan. When the mortgage is written, Ruven instructs that Ruven's minor son be named as the obligee. Thereafter, Shimon cannot oppose payment to Ruven on the grounds that it is the minor son, and not Ruven, who is named in the mortgage, since it is assumed that when the mortgage was written, the father was the guardian of the son and still continues in such capacity. However, if the son is no longer a minor when the instrument has to be paid, then the father must assign the instrument to the son unless the father can prove that it was really his money that was used to make the loan. If the father dies while the son is still a minor, then beth din will give the instrument to the son named therein, and the father's other heirs cannot legally plead that the instrument should be part of the estate.

A note of indebtedness names Ruven as the obligee, but just before the end of the note, it states that the money belonged to the community chest. Ruven pleads that the note belongs to him, since the community owed him money and it was for that reason that he was named in the note as the payee. The community denies Ruven's pleas. Judgment will be rendered in favor of the community, since the note stated that the money loaned belonged to the community. The community may assert any reason for naming Ruven as the obligee. If Ruven can prove his pleas with competent testimony of witnesses, then the note will be given to Ruven and he may sue on it.

A widow asserts that the land left her by her husband when he died was half hers, having been purchased with money that she had inherited from her father. The deeds name both the widow and the deceased husband as the owners. She will be judged to be the owner of half of the realty. If the widow is the sole grantee named in the deed, and she pleads that she furnished the funds for the entire realty, then judgment will be rendered in her favor. This mandate will be followed if the widow did not do business in the home, as defined in Chapter 62, or even if she did business in the home if the deed was written by the deceased husband to the wife. The beth din should examine every transaction very carefully, since many men write their assets in the names of their wives for any number of reasons.

# Chapter 61

## MISCELLANEOUS LAWS REGARDING INSTRUMENTS OF INDEBTEDNESS

### INTRODUCTION

This chapter, following Chapter 61 of the *Shulhan Aruch*, groups together various laws that were not included in other chapters regarding instruments of indebtedness. The most significant laws of this chapter deal with the practices of the community. If certain practices have developed in a community as to who may write and who may sign an instrument, what the contents of an instrument should be, or what effect should be given to certain terms, then such practices will often be followed.

### TEXT

#### Community practices to be followed in writing the instrument

The practices of the community regarding instruments should be followed unless following such practices would be in conflict with halachah.[1]

---

1. For example, a practice that conflicts with halachah would be if the community's practice is to include a provision that would permit the creditor to make his own levy in the form of self-help by seizing the debtor's assets without first having to resort to

Notes of indebtedness as well as all other documents, such as waivers of indebtedness, deeds of transfer, and other commercial documents, should follow the practices of the community, unless the parties have a reason for not following such practices.[2] Thus if an obligor authorizes a note of indebtedness to be written and accepts the associated obligations by a *kinyan*,[3,4] the draftsman may draft the instrument according to the practices of the community without the obligor's specifically so stating, even if the practice is to draft an instrument that is to be construed favorably to the obligee or grantee.[5] There is an opinion that even if the draftsman neglects to include all of the clauses favorable to the obligee that are ordinarily included by the community, the beth din will deem such clauses to be part of the instrument if it can be shown that the obligor was aware that such clauses were ordinarily inserted into instruments in that community.[6]

If the community enacted a law that all instruments must be drafted by the community scribe, then any instrument that is drafted by another scribe will not be enforced by beth din.[7] An exception would

---

beth din to obtain a judgment and an order permitting a levy. In the ordinary course of events, such levy cannot be made without a beth din order.

2. Unless otherwise specified by the parties, the community practice will be assumed.

3. No instrument may be drafted that obligates a person to be liable for something, or to give up any rights, or to part with ownership of anything unless the obligor authorizes the instrument to be drawn and delivered.

4. The obligor takes hold of a handkerchief or other object not belonging to him but given to him by the obligee or by an agent of the obligee and, by so doing, authorizes the obligation to take effect. In the case under discussion, the obligation undertaken by the obligor is to permit and authorize the note of indebtedness or other instrument to be drawn.

5. As noted in Chapter 207, there is the concept of *asmachta*, which is an obligation that is ordinarily not binding on the obligor, because it is an illusory undertaking of obligation. Certain exceptions make it binding, however. In some circumstances, if the instrument states that it is not an *asmachta*, then it will be presumed that it was drawn as an exception to the laws of *asmachta* and is binding. Unless the witnesses and draftsman were instructed otherwise, they may insert in the instrument that it was not an *asmachta*, if that is the community's practice.

6. There is a contrary opinion that since the instrument omitted the customary clauses, they were omitted intentionally.

7. A community may enact such legislation to prevent forgeries.

obtain if the instrument of obligation or deed were signed by the obligor, whether or not written by the obligor.[8]

There is a practice in some communities that when the obligor, by *kinyan*, authorizes the scribe and witnesses to write and execute an instrument, the scribe first writes a brief memorandum of the event, which would be signed by the witnesses. The intent of the parties, the scribe, and witnesses is that, when more time was available, the contents of the memorandum would be reproduced in another writing, which would have the effect of an instrument of indebtedness, a deed, or whatever instrument is intended. The memorandum is not to be afforded the status of an instrument unless it is the community's custom to afford a memorandum such status.

If an instrument says that the holder thereof may enforce payment thereof without a power of attorney from the payee in the instrument, then payment may be enforced unless there is a custom in the community against enforceability by a holder without a power of attorney.[9]

If an instrument states that it is payable to the bearer and does not name an obligee, then the holder may enforce collection even if it is known that he was not the lender who created the debt against the obligor.[10]

## Instruments are to be enforced according to their language

Instruments are to be enforced according to their plain language. The obligor's plea that he did not understand the terms thereof is no defense.[11] It does not matter whether the instrument is written in Hebrew or in some other language.

---

8. When the instrument is signed by the obligor, the concern about forgery, whether by the draftsman or by the witnesses, is alleviated.

9. If the instrument says "to the holder thereof," it makes no difference whether the holder is a Jew or non-Jew. If the holder was dead when the instrument was drawn, there is an opinion that he cannot be the holder.

10. See also Chapter 50 regarding bearer notes of indebtedness.

11. It is presumed that a person understood what he signed or instructed others to write to obligate himself. This holds true even if it is known that the obligor is illiterate.

There is an opinion that if the instrument contains a condition, then beth din must follow the intent of the clause rather than the literal language of the condition.

If the husband who is divorcing his wife pleads that he does not want to abide by the terms of the *kethubah* because he did not understand its terms when it was executed, he must still abide by its terms as written.[12] This holds true even if the husband can prove that he did not understand the *kethubah* because he was illiterate and lacked understanding of things legal.

## Instruments containing a clause that an amount will be agreed upon

Ruven and Shimon agree to dissolve their partnership. Shimon acknowledges that he owes Ruven money, but the exact amount is to be ascertained from their further examination of all relevant facts. To abide the event, Shimon authorizes the writing of an instrument signed by witnesses and stating that he acknowledges that he owes Ruven a sum not to exceed $1,000, the exact amount to be decided upon between the parties.[13] The instrument is executed on February 1. The fact that it is signed by witnesses causes Shimon's realty to be liened to Ruven.[14] On March 1, Ruven produces another writing signed by Shimon stating that Shimon owes him $100. If Shimon does

---

12. The *kethubah* is a writing executed at the time of a wedding ceremony. It is signed by two witnesses, as is any other instrument of indebtedness. The *kethubah* obligates the husband to make a certain payment to the wife in case he divorces her; in the case of his death, the *kethubah* obligates the estate to pay his widow a certain sum. The *kethubah* was instituted so that the wife would not be so unimportant in the eyes of the husband that he could divorce her with impunity. The *kethubah* document cannot be waived by the wife.

13. The sum of $1,000 was inserted into the instrument because both parties knew that the amount owing could not possibly exceed $1,000. It was necessary to insert some sum, for otherwise the instrument would have contained an unliquidated amount and would not have effected a lien on Shimon's realty. The fact that there was no lower limit did not affect the lien, since if there is an upper limit, it is not an unliquidated amount. Also, this instrument provided for a procedure to set the exact amount.

14. See Chapter 43.

not have assets to pay the $100, then Shimon can trace any real estate that Shimon owned on February 1, and that he thereafter sold.[15]

## Creditor alleges that the instrument was stolen and given to debtor

Ruven, without having an instrument of indebtedness in his possession, sues Shimon and pleads that Shimon admitted in the presence of witnesses that he owed Ruven $100 according to an instrument. Ruven further pleads that the instrument was stolen from him and given to Shimon. Shimon admits that he had made the admission alleged by Ruven, but states that Ruven had never lent Shimon money. Rather, Levi had asked Shimon to execute an instrument in favor of Ruven as if Ruven had loaned money to Shimon. Shimon continues that Levi took the instrument and promised to return it to him, and to ensure that delivery of the instrument would not cause Shimon any damage, Levi delivered to Shimon collateral security worth at least $100. Shimon further alleges that Levi returned the instrument to him, and that Shimon returned the security to Levi. If Shimon takes a *hesseth* oath that the facts are as related by him, he will win the case.[16,17]

## Instruments long past due

The obligor's heirs, in a note of indebtedness,[18] plead several defenses based on time: that the obligee waited until the obligor died so that the obligee could sue the obligor's heirs; that the amount of time that passed before the obligee made a claim on the note was inordinate;

---

15. The first instrument, dated February 1 and witnessed, created a lien on all of Shimon's realty up to $1,000, and thus any purchaser of realty from Shimon knew that there was a lien on the purchased realty.

16. See Volume III, Chapter 87, regarding different types of oaths.

17. Shimon is believed when he takes a *hesseth* oath, because he could plead that he repaid the instrument, since the instrument was not in Ruven's possession.

18. By "instrument of indebtedness" is meant an instrument that was witnessed by two witnesses and was delivered to the obligee in the presence of two witnesses. If the instrument was merely a promissory note signed by the obligor, then the obligor's defenses will be accepted.

and that the note is old.[19] If the obligee offers beth din sufficient explanation for waiting so long to sue, the defenses will be dismissed.[20] However, if beth din, after intensive examination, is not satisfied with the explanation, the defenses will be accepted and the complaint of the obligee will be dismissed. The defenses will be accepted even if the instrument states that the obligor will not raise any defense, and even if the instrument contains a credence clause stating that the presentation of the instrument was sufficient to enable the holder to collect thereon without further proof. If community practice prohibits suit on old instruments, then the prohibition is binding on the community. Also, if the defendant pleads that he paid the instrument before it became old, then the defendant may take a *hesseth* oath and be free of liability. Some commentaries set forth a rule which states that if the instrument does not bear interest it cannot be sued on after three years from its date, and if the instrument does bear interest it cannot be sued on after six years, depending upon the intent of the parties. What emerges from this law is a sort of statute of limitations that beth din should apply in each case, or else hold to the suggested three- and six-year rule. If the secular authorities have a

---

19. The actual reported case on which the law is based appeared in a decision of Asheri (1250–1327, Spain: *Responsa*, Chapter 68, par. 20), who was asked by a beth din to give advice on the following case. The obligee had waited for 30 years before suing on the instrument. The instrument had ten obligors, nine of whom had died. He sued only the heirs of the nine who had died and did not sue the tenth person, who was still alive, although the tenth person had the ability to pay the entire debt himself. The defendant heirs pleaded several defenses—that the instrument was written as an accommodation for a loan made to the community, and that the community had probably repaid the loan in the interim; that the plaintiff was not the type of person who would have loaned the large sum to these ten persons; that the plaintiff had waited too long to sue; and that the obligor who was alive was intentionally not sued, since he probably could have provided a defense. Asheri held that the fact that the obligee waited until the obligors had died and that he had waited a long time did not in and of itself invalidate the instrument. However, if the beth din believed that there was fraud involved, as evidenced by the inordinate delay, then beth din should find on behalf of the defendants. Asheri concludes that this was his practice when instruments were produced after considerable delay, and if he believed that there was fraud, then he gave a writing to the defendant to produce in the event that the plaintiff attempted to sue again on the instrument.

20. The plaintiff might, for example, allege that he had misplaced the instrument or had forgotten about it.

statute of limitations and this is the practice of the community, then such statute should be followed.[21]

## Memorandum not to be given status of an instrument

A writing contains the following: "This is an explanation of the admission made before us by Ruven that he is holding a certain sum left to Yaakov." It was held that there was not sufficient authority for the persons who heard the admission to take the statements of Ruven and reduce them to writing as a note of admission.[22] Had it been held to be a note of admission signed by two witnesses, the note would have placed a lien on the obligor's realty from the date of the admission, if a *kinyan* was made by the obligor. Also, if the witnesses' signatures could be authenticated, the instrument would be admissible into evidence without the witnesses having to appear. The lack of a *kinyan* also showed that the admission was not intended to be authority to write a note of admission. Beth din should investigate each case to determine whether the admission was intended to be authority to reduce the admission as a note of indebtedness. (See Chapter 40 for a discussion of circumstances under which an admission may be reduced to a note of admission.)

## Return of the instrument after it has been paid

The borrower should not repay a loan that is evidenced by an instrument of indebtedness unless he has obtained the instrument

---

21. See the comments of Mishpat Charutz, Chapter 61, comment 17, in *Mishpetai Emeth*, written by Rabbi Zechariah Shrebi and published in Tel Aviv, Israel in 1966. He also suggests that beth din seek to arbitrate the matter with a formula to be followed by beth din.

22. This law in the *Shulhan Aruch, Hoshen haMishpat*, Chapter 60, par. 10, also comes from a responsa of Asheri (Chapter 65, par. 3). Here, Asheri provides rules for when the witnesses may reduce the obligor's admissions to a note of admission, and when the admission may only be reduced to a memorandum, which the witnesses may later use to refresh their memories. Many of these laws appear in Volume III, Chapter 81.

itself, or at least until he has obtained a receipt of payment that sufficiently identifies the instrument that has been paid.

There may be situations, however, in which the loan has been repaid and the lender has not returned the instrument to the borrower. If, after the borrower has repaid the debt, the lender postpones returning the instrument of indebtedness, the lender may be put under a ban until he returns it. If the lender refuses to return the note, then beth din should use whatever method they believe advisable to obtain the return of the note to the borrower. For example, beth din might write a receipt for the borrower, which would serve as a complete defense if the lender sued on the instrument.[23] The prohibition against retaining a paid instrument is noted in Chapter 57.

---

23. There may be some problems if the lender assigned a paid instrument to an innocent purchaser. (See Chapter 66.)

# Chapter 62

## THE WIFE WHO MANAGES THE HOUSEHOLD

### INTRODUCTION

This chapter deals with a wife who manages her husband's property, and during the term of the management gains assets in her own name such as instruments of indebtedness, as well as other property. It deals also with a man who has amassed property in his own name while managing property for all his brothers. Whether the subject is the wife or the brother, the question arises, how did they amass this property when they were managing the property of others? Does the property really belong to the person or persons for whom they are managing the property?

The property that a wife brings into the marriage (the dowry) may be used by the husband, and all income therefrom belongs to the husband.[1] Therefore, if a wife who is managing her husband's property

---

1. Such property may be under the stewardship of the husband in one of two ways. In either case he keeps all of the profits of the property. According to the method known as *nichsai tzon barzel* (iron sheep property), the husband guarantees to the wife that the property will be returned to her upon divorce or upon his death at the same value as it had on the day he took possession, regardless of whether he makes a profit or loses money during the operation of the property. Alternatively, the property may be delivered by the wife to the husband as *nichsai melog* (milking property), in which case the husband does not guarantee the value of the property

now holds property in her name that she amassed *after* the marriage, it is presumed that the property, although in her name, is really property that she amassed for her husband. The deeds should have been in her husband's name, since she was using her husband's money to purchase the property since her own money had been turned over to her husband at the time of the marriage. However, if the wife can show that she inherited money of her own after marriage, then she is believed when she states that the property that now stands in her name was purchased with such money. By agreement, whether prenuptial or postnuptial, the parties can determine that the husband will not have the use of the property that the wife brought into the marriage. In return for the use of the property that the husband is given, the husband has certain obligations to the wife.[2] Brothers who have inherited property from their father stand in a relationship to each other similar to the relationship of wife to husband if they appoint one brother to manage the property. It may be assumed that the property that the managing brother has amassed should be owned by all the brothers. Certain presumptions are to be followed in all of these cases, and this chapter will deal with these laws.

---

when it is returned to the wife. In the latter case, all losses and gains are the wife's responsibility. In both cases the husband enjoys the profits of the property.

2. Maimonides, in *Laws Concerning Marriage*, Chapter 12, enumerates ten things for which a husband is obligated to his wife and four things for which a wife is obligated to her husband. According to Torah law, a husband is obligated to provide: (1) her food; (2) her clothing; (3) conjugal rights. The Rabbis instituted seven other obligations: (4) to heal her if she becomes ill, (5) to ransom her if she is captured, (6) to bury her if she dies, (7) to provide for her maintenance out of his estate, (8) to let her reside in his house after he dies as long as she is a widow, (9) to permit her daughters whom he has sired to receive their maintenance out of his estate until they become betrothed, and (10) to permit her male children whom he has sired to inherit her *kethubah*, in addition to sharing with their half-brothers in the father's estate. This is in addition to the statutory *kethubah* (which provides that the husband will pay to the wife a specified sum in case of divorce and that his estate will pay her a specified amount in case he dies). The four things to which a husband is entitled were all instituted by the Rabbis: (1) he is entitled to her earnings; (2) he is entitled to anything she finds; (3) he is entitled to the profits of the property she brought into the marriage; and (4) if she dies in his lifetime, he is entitled to be her sole heir. There are many laws governing whether some of these obligations may not be waived by the husband and/or the wife.

There is a difference between the laws that apply to the wife who manages her husband's property and the wife who does not manage her husband's property; if the wife who does not manage her husband's property amasses property in her own name, it cannot be said that she did this while she had stewardship of her husband's property, and thus the presumption in the husband's favor may not apply.

# TEXT

## The wife who manages her husband's property

Unless shown otherwise, it is presumed that a wife who is at home is managing her husband's property while she is at home.[3] There is also a presumption that since all of the wife's property was given over to the husband as part of the dowry, then all property in her possession is her husband's, even if she is named in the deed. There is also no presumption in favor of the wife if there is property standing in her name, since the husband may have any variety of reasons for putting the property in her name.

If a wife manages her husband's property and has instruments of indebtedness or deeds of real estate in her name, and she alleges that they belong to her and are not her husband's, and the husband alleges that she amassed the property while managing his money and his property, then the burden is on the wife to prove that she had her own funds that she received after the marriage, and to which her husband is therefore not entitled as part of the dowry. If she does not prove with two witnesses that the deeds and instruments of indebtedness and that are in her name are her own, then the presumption in favor of the husband will apply, and he or his heirs will inherit the properties represented by the deeds in her name and the instruments of indebtedness standing in her name.[4]

However, if the wife can prove that she had received independent

---

3. Most women are given money by their husbands for household expenses and other necessities, and thus they manage his money.
4. The result will be the same whether she is married or widowed.

moneys after the marriage, then she will obtain the deeds and instruments of indebtedness that stand in her name. She need not trace the moneys to the individual deeds, but if she can show independent moneys during the period after the marriage until the dates of the deeds, then she will be believed when she states that she bought the deeds in her own name from her own funds and also that she loaned the moneys from her own funds, which loans are evidenced by the instruments of indebtedness.[5]

The foregoing need for proof applies to instruments given to the wife by third parties. If the instruments are given by the husband, however, then she may keep them as her own without bringing proof of independent moneys after the marriage. If such instruments and deeds given by the husband are held by the husband, then it is presumed that they belong to the husband, and that he used his wife's name for his own purposes.[6]

If both the wife and the husband are dead when the case arises, then it is presumed that all of the deeds and instruments in the wife's name were hers, and the burden of proof is on those who contest this conclusion to prove otherwise.[7]

That which has been said regarding the wife also applies to the case in which a son manages his father's property, provided that the son is still dependent upon his father for his funds and thus could not possibly have amassed the deeds and instruments that stand in his name.

---

5. She may have to take an oath and keep the deeds and instruments of indebtedness. There is a usual presumption that that which a person possesses is his. In the case of the wife, that presumption is somewhat weakened by the fact that her own money and properties were entrusted to the husband at the time of the marriage. Thus it is assumed that everything she has amassed could not be from her own funds but rather is from funds she is managing for her husband. As soon as she can show that she had independent funds after the marriage, she is back under the usual presumption that if a woman possesses deeds or instruments or indebtedness in her name, then they must belong to her.

6. He may have done so in order to avoid paying creditors or taxes, or so that he could avoid communal obligations by pleading that he had no assets in his name.

7. If the husband is alive when his wife dies, he inherits her assets in all events, and the entire discussion is academic. Even if her heirs, who would inherit if there were no husband surviving her, allege that the husband waived his rights to inherit her assets by a prenuptial agreement, they have the burden of proof. If they plead this as a fact, then the husband may have to take an oath to offset this allegation.

## The wife who does not manage her husband's property

If the wife does not manage her husband's property, then all of the deeds and instruments in her name are presumed to belong to her, since she had no access to her husband's funds and therefore could not have been a trustee on his behalf. If the instruments or deeds are in the names of both the wife and the husband, then it is assumed that they belong to both of them equally.

## Cases involving brothers

If brothers who live together entrust one of them to manage their affairs from their home, and deeds or instruments are then amassed by the managing brother in his name, then it is presumed that they are the property of all of the brothers. If the managing brother alleges that he inherited money or deeds or instruments from his mother,[8] or that he found them or received them as a gift, then the burden of proof is on him to establish the facts. If he dies, then his heirs need not establish the facts; rather, the surviving brothers must establish the fact that they are entitled to their share of the deeds or instruments.[9] However, if it is generally known that the property had belonged to all of the brothers, and the deceased brother's deeds were dated subsequent thereto, then the deceased brother's heirs have the burden of proving that the property was their deceased father's.

That which has been said about the brother's bearing the burden of proof when he is alive applies when all the brothers' funds are pooled together. But if they had separate expense and income accounts, or if the brother had other business besides the business of the family, then he is believed when he alleges that the instruments and deeds in his name belong solely to him.[10]

---

8. In this case the brothers were the sons of another father.

9. While he is alive it is possible to question him about the deeds and instruments that stand in his name. After he dies, then the presumption that a deed or instrument is owned by the person named therein will prevail unless it can be proved otherwise.

10. If the brothers claim with certainty that the deeds and instruments were acquired with their joint moneys, then he may have to take an oath to sustain his allegations.

## Other persons

The laws that apply to wives or brothers do not apply to an unrelated person who manages the owner's property. All that is in his possession not applicable to the business of the owner belongs to the manager, including all personalty, deeds, and instruments in his name. However, if the personalty, deeds, or instruments are known to have once belonged to the owner, then the manager must prove that they now belong to him, such as through purchase or gift.

# Chapter 63

# A HOLDER WHO REQUESTS THE FORGERY OF AN INSTRUMENT

## INTRODUCTION

This chapter focuses on a person (the "holder") who presents an instrument of indebtedness. The debtor named in the instrument (the "debtor") produces witnesses who testify that the holder of the instrument sought witnesses who had not witnessed the loan either to forge the signatures of other persons or to sign that the holder had loaned money in their presence to a person named in the instrument as the debtor. The fact that a holder has sought people to become involved in such fraudulent practices renders his instrument suspect.

It is possible for a person to forge someone else's signature so artfully that he himself cannot tell that his signature was forged, and so he testifies that it is indeed his signature. There is a difference between a person's testimony that the signature on an instrument is his but he does not recollect signing it, and his testimony that he recollects signing the instrument.

An instrument of indebtedness has greater value to a lender than does an oral loan.[1] The loan described in the instrument may have taken place, but the borrower may not have provided authorization to reduce the loan to a writing subscribed by two witnesses.

---

1. See Chapter 43.

In beth din there are several alternatives for authenticating an instrument. The witnesses who signed may testify as to their signatures. Or, other persons who recognize their signatures may testify that they are the signatures of the witnesses. Beth din may recognize the signatures, or they may have another authenticated document with which to compare the signatures on the instrument.[2] Witnesses who were present when the loan was made may testify that they saw the loan, but that they do not recall signing the instrument. In all of these situations, the person named in the instrument as the debtor denies the loan.

What is the effect of testimony by two valid witnesses that the holder of the instrument sought persons to sign an instrument against the debtor, insofar as the contested instrument is concerned and also insofar as any other instruments the holder may have against the debtor are concerned? And what, if any, effect does the holder's attempt to secure the services of perjurors have on other instruments that he has in his possession?

# TEXT

## Invalidation of instruments if the holder sought the services of forgers

If witnesses testified that Ruven sought witnesses to forge an instrument against Shimon in the sum of $100, then the instrument that he produced against Shimon in that sum may not be used by Ruven to collect money from Shimon. Ruven's claim is now a claim on an oral loan. The fact that beth din has authenticated the instrument does not alter the situation, since it is assumed that the forgery was so well done that even the alleged witnesses cannot tell that their signatures were forged. If the witnesses recollect the loan and also testify that they recognize their signatures, then the instrument will be authenticated.

If the witnesses testify that they recollect signing the instrument, or if other persons testify that they recollect that the witnesses signed the instrument, then the instrument will be valid.

---

2. See Chapter 46.

## Effect on other instruments in the holder's possession

Other instruments against the debtor that the holder has in his possession will be deemed to be subject to authentication if they are in an amount other than that for which the holder sought forgers.[3] However, the beth din should scrutinize such instruments with a greater degree of care than instruments produced by other holders. If the witnesses testify that the holder sought to have them forge the instrument without specifying a sum, then all instruments that the holder has against the debtor will be invalidated.

If the witnesses testify that the holder sought to have them forge signatures on the instrument without naming a debtor, then all of the instruments in the holder's possession are invalidated.

If the instrument predates the time that the holder was seeking forgers, and the instrument has been authenticated in beth din, then the instrument is valid.

## Disposition of the invalidated instruments

The invalidated instruments are not destroyed but rather are placed in a depository or with the beth din itself.[4]

---

3. The reason is that all persons are presumed honest, and the second instrument is assumed to represent a valid loan. The holder sought forgers because he really had lent the debtor money, but the loan was an oral one, and the holder wanted to convert it to a written one.

4. The instruments are not destroyed because witnesses may come and testify that they saw the witnesses sign the instrument. The instruments are not left in the holder's possession because he may institute an action on the instruments in some distant beth din where there will be no witnesses to testify that the holder had sought forgers.

# Chapter 64

## LEVY MADE BY A CREDITOR/BAILEE ON INSTRUMENTS IN HIS POSSESSION

### INTRODUCTION

According to Torah law, personal property inherited by heirs cannot be traced by the decedent's creditors.[1] According to a Geonic decree, however, the decedent's creditors can trace not only personal property to the debtor's heirs, but also instruments of indebtedness that the decedent possessed. If a creditor uses self-help and seizes personalty or instruments of indebtedness from the decedent, such seizure is valid.[2] Is the situation in which the creditor, as a bailee, is holding instruments of the debtor subject to a similar levy?

### TEXT

#### Levy on instruments made by the bailee to pay the bailor's debt

The debtor had deposited with the creditor instruments that belonged to him, and this was known. Thereafter the debtor died. There were

---

1. See Chapter 107 in Volume IV.

2. As discussed in Chapter 66, the ownership of an instrument of indebtedness cannot be transferred except through the delivery of the instrument together with a written assignment thereof. If the creditor has seized instruments, he may keep them until the heirs repay the moneys due him from the decedent.

witnesses both to the delivery of the instruments to the creditor and to the fact that the instruments were in the creditor's hands before the lawsuit was instituted by the heirs for their return.[3] The creditor alleges that he levied on these instruments to repay the debt while the debtor was still alive. If there are witnesses to subtantiate the creditor's allegation that the debtor, while he was still alive, demanded that the creditor return the instruments to him, and the creditor refused to do so, then the levy is valid, without the creditor's having to take an oath. If there are no witnesses to testify to such facts, then the alleged seizure by the creditor is not valid against the heirs.

There is an opinion, however, that the creditor may allege that he seized the instruments as collateral security for repayment of the loan.

If it was not known that the bailor/decedent was indebted to the bailee, then the bailee is not believed when he merely alleges that he levied on the instruments that the bailor deposited with him for a debt that the bailor owed to him. The bailee must turn the instruments over to the heirs of the decedent/bailor.

---

3. If there are no witnesses that the creditor had the instruments in his possession immediately prior to the lawsuit, then the creditor, although admitting that he once had possession of the instruments, as testified to by the witnesses of delivery, could have claimed that the instruments were lost by an Act of God. In such a case he would not be responsible for them. But if there are witnesses that he had the instruments in his possession immediately prior to the lawsuit, then he cannot allege an Act of God, and thus arises the necessity of his refusing to return the instruments to the debtor during the debtor's lifetime.

# Chapter 65

## FOUND INSTRUMENTS AND RECEIPTS

### INTRODUCTION

It occasionally happens that an instrument or a receipt of payment is found by a person who is neither the lender/payee nor the borrower. The finder may discover it among his own papers or in the street, or heirs may come across it among the decedent's papers.

When a person finds an instrument among his own papers, he will usually know something about its nature and origin; he will know, for example, whether the instrument was given to him by a borrower to hold for a loan not originating with the finder, or was given to him by a lender for safe-keeping or as an escrowee. When the nature and origin of the instrument are not known, or not remembered, however, many questions may arise.

There is a concept in halachah known as "setting the matter aside until the prophet Elijah appears." The prophet Elijah is the harbinger of the coming of the Messiah. When there are matters that the beth din cannot decide because they cannot ascertain the facts, such matters are held in abeyance, with neither party to the dispute obtaining judgment. In the case of an instrument or receipt, this means that neither the lender nor the borrower will be given possession.

# TEXT

## An instrument found among one's documents

A person finds an instrument among his documents and does not know its nature or origin.[1] Perhaps it was given to him by the lender for safekeeping; or perhaps the borrower gave it to him to hold after he had paid the lender named therein; or perhaps it was given to him to hold as an escrowee, and all or part of it had been paid. In all of these cases the instrument should remain with him until Elijah the prophet appears. If he fails to keep the instrument and instead returns it to the lender named therein, then he has transgressed the instructions of the Sages. If the finder has transgressed by returning the instrument to the lender, and the lender contradicts the finder and states that he always had possession of the instrument, and there is no independent testimony that it was the finder who gave him the instrument, then the lender may collect on the instrument. But if there were witnesses, or if the lender admits that it was the finder who turned the instrument over to him, then the lender must return the instrument to the finder and it will remain with him until the coming of Elijah the prophet.

If the finder has the instrument in his possession and now remembers that he was the escrowee and claims that he now remembers the terms thereof, his statement is believed.[2]

If independent proof arises as to who should get the instrument, then that proof will be controlling. Also the parties, the borrower and the lender, may decide between themselves who should get the instrument, and the finder shall then give the instrument to the agreed-upon party.[3] However, if beth din suspects fraud, then the agreement between the lender and the borrower may be disregarded. If they have

---

1. All that is said about an instrument of indebtedness applies equally to mortgage instruments, deeds, deeds of gift, and all other types of documents.

2. This is not similar to the situation in which a witness states that he does not remember the facts, and he may not thereafter claim that he now remembers the facts. In the case of a witness, he may not recant his testimony. (See Volume I, Chapter 29.)

3. This is the case so long as beth din does not fear that the parties are conniving to perpetrate a fraud on the borrower's creditors or on persons who purchased real estate from the borrower after the date of the instrument. (See Chapter 39.) In the case in which the instrument was found in the street, there is concern that the parties

agreed to destroy the instrument, then their agreement will be followed, since the torn instrument cannot be used to defraud creditors.

If there is one witness who testifies that the instrument belongs to the lender, then the borrower, if he disputes this, must take a Torah oath, just as he would in any case in which there is one witness who testifies on behalf of the lender. If he takes the oath, the instrument will remain with the finder until the prophet Elijah appears.[4] However, if the sole witness testifies that the instrument belongs to the borrower, then there are several options available to the borrower. He may request that the lender take an oath to contradict the witness, and if he does, then the lender will obtain the instrument. If the lender refuses to take such an oath, then the instrument will be destroyed. If the borrower remains silent and does not demand that the lender take an oath, then the instrument will remain in the hands of the finder.[5]

If the found instrument is a mortgage document and the finder does not know its status,[6] then even if the mortgagee named therein is occupying the land described in the mortgage as a mortgagee in

---

may be perpetrating a fraud on creditors or purchasers. The latter case can be distinguished because in that situation the instrument was found in the street, and the lender apparently failed to take adequate care of the instrument because it was paid. Some authorities hold that the person to whom the instrument will be returned must take an oath before the instrument is legally returned to him.

4. See Volume III, Chapter 87, regarding Torah oaths. If the borrower admits that he owed the money when the instrument was escrowed with the finder, and he now alleges that he paid the instrument in the interim or that new conditions were entered into after the instrument was deposited with the finder as escrowee, then the borrower is now in a position of one who cannot take an oath, and he must therefore pay. He cannot take an oath because if one witness testifies against him, the defendant can take an oath to deny the facts testified to by the witness. In this case the borrower admits the facts testified to by the witness—namely, that the instrument was valid. However, he alleges additional facts that alter the liability, but these additional facts do not contradict the witness.

5. The lender may not impose an obligation on the borrower to take an oath and obtain the instrument.

6. The property owner who is borrowing money is known as the mortgagor. The lender of the money is known as the mortgagee. The mortgage instrument can be of two kinds. It may be security for the loan from the lender/mortgagee to the owner/mortgagor, and the owner will remain in possession of the land that is the security for the mortgage until the loan has been paid. Or, the mortgage may permit the lender/mortgagee to take possession of the land, and the profits from the land will be used to pay off the loan. The case discussed in the text falls into the latter category.

possession, such occupier in possession must vacate the land if he relies solely on the found document,[7] and the instrument must remain with the finder until the coming of Elijah the prophet.[8]

If a found instrument names the finder's son or father as the creditor, then none of the foregoing applies, and the instrument is deemed to be that of the finder's father or son, and not that of a stranger.[9] Thus, if the instrument was found by the son of the person named as the lender, the father is given the instrument and may enforce collection thereof.

## Instruments found by heirs of the possessor

Heirs may not return an instrument that they find among the decedent's belongings to its rightful owner unless they are certain of the legal status of the instrument. Some authorities hold that if the lender named in the instrument seizes the instrument from the

---

7. The fact that the lender/mortgagee is in possession does not overcome the fact that land is always presumed to be in the ownership of the last known owner. (See Chapter 140 in Volume V.)

8. The fact that the mortgage was found in the hands of the finder negates the presumption that the occupier of the land may have had that the mortgage was his and had merely been deposited with the escrowee/finder. It could well have been that the borrower/mortgagor deposited the mortgage instrument with the escrowee for safekeeping after the mortgagor had paid off the mortgage, or that most of the loan had been repaid by the mortgagor, and to return the instrument to the mortgagee/lender would prejudice the mortgagor/borrower.

9. As stated in Chapter 140, if a person occupies land known to belong to the last owner and the occupier alleges that he had purchased the land but lost the deed, and the owner did not lodge a protest during the three years of occupation by the occupier, the beth din will presume that the occupier is telling the truth and will award the occupier possession of the land. Chapter 149 names persons who may not rely on this presumption. Because of the special relationship between the owner and the occupier, there was no need for the owner to protest the presence of the occupier, since he assumed that the occupier would not allege that he purchased the land from the owner. An example would be the son who occupies property belonging to his father for three years. The father does not lodge a protest during this period, but after three years, the father moves to evict his son. The son alleges that he purchased the land from his father before the three-year occupation began, but he lost the deed. The son relies on this time frame so that there will be a presumption that he purchased the land. However, there is no such presumption in such a case, since it is assumed that the father permitted the son the use of the land and saw no necessity to protest. The foregoing applies to a son who is living at home and is supported by his father.

decedent's home before the heirs take possession of the instrument, then he may retain the instrument.[10] If the instrument found among the decedent's papers is a *kethubah* document,[11] then it must be returned to the woman named therein, if she is married to the husband therein named, and if it is not suspected that the instrument had already been paid and was left with the escrowee for safekeeping by the husband or his heirs.[12]

If the heirs of a decedent allege that an instrument found in the decedent's belongings was given to him as collateral security for a loan, then the instrument will remain with the heirs as their possession. They cannot enforce collection of the instrument against the debtor named therein because they have no assignment of the instrument to the decedent.[13] If the heirs do not make the allegation, the beth din will not make it on their behalf.[14] However, if the instrument does not require an assignment, then the beth din may raise the allegation on its own even if the heirs do not raise it.[15]

If among the documents of the decedent there is an instrument in his favor, and it has written across it in his handwriting a notation that

10. The lender may retain the instrument even if the heirs had already taken possession of it, whether in the decedent's home or in the heirs' home, until such time as the heirs have stated that they do not know the legal status of the instrument. If the lender takes the instrument after the heirs have declared that they do not know the legal status, then the instrument must be returned to the heirs and left with them until the prophet Elijah comes.

11. The *kethubah* is an instrument written by the husband in favor of his wife at the time of the wedding ceremony. It states that in the event of a divorce, he will pay a sum specified in the *kethubah,* and that in the event of his death, his estate will pay that sum to the widow.

12. It is unlikely that the husband paid off the *kethubah* while he was still married to his wife. It is therefore assumed that the wife left the *kethubah* with the decedent for safekeeping. This reasoning may apply to all instruments found in the decedent's belongings, including instruments whose time for payment has not arrived, since it is generally presumed that an instrument is not paid before its due date.

13. See Chapter 66 regarding assignment and transfer of instruments. If after the heirs have alleged that the instrument was held as collateral security by the decedent, the lender named in the instrument desires to obtain possession of the instrument to collect from the borrower therein named, he will have to negotiate with the heirs of the decedent.

14. The beth din will often raise pleas on behalf of heirs that the heirs themselves should have raised; beth din does this because heirs are rarely in a position to know the facts of the decedent's property.

15. An instrument of indebtedness that states that it is payable to the bearer thereof does not require a separate assignment.

another person has a one-half interest in the document, the other person does not obtain an interest in the document.[16]

The heirs find among the decedent's documents a tied bundle of documents belonging to the decedent's sister. Some of the documents are favorable to the sister, such as documents of dowry gifts to her and deeds for real estate naming her as the grantee; and others are liabilities to her, such as deeds of gift from her to her husband. It is presumed that she had deposited the entire bundle of documents with her brother, who later died, and all of the documents are returned to her, including the ones that are liabilities, because it is presumed that she did not as yet make the gift to her husband.[17] Although the instrument of dowry is similar to an instrument of indebtedness in her favor and should really be left with the escrowee until the coming of the prophet Elijah, in this case because it was tied together with other documents favorable to her, it is presumed that this too belonged to her and was not merely given to the decedent/brother for safe-keeping by her father-in-law.

## Instruments found in a public place

An instrument found in a public place should not be returned to the lender. This holds true even if (1) the instrument contains a credence clause[18] or (2) is not yet due,[19] or (3) does not contain a lien

---

16. The reason is that even if the decedent were alive and so stated, there would not be a transfer of interest unless he stated it to witnesses and instructed them to be witnesses to the fact. He could have stated that he made the admission so that people would not think him a wealthy man.

17. There is an opinion that if the deed of gift from a wife to her husband contained a clause stating that this was a transfer of title (a *kinyan* clause; see Chapter 195), then the result would be the same, since the wife wanted the deed to so state after she delivered it to her husband. There is also authority that states that a deed that contains a *kinyan* clause is given to the husband.

18. The credence clause states that if the instrument is presented for payment, then the borrower will not raise any defense, and if the lender sues on the instrument, then beth din may enter judgment without having to investigate the facts of the making and giving of the instrument. The defense of forgery, however, is available in such a case since this goes to the essence of whether it is an instrument. One might assume that since the instrument contains a credence clause, it should be given to the lender, since the borrower must have had faith in the lender's integrity if he put such a clause in the instrument; therefore, the law states that the instrument may not be returned to either of the parties.

19. There is a presumption that an instrument is not paid before due. (See Volume

clause,[20] or (4) even if the borrower admits that the instrument has not been paid. In all of these cases, there is a suspicion that the lost instrument is flawed, and thus the lender and borrower have entered into a conspiracy to perpetrate a fraud on the persons who purchased real estate from the borrower. Even if either of the parties were to identify the physical characteristics of the instrument, it would not be returned.[21]

However, if the borrower admits that the instrument is authentic and has not yet been paid, and (1) the instrument specifically excluded a lien on the real estate of the borrower or (2) the borrower has sufficient assets to pay the loan, then in any of such events the instrument should be turned over to the lender.[22] Even if the

---

III, Chapter 78.) Thus if the instrument that is found in a public place is not yet due, it might be presumed that it was not yet paid, and should be turned over to the lender. The law teaches that the instrument may have been lost because there was something wrong with it, and the lender therefore failed to take adequate care of it. The fact that it was lost flaws the instrument sufficiently to overcome the presumption that an instrument isn't paid before its due date.

20. A lien clause in an instrument that is subscribed by at least two witnesses and given to the lender in the presence of witnesses creates a lien on the real property of the borrower. (See Chapter 43.) Thus if the borrower owned real estate at the time the loan was made, then all of the real estate then owned by him was subject to the lien of the lender. If the borrower thereafter sold any of such real estate, and the borrower lacks the means to pay the lender, then the lender may levy on the real estate that the borrower sold. The absence of a lien clause does not imply that the borrower's real estate is free of the lien, since it is presumed that the lien was inadvertently omitted, and the instrument will be treated as if it contained a lien clause. Because the lender failed to take adequate care of the instrument, it is presumed flawed. In order to exclude the borrower's real estate from the lien of the lender, there must be a specific clause so stating.

21. For example, either party may state that there was a hole in the instrument. Since both of the parties at one time or another had the instrument in their possession—the borrower before the instrument was delivered, and the lender upon delivery—the fact that each one can identify the instrument is not sufficient proof to justify turning the instrument over to such party. However, if the borrower alleges that there was never a loan, and then the lender is able to identify the physical characteristics of the instrument, then the instrument will be given to him since he had it at one time, contrary to what the borrower has alleged.

22. In either of these cases it is not possible to perpetrate a fraud on the purchasers of the borrower's real estate. In the first case, the purchasers are specifically excluded from the lien of the lender. In the second case, the borrower has sufficient real estate to pay off the loan. Even if he should thereafter dispose of his remaining real estate,

borrower does not admit the loan, if the instrument was found on the date it was made and had annexed to it an authentication of the beth din, then it should be turned over to the lender.[23] There is an opinion that in the latter situation, if the borrower is available to be questioned, then the instrument should not be turned over to the lender if the borrower alleges that he paid the loan and it was he who lost the instrument.

If an instrument of indebtedness that contains a clause imposing interest payments on the borrower is found, beth din may order the instrument destroyed.[24]

If one finds in the marketplace an untorn instrument among torn instruments, all of them naming one lender and one borrower, then the instruments should not be returned to the borrower named therein. However, if a receipt naming the borrower is found among the torn documents, then the instruments should be returned to the borrower.[25]

If instruments are found in a receptacle, then the receptacle and the instruments therein should be given to the party who can identify the receptacle, unless it is the custom in that community that all persons deposit their instruments in such receptacles.[26]

If one finds at least three instruments firmly rolled together, either end to end or placed one on top of the other and then rolled together, and all the instruments have the same lender and the same borrower, then one should announce that one has found documents. Whoever

---

the earlier purchasers would be protected, since the lender must levy in the inverse order of the purchasers of the real estate.

23. The lender, in order to protect himself, brought the witnesses to the loan to beth din, and they testified that they saw the loan, and the beth din then authenticated the instrument. The lender is now spared the trouble of finding the witnesses or persons who recognize the witnesses' signatures to testify if the borrower later raises a defense as to the instrument's authenticity. There is also a presumption that an instrument that has been authenticated by a beth din is not paid on the date on which the loan was made.

24. It is a transgression of Torah law to take interest and to give interest for the extension of credit or for lending money. (See Leviticus 25:36.)

25. This would hold true even if the receipt did not contain the signatures of witnesses or even the signature of the lender. This entire law may hold true, according to one opinion, even if the torn instruments together with a receipt were found in the lender's house.

26. If the custom was not to safeguard instruments in such a receptacle, then so long as the party provided some sort of identification, even if he did not do so with great particularity, he would obtain the receptacle with the instruments.

claims them must state the number of documents that he lost and the manner in which they were rolled or tied together.[27-29]

If one finds three authenticated instruments together, with one common borrower and different lenders, then the instruments are to be turned over to the borrower, even if he cannot furnish any identifying marks, and not to the lender, even if he offers identifying marks.[30] If the instruments are not authenticated, they should be turned over to the party who offers identifying marks.[31]

---

27. The manner and style of rolling the documents serves as an identifying mark.

28. Since the lender and the borrower are the same in each of the instruments, then it is assumed that the instruments were lost either by the lender, because they have not yet been paid, or by the borrower, who took possession of the instruments after he paid them.

29. It should be remembered that identifying the instruments as to dates and amounts will be of little value, since it is assumed that both the lender and the borrower know the contents of the instruments. Both claim the instruments, the lender because they have not yet been paid, and the borrower because, as he alleges, they were paid. The commentaries on the *Shulhan Aruch* provide many rules regarding these rolled-up instruments. A few of them are as follows: (1) If instruments are tied together, then even if there are only two, they can be identified by their amounts and by the manner in which they are tied. There is also opinion that if there were only two instruments, then the mere identification of the number and manner of rolling the instruments should not entitle either party to possession. (2) If there are three or more instruments, and one party knows the number, or the manner of rolling them together, or the way in which they were tied together, and the other party knows none of these things, then the former party will be given possession. (3) If one of the parties knows the manner in which the instruments were rolled together, and the other party knows the number, then the instruments should go to the party who identifies the number. There is also contrary opinion stating that neither party should be given the instruments. (4) If only one of the parties is before the beth din and he knows two of the categories (the number, or the manner in which the instruments are rolled together, or the manner in which they were tied), then he will be given possession.

30. The reason is that often the lender will take the instrument (and the witnesses where necessary, as where the beth din does not recognize witnesses' signatures on an instrument) to have it authenticated as soon as the loan transaction has been completed. Thereafter the lender will take care of the authenticated instrument. The fact that three such instruments were found naming different lenders and one borrower is evidence that the lost instruments did not belong to three individual lenders; the idea that they were all lost and somehow managed to come together is too great a coincidence. It must have been the borrower who paid them and then tied them together and thereafter lost them.

31. If the instruments have not been authenticated, then perhaps the three lenders all went together to beth din to have the instruments authenticated, and beth din tied

If one finds three instruments together, and they have one common lender and three different borrowers and were writtten by three different scribes, then they are to be turned over to the lender even if he does not furnish any identifying marks.[32] However, if all three instruments were written by the same scribe, they are to be turned over to the party who can furnish identifying marks.[33]

There is an opinion that the foregoing three paragraphs would also apply if only two instruments were found.[34]

If one finds writs of appraisal,[35] deeds relating to feeding one's stepchildren,[36] documents of halizah,[37] documents of mi'un,[38] documents relating to selection of arbitrators,[39] or any other documents

---

them together and lost them before they were authenticated. Or perhaps the borrower prepared the instruments hoping to borrow from the three lenders, and then the loans did not take place. In such a case, the instruments will be given to any of the parties who can furnish an identifying sign, such as the number of the instruments or a description of the manner in which they were tied together.

32. The only plausible explanation is that the lender lost the instruments after he had made the three loans and tied the documents together, for if these were instruments returned to the three borrowers after they had paid off the loans, why would they have been tied together and lost by one person?

33. Perhaps the lender gave the documents to the scribe to take to the beth din for authentication. Or perhaps the lender or the borrower had asked the scribe to have the instruments ready in the event that he planned to make the loans to the three borrowers. If this is the possibility that the beth din considers, then this law would apply only if the instruments were not authenticated.

34. This opinion holds that the number three is specified in the codes regarding these laws because the number three can be an identifying mark, but the number two cannot.

35. When the debtor does not have money to pay his creditor, the beth din will appraise the debtor's real estate so that the creditor can levy on it. The writ of appraisal contains the appraisal.

36. This is an instrument whereby the husband undertakes to feed his wife's children from her prior marriage.

37. If a married man died and left no surviving issue, his widow must marry the decedent's brother. However, the decedent's brother may perform an act of halizah instead of marrying his deceased brother's wife.

38. Under Torah law, a minor girl's father may betroth her to a man of his choosing. If the father died while she was still a minor, the Rabbis ordained that her mother, or brothers who have attained their majority, may betroth her to a man of their choosing. When the girl reaches the age of majority, she may declare that she does not want the marriage arranged by her mother or brothers; the beth din will then write an instrument of mi'un for her, and she will not require a divorce to marry.

39. Two interpretations are given in the Talmud in defining documents of berrurin.

issued by a beth din, the documents shall be given to the parties on whose behalf they were prepared.[40]

If one finds deeds of gift made by a person who was not on his deathbed, or deeds of sale of property, such deeds are not given to the donee or grantee named therein even if the donor states that he wants the named donee or grantee to obtain the deed.[41] An exception is made if the deed of gift reserves to the donor the right to retract the gift at any time.[42]

If a deed of current transfer is found (that is, a document stating that the grantor transfers to the grantee his property by *kinyan*), even if it is admitted that the instrument did not yet reach the grantee,[43] the

---

One definition is that they are instruments whereby parties to a dispute agree to submit the dispute to arbitration by each selecting one arbitrator and having the two selected arbitrators choose a third arbitrator. The documents naming the arbitrators selected are instruments of *berrurin*. Another interpretation defines them as instruments containing a record of pleadings.

40. In all of these situations there is no reason to suspect that the documents were drawn up but the act did not take place. The fact that the beth din has issued the documents is evidence that the transactions were completed. In addition, these are not the kinds of documents that might lend themselves to a plea of payment. The *Shulhan Aruch*, after discussing the laws contained in this last paragraph, also discusses documents freeing slaves.

41. A deed of sale or gift takes effect when it is delivered to the donee or grantee or their agents. Since these documents have been lost, they are suspect in that there were not actually delivered on the date stated therein. There is concern that there might have been a conspiracy between the named donor or grantor and the alleged donee or grantee. The donor made a gift of a field to a Mr. A on February 1. The deed of gift to Mr. Donee, which was later found by a third party, is dated January 1. If the January 1 deed of gift to Mr. Donee is given effect, it will wipe out the gift of February 1. The reason is that there may have been a fraudulent agreement between the donor and Mr. Donee to write a predated deed of gift to wipe out the deed of gift to Mr. A. The same procedure would apply to deeds of sale of real estate. If it can be proved by witnesses that the deed of gift reached the donee on the date named therein, then the deed should be given to the donee.

42. The deed of gift contains a condition subsequent; that is, it states that "the gift shall become effective immediately from this day unless I retract at any time before my death." Because the deed of gift can be canceled by the donor at any time, the turning over of the deed to the donee is of no significance, since fraud cannot be perpetrated on a legitimate buyer of the property. In the example given in the previous note, since the donor sold or gave the property to Mr. A on a date subsequent to the date in the lost deed, the lost deed was wiped out by implication of the sale to Mr. A.

43. The *kinyan* effected immediate transfer of title. (See Chapter 195.)

found instrument is to be given to the grantee named therein, even if the grantor objects.[44]

If a deed of gift *causa mortis* is found, and the donor says to deliver it to the donee, then it is given to the donee.[45] If the donor is dead, then even if the heirs say to give the deed to the donee named therein, the deed is not so delivered to the donee, unless it was a deed of current transfer.[46]

A lender and a borrower come to beth din; both are holding onto an instrument, and each is claiming title to it.[47,48] The lender alleges that the instrument is his; he had taken it out to collect on it and was carrying it when he lost it. The borrower alleges that he paid the instrument and it was returned to him, and he lost it. If the instrument has not been authenticated, or is a promissory note containing only the signature of the borrower, then the borrower takes a *hesseth* oath and is free of payment under the instrument.[49] However, if the instrument contains two witnesses and has been authenticated or is capable of being authenticated, and each party takes an oath—the lender that at least half of the amount is due to him, and the borrower that not more than half

---

44. Since the deed of current transfer was effective from the date named therein, there is no room for the parties to perpetrate a fraud.

45. A gift *causa mortis* is a gift made in contemplation of death. Such gifts are sustained even though they lack some of the formal requisites for a transfer of interest by gift. The reason is that it is believed that a person on his deathbed should have the peace of mind of knowing that his wishes for the disposal of his property will be followed. The persons who hear the dying donor's declaration may draw up the deed according to his instructions without the formal requisites of a *kinyan* or other formality. If the dying person recovers, he may cancel the gift. If he dies, the gift is carried out.

46. In this situation it is suspected that there may be fraud. The deed was not meant to be given by the donor, and the son of the donor sold the property to a third party and now wants a prior dated deed of gift to usurp the other deed.

47. See Chapter 138 in Volume V regarding found objects held by two persons, each alleging to be the finder.

48. In this case it is the parties who are the finders. They both picked up the instrument simultaneously or nearly so, such that neither has more proof than the other that he picked up the instrument first.

49. Since the instrument was not authenticated, the borrower could have pleaded that it was a forgery. Therefore, his admission that it was a valid, paid instrument is accepted on condition that he take a *hesseth* oath. As for the instrument that bears the borrower's signature, the borrower could have alleged that he paid the instrument, and his plea would have been believed. (See Chapter 69.) Thus here too he may take a *hesseth* oath and be relieved of liability under the instrument.

of the amount stated in the instrument is due—then the borrower will pay to the lender one-half of the current value of the instrument.[50]

A lender sues a borrower on an instrument and produces the instrument in beth din. Beth din grants the lender a judgment. Before the borrower pays the judgment, the lender loses the instrument, and it becomes known that the lender has lost the instrument. The borrower thereupon alleges that he had paid the instrument and states that if anyone should find the instrument, it should be returned to him. Under the circumstances of the case, beth din assumes that the instrument was not paid and that the the borrower's allegations of payment came about only because he had heard that the lender was looking for the instrument. Beth din will thereupon write a new instrument for the creditor and endorse thereon that it has examined the original instrument; it will further note the name of the lender, the amount of the instrument, and the names of the witnesses, and state that the lender lost the instrument and that it is incumbent upon the named borrower to pay it.[51]

## Found receipts of payment

A receipt may be presented that was found in any one of three circumstances: it may have been found in a public place; it may have been in the possession of the lender; or it may have been held by a third party.[52]

**If a receipt was found in a public place,** then there are three possible situations: (1) the receipt is authenticated in beth din; (2) the receipt is not authenticated in beth din, but can be authenticated; or (3) the receipt is not authenticated, and it is not possible to authenticate it.

(1) If the receipt has been authenticated in beth din, then it will be turned over to the borrower, even if the lender does not admit that the loan has been repaid.[53]

---

50. The current value of the instrument depends upon the lender's prospects of recovering the full value of the instrument, taking into account the borrower's financial strength.

51. Beth din plays a similar role when the instrument that the lender has in his possession is partially obliterated.

52. The laws covering escrowees are found in Chapter 56.

53. It is presumed that beth din would not have authenticated the receipt if they had not known that the loan was repaid.

(2) If the receipt is not authenticated but is capable of being authenticated, and if the lender admits that it is genuine, then the receipt will be turned over to the borrower.[54] If the lender does not admit that the loan has been repaid, then the receipt is not turned over to either party, and the original instrument may be enforced by the lender.[55] In addition, the lender's creditors may levy on the instrument and enforce collection against the borrower.[56] The borrower may insist that the lender take an oath that the loan has not been repaid. The lender's creditors may not, however, trace the borrower's assets to purchasers of the borrower's real estate.

**If the lender had the original instrument** and it is endorsed thereon that the instrument was fully or partially paid, then the receipt is given full effect.[57,58] However, if the notation thereon is that another person had an interest in the instrument, then the notation is not independently given effect.[59] If a nonauthenticated receipt, not attached to the instrument, is found in the lender's possession, then the receipt is given no effect.[60] If the receipt is authenticated, it is to

---

54. The receipt will be turned over to the borrower even if the lender has creditors and they might thus be deprived of another of the lender's asset to levy upon in the event that the lender does not pay his creditors. Fraud is not suspected, for even if the lender's creditors were to take possession of the receipt, they still could not collect on the loan from the lender to the borrower because there is a legitimate receipt, the lender admits payment, and the borrower alleges that he repaid the loan.

55. The lender alleges that he prepared the receipt in anticipation that the loan was going to be repaid, and he therefore did not have it authenticated.

56. The reason is that the instrument has been authenticated or is capable of being authenticated, and the receipt is not authenticated and has the additional flaw of having been lost, and the creditor denies that the loan has been repaid.

57. It does not matter if the receipt was witnessed or even if the receipt was not in the handwriting of or signed by the lender.

58. It is presumed that the lender would not have permitted the instrument to be altered with a receipt endorsed thereon if no payment had been made.

59. This is similar to the situation in which a person, in the presence of others, admits that he owes money; the admission is not given effect unless he specifies that he wants the persons to serve as witnesses to the admission. (See Volume III, Chapter 81.) This holds true if the holder of the instrument is alive and denies the truth of the notation on the grounds that he wanted people to believe that he had fewer assets than he actually has. Even if the holder is dead, however, this plea is offered by the beth din on behalf of the heirs. There is also an opinion that if the notation was on a separate instrument it might be valid, since the reason previously given would not apply.

60. This is so even if the receipt is in the handwriting of the lender or the borrower. Perhaps it was prepared in anticipation of payment. Even if there are signatures of

be turned over to the borrower, even if it was found in the lender's possession.

If the untorn instrument to which the receipt refers is found among the torn instruments of the lender, the receipt is given effect.[61] If there is no receipt and the untorn instrument is found among the lender's torn instruments, the untorn instrument is presumed to be still valid. Also, if the instrument is found among the lender's paid, untorn instruments, then it is presumed to be paid.

An entry made on the lender's books indicating that a certain instrument was fully or partially paid will be given effect as recorded.

**If a receipt is presented** by an escrowee, and (1) the escrowee also holds the instrument, or (2) there are witnesses on the receipt whose signatures can be authenticated in beth din, or (3) the receipt is in the lender's handwriting, then the escrowee will be believed if he states that the loan was repaid. If none of these three criteria is fulfilled, then the escrowee's word as to the status of the loan is not believed.[62]

If the escrowee dies or does not know the status of the loan, but he holds both the instrument and the receipt, then it is presumed that the instrument was paid and it is therefore destroyed.[63] If a person holding an alleged receipt does not hold the instrument, and the receipt is not signed, then it has no effect.[64] If the receipt is signed and authenticated in beth din, then it is presumed that the receipt is authentic; therefore, when the lender produces the instrument, beth din will destroy it.

## Notations of payment on the instrument

If the lender dies, and there is found on one of the instruments in his possession a notation that the instrument was partially or fully paid,

---

witnesses thereon, the receipt is not given effect unless it was delivered to the borrower or authenticated in beth din.

61. The fact that the receipt was found together with the instrument among the torn instruments of the lender indicates that the loan was repaid.

62. Under these circumstances, even if the borrower would have had possession of the receipt, the receipt would not be given effect if the lender alleged nonpayment.

63. Since the parties trusted the escrowee with the instrument, there was no reason for a receipt. It is therefore presumed that the receipt was given when the instrument was paid.

64. The person holding the receipt is not even regarded as an escrowee.

then it is presumed that the notation reflects the true status of the instrument.[65] Similarly, if the deceased lender's book contain entries that instruments have been paid, the entries will be given effect. But an unauthenticated receipt found among the decedent's papers will not be given effect, since it is possible that he prepared the receipt in anticipation of payment.[66]

If a father before his death tells his son that one of the instruments in his possession was paid, but he either does not remember which one it was or fails to specify which one it was, then the son may not collect payment on any of the instruments that he inherited from his father.[67,68] However, if a receipt is found, whether among the decedent's papers or in the hands of a third person or in the hands of a borrower, then it is presumed that this is the payment referred to, and all the other instruments may be collected upon. If the decedent leaves more than one instrument from any borrower, it is only the largest of these instruments that may not be collected upon, and the other instruments are enforceable.

---

65. In many situations beth din would, *sua sponta* (on its own motion), plead on behalf of minor heirs; in this case the presumption is that the notation reflects the true situation. It is pleaded on their behalf, not that the notation might have been placed on the instrument in anticipation of payment, but that it might have been written before payment was actually made.

66. This is true even if the receipt is in the handwriting of the lender and even if it contains signatures of witnesses.

67. If before his death he remembers which instrument was paid, then his statement is believed.

68. Each borrower may plead that the instrument referred to by the decedent was his instrument. If any of the borrowers admits that his was not the instrument referred to, then they will have to pay. However, the son may impose an oath on any borrower who states that it was his instrument that the decedent meant.

# Chapter 66

# ASSIGNMENT
# OF INSTRUMENTS
# OF INDEBTEDNESS

## INTRODUCTION

Most of the chapters in this volume have thus far dealt with a creditor/lender who holds an instrument of indebtedness against a debtor/borrower. The creditor wants to dispose of the instrument for any number of reasons. For example, he may need money and may therefore want to sell the instrument. If the instrument is for $100 to be paid six months from the time when the creditor needs money, he may prefer to sell the instrument to a purchaser who offers him $80. Or, if he feels that his estate is too large for tax purposes, he may want to give the $100 instrument to his friend or child as a gift. The creditor who is transferring the instrument, whether by gift or sale, is assigning the instrument to the donee or purchaser. The creditor who is transferring the instrument is designated the "assignor," and the person to whom he is transferring the instrument is designated the "assignee." The transfer is effected by an "assignment" of the instrument, which is usually made by a writing.

The term *instrument*, as used in this chapter, may apply to an instrument of indebtedness (a note of indebtedness, a note of admission, or a note of confession) or a promissory note.[1] The

1. The instrument of indebtedness is a writing subscribed by at least two witnesses,

instrument consists of the paper on which it is written and the written letters on the paper. The assignee is not interested in the paper for its own sake.[2] The assignor desires to sell the obligations that the words on the paper enforce. But the letters are not a tangible thing that can be acquired in the manner in which tangible things are customarily acquired.[3] Thus there must thus be another method by which the rights that accompany the instrument can be acquired. As this chapter describes, that method is for the assignor to deliver the instrument to the assignee together with a written assignment. This chapter discusses the things that can be thus assigned, the method of assignment, and related matters, such as the residual power of the assignor to forgive the underlying debt after the assignment is made.

# TEXT

## Things that are assignable

All that will be said about the assignment of an instrument applies whether the assignment is a gift or results from a sale. An instrument, as defined in the Introduction, is assignable. The language in which the instrument is written does not matter. The instrument may even have been prepared in a Gentile court, so long as it meets the conditions for recognition of such instruments in beth din.[4]

A bearer instrument, by contrast, does not require a separate

---

whether or not it is also subscribed by the debtor. A promissory note is subscribed by the debtor; it is usually not subscribed by any witness, although it may be subscribed by one witness.

2. We are not discussing the remote case in which the assignee wants the paper for its utilitarian use, such as to cover a bottle.

3. See Chapter 198 for the method of acquisition of personalty.

4. The requirement that the instrument meet the criteria of the beth din applies only if both the assignor and the assignee are Jews. But if the assignor is a Gentile, whether the debtor is Jewish or a Gentile, then under the conflict-of-laws doctrine, the laws of the Gentile courts apply, and whatever rights the Gentile would have had in the Gentile courts, the Jewish assignee has in the beth din. Thus if the Gentile courts do not require both a written assignment and delivery of the assignment together with the delivery of the instrument, then the beth din will apply such law. Also, if the assignor cannot forgive the debt under Gentile law, then he would not be able to forgive the debt in this case. If the assignor was a Jew and the assignee a Gentile, the Gentile has all of the rights of the Jewish assignor.

assignment; mere delivery by the assignor to the assignee is sufficient to pass title to it.[5] If the instrument is made payable to the lender and to his order, then there are conflicting opinions as to whether it requires a separate assignment or just delivery of the instrument.[6]

If when the instrument was drafted the lender ordered it to be made payable to a third party, but the lender retains possession of the instrument, then the transfer of title to the third party requires an assignment. However, if the lender instructs the maker of the instrument to name the third party and to deliver same to the third party, then the delivery of the instrument alone is sufficient to render the third party the owner of the instrument.

Enforceable contracts are also assignable, as are obligations of the government and of corporations, such as their bonds and licenses.[7-9] Insurance policies are not assignable, since they represent a future interest in the event of a loss. However, insurance contracts are assignable together with the sale of the merchandise that they insure. Lottery tickets are assignable by delivery alone and need not comply with the laws of this chapter. Mortgagee-in-possession types of mortgages are subject to the laws of this chapter.[10] There is an opinion

---

5. A bearer instrument is an instrument wherein it is stated that it is payable to the person (or his representative) who bears, or carries, it to the place where it is to be paid. The instrument may be any of the instruments named in the Introduction to this chapter, or any other instrument that evidences a debt or obligation. The promissor, or obligor, will pay the amount due to the person who presents the instrument. Promissory notes often state that "The payor will pay One Hundred Dollars ($100.00) to the bearer hereof," and the name of the payor will be signed thereto.

6. The instrument will read "Pay $100 to Mr. A or his order" or, as many checks in the United States state, "Pay to the order of Mr. A."

7. If the government gave partners a contract to obtain certain rights, and the partner who is holding the contract alleges that the other partner assigned all his rights thereunder to him, the allegation is of no avail, since there was no compliance with the laws of this chapter.

8. Bearer bonds issued by a government or corporation need not comply with the laws of this chapter. Mere delivery by the assignor to the assignee is sufficient to pass title.

9. Licenses granted by the government that may be revoked at will may not be assignable in the manner discussed in this chapter. They may have to be assigned with the permission of the licensing government.

10. The mortgagor is both the borrower and the owner of the real estate. The lender is the mortgagee; that is, he lends money to the owner, who gives the lender a mortgage on the real estate owned by the borrower. This type of mortgage provides that the mortgagee takes possession of the mortgagor's realty for a time certain, and has the use of and the profits of the real estate. On the termination date of the

that delivery of an assignment by itself is sufficient to transfer title to the mortgage.[11]

A warehouse receipt cannot be assigned by the methods provided for in this chapter.[12]

The property that a wife brings to a marriage may be used and controlled by the husband during the marriage and does not require an assignment from the wife to the husband if the property includes instruments.[13]

## The assignment

The assignment must be made in the form of a written deed that transfers title to the instrument being assigned. Even a *kinyan* with witnesses who sign that they witnessed the assignment of the rights would not suffice, since such a writing would serve only as proof of the assignment; it is not itself an assignment.

The assignment must state that it assigns the instrument and all of the rights that flow therefrom. Like any other instrument, the assignment must be signed by the assignor or by subscribing witnesses. If witnesses sign, they must write that they were instructed by the assignor to write the assignment that conveys the instrument and the rights thereunder.

## Method of assignment

An instrument must be assigned in two parts: the delivery of the instrument assigned, and the delivery of the assignment. Neither element is sufficient without the other. The assignment may be endorsed on the instrument, or it may be made by a separate writing.

---

mortgage, the debt of the mortgagor is cancelled. Or else the mortgagee takes the profits of the mortgaged realty until the debt is paid, at which time he returns the realty to the mortgagor.

Under this type of mortgage, the mortgagor has the right to pay off the loan and retake his realty. This type of mortgage may be assigned by the mortgagee to the assignee by complying with the provisions of this chapter.

11. Since the assignor is in possession of the realty, the assignment is similar to an assignment of realty owned by the assignor, and a deed alone would effect the transfer.

12. The warehouse receipt does not contain any rights. It is merely proof that the bailor has deposited something with the bailee/warehouseman.

13. See Maimonides' *Laws of Marriage*, Chapter 16. The parties may by agreement remove the wife's property from her husband's control.

The assignment must state that it assigns the instrument and all of its obligations to the assignee. There is an opinion that the delivery of the instrument must precede the delivery of the assignment, unless the assignment is endorsed on the instrument.

The assignee must physically take the assignment and the instrument into his hands and lift it up to show that he has acquired them.[14]

If the assignee paid for the assignment, and the assignor reneged on the agreement before he delivered the instrument and the assignment and returned the assignee's payment to him, then the assignor is subject to being called a person of questionable trust.[15] However, if the agreement contains a clause backed by placing a lien on the real estate of the assignor that he would not renege on the agreement, and if he still reneged and failed to deliver the instrument and the assignment, then the assignor must pay to the assignee the full value of the instrument even if the assignee paid less than the full value of the instrument. Similarly, if the agreement of assignment is made with a warranty that the assignor will make good the underlying debt if the debtor fails to deal with the assignee, then the assignor must pay to the assignee the full value of the instrument even if the assignee paid less than the full value of the instrument.[16] The assignee may retain the assignment until he receives his money back from the assignor. And if the assignor cannot repay the money, the assignee may collect the amount due to the assignor from the debtor to the extent of the money owing from the debtor.[17]

---

14. See Chapter 198 regarding acquisition of personalty and instruments by lifting. Where there are many instruments being assigned and it is not feasible to lift them up, they can be acquired by drawing them to the assignee as stated in that chapter. The act of acquisition can be made only with the instructions of the assignor to the assignee to acquire the instrument.

15. He is not, however, subject to the curse of "he who has punished" stated in Chapter 198. The reason is that the curse applies only to sales of personal property where part or all of the sales price has been paid and then one of the parties reneges on the deal before a legal acquisition of the personal property has been concluded. The sale of instruments is not tantamount to the sale of personal property.

16. If the agreement contained a provision that the assignor would make good the value of the instrument if the debtor could not pay, and if the assignee paid less than the full value of the instrument, then the assignor need not abide by the part of the agreement that provided for the overage, since that would represent gain in the nature of interest, which is prohibited.

17. See Volume III, Chapter 86, where it is shown that a creditor of a second creditor may levy on the second creditor's debtor.

The assignor may transfer to the assignee title to a piece of realty, and the title to the instrument may be transferred simultaneously.[18]

If the assignee reassigns the instrument to the lender named in the instrument, delivery of the instrument suffices to effect the transfer, and there need not be a separate assignment.[19]

## Possible conflicts of interest among the parties

If one of the witnesses on the instrument is the assignee, there is no fear of a conflict of interest.[20] Once he has purchased the instrument, however, he may no longer be a witness to anything pertaining to the amendment or correction of the instrument. Furthermore, he may not testify as to any ambiguity in the instrument. If the debtor pleads forgery, then the facts of the transaction will have to be proved by the assignee.

If the assignor admits the writing of the assignment, then the assignment is valid even if he is one of the subscribing witnesses on the assignment.[21] However, if the assignor denies assigning the instrument to the assignee and claims that the debtor forged the assignment, then beth din must examine the facts of the case.[22]

---

18. Chapter 202 discusses this type of transfer of title to personalty by the method known as *agav*, or "along with." Along with the transfer of title to realty, there is also transferred title to personalty—in this case, the instrument. In this situation, there is no necessity for delivery of the instrument and no necessity for an assignment. The instrument is acquired when the realty is acquired, regardless of where the instrument is located. There are some who hold that there must still be an assignment and a delivery of the assignment, and the transfer "along with" only obviates the necessity of delivery of the instrument. If a seller sold all of his personalty "along with" his realty and transferred title to the realty, he does not necessarily transfer title to his instruments, unless he specifically told the purchaser to acquire the instruments.

19. The reason is that since the assignor had retained the personal obligation of the debtor, he needs only the instrument for the retransfer of the security aspect of the loan.

20. There is no suspicion that he signed on a falsified instrument so that he could later purchase the instrument. If that were the case, the second witness would not have signed, and, furthermore, it is a suspicion of a remote happening. However, the instrument should not be purchased by both subscribing witnesses together.

21. There is no suspicion that the debtor preferred to have the instrument in the hands of the assignee, with whom he could deal more easily, than in the hands of the assignor. Since the assignor admits that he wrote the assignment and delivered it together with the instrument to the assignee, there is no suspicion.

22. It is possible that the debtor wanted to deal with the assignee and not with the assignor.

## Forgiveness of the underlying debt
## after assignment

Even after the lender has sold or assigned the instrument to the assignee, the lender, or even his heirs, may forgive all or part of the underlying debt to the obligor.[23-27] Alternatively, the assignor may write a receipt of payment to the debtor, or he can extend the time for payment. However, if the debtor endorses the instrument and states thereon that he is obligated to the lender and to all of his assigns, and then the assignor assigns the instrument to the assignee by delivery of the instrument together with an assignment, then, according to one

---

23. Only the original lender may forgive the underlying debt. Neither the original assignee from the lender nor any subsequent assignee may forgive the underlying debt, since they do not have the rights to the debtor's personal obligation.

24. The reason for this is that according to one opinion, Torah law prohibits the assignment of instruments because they have no intrinsic value, and it is only by Rabbinic enactment that they are assignable. Even according to the opinion that Torah law permitted assignment, the assignor can still forgive the debt even after the assignment, since each indebtedness carries with it two distinct obligations: the personal obligation to repay the loan and the lien on the property of the debtor as surety for repayment. When the assignor sells the instrument, he can sell only the lien on the debtor's property; he cannot transfer the personal obligation of the debtor because such obligation is not transferable. The assignor retains the personal obligation of the debtor, and this he can forgive. The surety automatically falls when he forgives the personal obligation, since it was surety for a debt that no longer exists.

25. If the lender at the time of the loan asked that the instrument be made out to a third party, and the lender still had the instrument in his possession at the time of the assignment, it is the lender and not the third party who may forgive the instrument because it is the lender who has the real interest in the debt.

26. Opinions differ on the question of whether the heir can forgive the debt if the instrument is against him. Say, for example, that a father loaned money to his son and has an instrument for the debt. The father assigned the instrument to a purchaser and then died before the due date. The son now wants to forgive the debt and would thus be freeing himself of it. Opinions conflict as to whether the son may do so. If the assignment was made by a gift *causa mortis*, then the heirs cannot forgive the underlying debt. The Rabbis, in establishing gifts *causa mortis*, wanted the dying declarant to spend his last moments peacefully, without having to wonder whether his intentions would be carried out. (See Chapter 250.)

27. The lender may forgive the underlying debt even if he agreed with the assignee that he would not do so, because the debtor always has the right to have his debt forgiven and the lender would be giving away a right of the debtor by this agreement.

opinion, the assignor can no longer forgive the debt.[28] Another opinion holds that even in the latter case the assignor can forgive the debt, but if the instrument is made payable to the bearer, then the assignor cannot forgive the debt.

The assignor cannot forgive the debt if the assignor was indebted to the assignee at the time of the assignment and did not have any other assets with which to pay the debt.[29]

The assignee can protect himself by persuading the debtor to write a new instrument in the name of the assignee. In such case the assignee should not give up the first instrument; to do so would be to relinquish his priorities as a creditor from the date of the first instrument until the time the second instrument was written.[30] The second instrument should state that it is collectible only if the assignor forgives the debt of the first instrument. Another method would be for the debtor to admit before witnesses, in compliance with rules of admissions made by debtors, that he agrees that the instrument that is being assigned by the assignor to the assignee will be a binding obligation upon the debtor.[31]

Chapter 126 states that if the creditor, the debtor, and the assignee are present, the creditor can even orally assign the debt to the assignee without the necessity of a writing.[32] If this procedure is

---

28. In this case the assignor is able to transfer the personal obligation of the debtor together with the lien on the property of the debtor. This transfer can be made only to someone who is alive when the debtor endorses the instrument, since the debtor's personal obligation can be given only to a person who is in existence at the time it was made.

29. The reason is that even without the assignment the instrument stood as security for the debt owed by the assignor to the assignee, and the assignee could have collected the instrument from the debtor even without an assignment, since the assignee could levy in any place where he could find assets of the assignor. (See Volume III, Chapter 86.) This law applies only if the assignor was indebted to the assignee prior to the assignment. But if the debt resulted from the assignment of the debtor's instrument by the assignor to the assignee, then the assignor can forgive the instrument to the debtor.

30. If the second instrument were predated, it would be invalid. (See Chapter 46.)

31. In such a situation the assignor has nothing left to forgive, since the debtor's obligation is now in the hands of the assignee.

32. Once so orally assigned, none of the parties may cancel the assignment. The purchasers from the debtor are now in the same position with respect to the assignee as they were with respect to the assignor; that is, if the debtor does not have the assets to pay the debt, the assignee can proceed against those who purchased the

followed, the assignor can no longer forgive the debt to the debtor.[33] However, the assignee cannot in such a case bring an action to compel the assignor to turn over the instrument to him.[34] If, instead of the debtor, the creditor, and a third party being present, the creditor as bailor and the bailee of the instrument are present together with a third party, and the creditor instructed the bailee to transfer the note to the third party, the creditor can renege until the bailee makes actual delivery of the instrument to the third party.[35]

If the underlying debt is secured by collateral and the collateral is assigned together with the instrument, the assignor can no longer forgive the debt.[36]

In the event that the assignor forgives the underlying debt, he must make restitution to the original assignee or to the ultimate assignee who is holding the instrument when the note is forgiven.[37] He must pay the value of the instrument at the time of the forgiveness.[38] If the

debtor's realty after the debt was made, provided that the realty was owned by the debtor on the date the loan was made.

33. The assignor, at the moment of the assignment in this method, relinquishes any rights he had against the debtor and thus has nothing to forgive.

34. This type of an assignment, without the delivery of the assignment and the original instrument, transfers the debtor's personal obligation and the lien on his realty, but does not act as a transfer of the instrument itself. Thus the debtor may not plead that he paid the debt to the assignee. However, beth din may subpoena the assignor to produce the instrument and admit the instrument as if it had been produced by the assignee.

35. However, if the creditor/bailor gave the third party an assignment of the instrument, then the bailee must transfer the instrument to the third party; the creditor cannot renege even though he has not delivered the instrument to the third party.

36. The collateral could consist of personalty or realty of which the assignor had taken possession and that he now transfers to the assignee together with the instrument and assignment.

37. The liability results from the fact that the lender is the indirect cause for the assignee's loss and as such is liable, as would be one who tore or burned an instrument belonging to a lender. See Chapter 385 regarding indirect causes of damage.

38. If the debtor is in a strong financial position, then the instrument may be worth nearly, or exactly, its face value. If the debtor is not financially strong or is a difficult litigant, then the value of the instrument might be less. It is assumed when the assignee purchases the instrument that these factors are taken into account. The laws are the same whether the debtor is a Jew or Gentile. If the debtor is a Gentile and the instrument provided for interest, the lender must also pay the value of the interest to the assignee. But the lender is not liable for anticipated profits that may accrue to the

lender dies, his heirs are liable to repay the assignee.[39]

## Warranties made together with the assignment

Chapter 39 stated that the absence of a warranty in an instrument is deemed a mistake of the draftsman, and the instrument may be amended by motion of the holder. This rule also applies to the assignment. Thus, unless stated otherwise, every assignment of an instrument is deemed to contain a warranty that the instrument that is being assigned will be paid. Thus if the creditor of the assignor levies on the instrument in the hands of the assignee, or if another person claims and proves that the instrument is really his and not the property of the assignor,[40] or the third party purchased the instrument from the assignor before the assignee purchased it, then the assignor must make restitution to the assignee for the market value of the instrument as of the time that the instrument was taken from the assignee. If the assignor does not have funds with which to make restitution to the assignee, the assignee can levy against purchasers of real property from the assignor that he owned when he assigned the instrument and that he sold after the assignment.

If the assignor at the time of making the assignment warranted to the assignee that the instrument would be paid by the debtor, and if the instrument that was assigned was paid prior to the assignment or was forgiven by the assignor prior to the assignment, then it is a sale made in error and voidable by the assignee. The assignee is entitled to the return of his money rather than the market value of the instrument.[41]

If the debtor under the instrument pleads that the instrument is a forgery, and the assignor alleges that the note is not a forgery, and there is no way to confirm the authenticity of the instrument, or if the

---

assignee. A dissenting opinion holds that the lender need pay only the purchase price of the instrument paid by the assignee.

39. Chapter 385 notes an opinion that the person who indirectly causes damage is legally not liable, and it is only a Rabbinic penalty that is placed on such person to pay for the damage. According to this view, the heirs would not be liable to the assignee.

40. The third party shows proofs to the beth din that the instrument was mistakenly given to the assignor and was really intended for him.

41. This is not technically a breach of warranty, since the assignor was not assigning anything because the instrument was not in existence as an instrument.

debtor is a very strong and intimidating person and the assignee is afraid to sue him, then the assignor need not make restitution to the assignee, since he brought the inability to collect upon himself.[42] If the instrument is proven to be a forgery, the sale is voidable and the assignee is entitled to the return of his money. If the debtor alleges that the instrument was paid and the assignor alleges that it was not paid, then the assignor must take an oath it was not paid, and if he refuses to take the oath, he must return the assignee's money.

If at the time of the assignment the debtor is without assets to pay, whether the assignee knows of this or not, it is a voidable sale.[43] However, if the debtor becomes impoverished after the assignment, then the assignee has no redress against the assignor.[44]

## Debtor's plea of payment to the assignor or the assignee

If the debtor alleges that he repaid the loan to the assignor, he must still pay the loan to the assignee, since the assignee has both the instrument and the assignment. However, unless the instrument had a credence clause that provided that it would be paid upon presentation and without defense, the debtor can insist that the assignor take an oath that he was not paid. If the assignor refuses to take an oath, he must pay to the assignee the value of the instrument.

If the debtor is deceased, then, unless he died before the due date of the instrument, both the assignor and the assignee must take oaths that they were not paid.[45,46] If the debtor alleges that he paid the heirs

---

42. The assignee should have made a thorough investigation of the instrument before he agreed to purchase it.

43. It is a voidable sale according to the view set forth in the text following that overreaching applies to instruments if it exceeds 50 percent. This would apply even if the assignee had some idea about the debtor's financial condition.

44. The assignor would be liable if he warranted that if the debtor did not have the assets to make payment, then the assignor would pay to the assignee. In all cases the beth din must ascertain whether there was a mutual mistake, in which event the sale is voidable, or if the facts were known or should have been known, in which event the sale is not voidable.

45. In all situations, if a creditor comes to enforce a claim against the defendant's heirs then the plaintiff must take an oath that he was not paid.

46. See Volume III, Chapter 78, regarding a debtor's pleading that he paid the instrument before its due date.

of the assignor, then they must take an oath that they were not paid, and if they refuse to take the oath, they must pay to the assignee the full amount of the loan. If both the debtor and the assignor died before the loan was paid, the assignee must take an oath that he was not paid, that the assignor did not tell him that the loan was paid, and that he has no information that the loan was repaid. The heirs of the assignor also have to take an oath that they have no information that the loan was repaid. If the assignor's heirs refuse to take such an oath, then the assignee collects the instrument from the assignor's heirs if they inherited enough from their father to pay the instrument. If they do take the oath, the assignee collects the instrument from the heirs of the debtor.

If the assignor gave the instrument to the assignee without a written assignment, but with an oral assignment, and the debtor paid the instrument to the assignee, then the assignor has no claim against the others.[47]

If there had not been a written assignment together with the delivery of the instrument to the assignee, then the debtor, before he pays the assignor, can insist that he will pay only if the assignor delivers the instrument to the debtor.[48]

## If the assignee does not produce the assignment[49]

If the assignee has the instrument that he alleges was assigned to him by the assignor, but the assignee does not have in his possession the assignment from the assignor, then the assignee's position is weakened in his relationship to the assignor and the debtor.

There are two opinions regarding his relationship to the assignor. One opinion is that the assignee is believed that he received the instrument from the assignor without even the necessity of having

---

47. Had there not been the oral assignment, the assignor would be able to recover the payment from the debtor even though he had given the instrument to the assignee. The debtor could recover from the assignee what he paid to the assignee.

48. An offer by the assignor to issue a receipt to the debtor is not adequate, since it puts the burden on the debtor to watch his receipt.

49. There are several situations in which the assignee may produce the instrument but may not have the assignment. For example, he may have lost the assignment, or he may never have had an assignment if he purchased the instrument along with realty.

witnesses to testify to what he pleads. Dissenting opinions hold that the assignee is not believed against the assignor without proof, since there is a weakness in the assignee's position because he does not have the assignment.

Regarding his relationship to the debtor, if the debtor pleads that before he pays the instrument the assignee produce witnesses that the instrument was transferred to the assignee by the assignor, then the assignee must comply with such a request. If the assignee does not comply, he cannot collect the debt from the debtor.[50] On the other hand, the debtor may decide to pay the assignee, and the assignor cannot prevent such payment, except that he may intervene to demand that the assignee take an oath that he received the instrument from the assignor by valid assignment.[51] If the debtor pleads that he has paid the instrument to the assignor, and the assignee demands that the assignor take an oath that he was not paid, then the assignor may take such an oath that he was not paid, in which event the assignee will collect the debt from the debtor. If the assignor does not wish to take such an oath, then the debtor need not pay the assignee, and the assignor must pay to the assignee the value of the instrument.[52] If the assignor has no assets with which to pay the assignee, then the assignee bears the loss, since he has put himself into the position of not having proof that he is the lawful assignee of the instrument.[53]

If the assignee who does not have the assignment is able to prove with witnesses that the assignment was made, then the debtor must pay the instrument to the assignee.

---

50. There is no reason that the debtor should put himself into the position of paying a person who alleges that he is an assignee when in reality he may have found, or even stolen, the instrument.

51. The assignee alleges he lost the valid written assignment, or he alleges he obtained the instrument along with realty that the assignee received from the assignor. The receipt of the realty may be by purchase or by gift.

52. Of course, the same result would follow if the assignor admitted that the debtor had paid him for the instrument: the assignor would have to pay to the assignee the value of the instrument.

53. He has put himself into that position by having lost his assignment, or by purchasing the instrument along with realty, which left him without any evidence of purchase of the instrument.

## Lawsuits by both the assignor and the assignee against the debtor on the same instrument

If the instrument was properly assigned and both the assignor and the assignee sue the debtor, then beth din will direct and compel the debtor to pay to the assignee. If the debtor nevertheless paid the assignor, then the beth din will compel the assignor to pay the amount collected to the assignee. The assignee has no legal claim against the debtor,[54] except if the debtor knew that the assignor was a spendthrift and was quickly disposing of his assets, or that the assignor was a powerful person and the assignee could not win a lawsuit against him and/or enforce a judgment against him.[55] In the latter event the debtor would have to reimburse the assignee for the loss that the debtor occasioned by paying the debt to the assignor.[56]

## Overreaching in sales of instruments, and other miscellaneous laws regarding instruments

The laws of overreaching are found in Chapter 227. These laws do not generally apply to the sale of instruments.[57] Thus the assignor may sell to the assignee an instrument the value of which is $1,000 for $1, or an instrument whose value is $1 for a $1,000.

---

54. The assignee has no legal claim against the debtor because he has no legal connection with the debtor, since the assignor could have forgiven the claim after the assignment. When the debtor paid the assignor, it was the equivalent of the assignor's forgiving the debt, in which event the assignee could claim only against the assignor. The assignor's ability to forgive the debt even extends beyond the time of the beth din's rendering a decision in favor of the assignee against the debtor.

55. If the debtor was not aware of these facts, he would not have to pay the assignee.

56. This presupposes that the debtor was not intimidated by the assignor but paid the assignor despite his fear.

57. The laws of overreaching generally apply to sales of matters that have their own intrinsic value. An instrument has no intrinsic value (except possibly the value of its paper, but it is not purchased for its paper value), and thus the laws of overreaching do not apply. There is an opinion that if the disparity between the value of the instrument and the sales price exceeded 50 percent, then the laws of overreaching would apply. However, if the instrument is sold for its paper value, the laws of overreaching would apply.

Just as the laws of overreaching do not apply to the sale of instruments, the laws of oaths also generally do not apply to claims made for the sale of instruments.[58]

If partners or heirs want to divide instruments due to them, beth din will appraise each instrument individually and then take a sum of the current value of all the instruments and divide them equitably by lot. If there is only one instrument, then they follow the rules of partition as stated in Chapter 171.[59] There is no necessity for assignments and delivery in such divisions.

If as a gift *causa mortis* a decedent leaves "all [his] possessions to Mr. A," the donee also gets possession of the instruments belonging to the grantor. If the decedent leaves "all [his] personalty to Mr. A," then the instruments are not included.[60] In all other gifts the grantor must both employ an act that will effect a transfer and use language transferring the instruments, such as "the instruments and all of the rights thereunder are transferred."

---

58. For example, if the assignor pleads that he transferred 100 instruments to the assignee, and the assignee admits receiving only 60, then he need not take an oath regarding the remaining 40. Similarly, if the assignor produces one witness to back his plea that he transferred 100 instruments, and the assignee denies the transfer, then the assignee need not take an oath. Furthermore, a bailee need not take an oath regarding instruments that were given to him as a bailment. Such oaths would be Torah oaths, and they are discussed in Volume III, Chapter 87. The parties may, by agreement entered into with a *kinyan*, vary the responsibilities under these laws.

59. There is an opinion in Chapter 171 that the laws of partition do not apply to the division of instruments.

60. Thus if a husband waives "all rights to the property of the wife," he has waived his rights to the instruments owned by her. However, if he waives "all of his rights to her personalty," he does not waive his rights to manage her instruments.

# Chapter 67

## LAWS CONCERNING SHEMITAH AND PROSBUL

### INTRODUCTION

The title of this chapter as it appears in *Shulhan Aruch* is much broader than is actually discussed in the chapter. *Shemitah* covers two topics: (1) the cessation of work on the land during the seventh year and (2) the cancellation, or cessation of enforcing collection, of loans during that year.[1] The chapter discusses only the cancellation of debts. Interrelated with these two topics is the subject of the jubilee year.

There is no concept of bankruptcy in halachah. Thus an indebtedness is never cancelled just because the debtor does not have the ability to pay. According to Torah law, however, all debts were cancelled at the end of the *shemitah* year.[2] It was then considered that people might hesitate to lend close to the *shemitah* year because the repayment of the loan would be cancelled. Therefore, Hillel instituted the *prosbul*, pursuant to which loans would not be cancelled, so that

---

1. In Rabbinic literature, the seventh year is often referred to as *shevi'ith*. But since Rabbi Joseph Karo called the chapter "Laws of *Shemitah* and *Prosbul*," the term *shemitah* has been retained here in referring to the seventh year.

2. The Torah states: "At the end of every seven years thou shalt make a release. And this is the manner of the release: every creditor shall release that which he hath lent unto his neighbor; he shall not exact it of his neighbor and his brother; because the Lord's release hath been proclaimed" (Deuteronomy 15:1–2).

people would not be reluctant to make loans by reason of the approach of *shemitah*.³

On the subject of refraining from lending before the *shemitah* year, Maimonides writes: "If a person refrains from lending money before the *shemitah* year because he fears that there may be delay in repaying the loan, and in the meantime that *shemitah* will intervene and cancel the loan, he transgresses a negative commandment, as it is written, 'Beware that there be not a base thought in your heart' [Deuteronomy 15:9]. This is a serious transgression for the Torah has warned against it with a double injunction.... The Torah is very particular regarding this evil thought and calls it a base thought."⁴

*Prosbul* is a device enacted by Hillel in the first century B.C.E. to encourage loans and commerce by enabling the lender to enforce collection of the loan even after the *shemitah* year.

The Jewish agricultural calendar cycle consists of seven years. A farmer must follow this calendar in tithing his produce and in letting his land lie fallow during certain times. The cycles commenced with the entry of the Jewish people, led by Joshua, into the land of Israel. The conquest and division of the land took fourteen years. Beginning with the fifteenth year, the agricultural cycles were counted in seven-year cycles. Thus the twenty-first year after the entrance into Israel was the first *shemitah*, and the 64th year was the first jubilee year. The effectiveness of the jubilee year ceased when the first two tribes, Reuben and Gad, were driven from the Land of Israel by the Assyrians around 722 B.C.E. The procedure for counting the jubilee year continued, however, so that the *shemitah* year would be correctly reckoned. In modern times, the *shemitah* years are counted without the jubilee year. The year 5747 (autumn 1986 to autumn 1987) was a *shemitah* year. This year 5751 is the fourth year of the *shemitah* cycle.⁵

---

3. The term *prosbul* may come from Greek meaning a decree made to benefit the rich so that they will not refrain from lending and thus transgress the commandment not to refrain from lending.

4. Maimonides, *Laws Concerning the Sabbatical Year and the Year of the Jubilee*, Chapter 9, Law 30.

5. Maimonides cites the opinion of the Geonim that the years of *shemitah* are counted according to a tradition handed down from person to person. This tradition was that during the seventy years between the destruction of the First Temple and the building of the Second Temple, only *shemitah* years were counted and not jubilee years. Maimonides himself holds that the jubilee years were counted during these

During the first six of the seven years of the cycle, the farmer has to give approximately one-fiftieth of his produce to the priest (*kohen*).[6] Thus if a farmer had 100 bushels of wheat, he gives approximately two bushels to the priest, leaving approximately ninety-eight bushels. During all six years of the seven-year cycle, he then measures one-tenth and gives this to the Levite as the first tithe (*maaser*). Thus he gives 9 and 8/10 bushels to the Levite, leaving 88 2/10 bushels. During the first, second, fourth and fifth years of the seven-year cycle he separates another 10 percent from the remaining amount—that is, 8 8/10's—and these were taken to be eaten in Jerusalem. This is known as the second tithe (*maaser sheni*). If the amount is too large to take, there are procedures for redeeming the second tithe. During the third and sixth years of the seven-year cycle, the farmer gives the 8 8/10 bushels to the poor. This is known as *maaser ani* (the tithe for the poor).[7] During the 7th year, the farmer can neither sow nor harvest.[8] The 7-year cycles were continued for 7 cycles, and at the end of the 49 years there was a jubilee year. According to Torah law, the cancellation of debts is in force only when the jubilee year is in force. This cancellation was in effect both within and outside the Land of Israel. Thus when the force of the jubilee year had ceased, the Torah requirement for cancellation of debts also ceased. The Rabbis, however, decreed that the cancellation of debts should

---

periods. Maimonides, writing in 1176 C.E. states that it was the *shemitah* year and the twenty-first year of the jubilee. According to the Geonic counting, which is now followed, that year was the year after the *shemitah* year.

6. According to Torah law, any amount that the farmer gives to the priest as *terumah* will suffice. The Rabbis, however, set standards for this giving. A generous person gives approximately one in forty, while an average person gives approximately one in fifty, and a stingy person gives approximately one in sixty. The farmer need not measure an exact amount for *terumah* but should approximate the amount, whether by volume, weight, or count.

7. In addition to these tithes, the farmer also had to set aside a portion of his field for the poor to harvest. The poor were also entitled to all sheaves that were left in the fields and to any grain that fell from the hands of the farmer while he was reaping the grains. For a full discussion of these laws, see Maimonides, *Laws of Agriculture*.

8. In the State of Israel there are currently many farmers who observe these laws and many people who eat produce that is only grown in conformity with these laws. The Chief Rabbis have devised a method for permitting farmers to grow and consumers to eat from produce grown during the seventh year, and many people rely on this device. With the coming of the Messiah speedily in our days, we can hope that there will once again be counting not only of *shemitah* years, but also of jubilee years.

be in force in all places so that the law of the cancellation of debts would not be forgotten.[9] Some authorities hold that the cancellation of debts is not practiced nowadays outside Israel, but only in the Land of Israel.

Maimonides, in *Book of Agriculture*, Treatise 7, Laws Concerning the Sabbatical Year and the Year of the Jubilee, lists twenty-two Torah commandments regarding these topics, nine of which are positive and thirteen, negative.[10] The topics are divided into three main categories:

---

9. The question arose in the Talmud (*Gittin* 36a) of how Hillel could make a decree that seemed to violate the Torah law. The Torah states that the cancellation was not in force because the jubilees were not in force, yet Hillel decreed that there would be a cancellation of debts. It was answered that there had already been a decree by the Rabbis that the *shemitah* year should effect a cancellation of the debts, and Hillel, in order to promote commerce, enacted the *prosbul*, which affected only a Rabbinic decree. However, at such times that the cancellation of the debts would be of Torah origin, then the *prosbul* would not be effective.

A more basic question was also asked: how could the Rabbis decree that there should be cancellation of debts when according to Torah law the debts should have been paid? One answer given is that the Rabbis have the authority to make decrees enjoining people from acting—in this case, enjoining people from collecting debts—and thus it was acceptable for Hillel to decree that debts could be enforced. Another answer given is that the beth din has the right to expropriate property, and thus they could decree that the debts should be cancelled. In all events the decree of Hillel instituting the procedure of *prosbul* enabled the lender to collect his debts.

10. The positive commandments are as follows: to cease from tilling the land in the *shemitah* year; to permit the land to lie fallow in the *shemitah* year; to cancel loans in the *shemitah* year; to count the jubilee years and by cycles of seven years; to sanctify the jubilee year by letting the fields lie fallow; to sound the *shofar* (ram's horn) in the jubilee year; to grant the right of redemption of sold land in the jubilee year; to grant the right to redeem houses sold within a walled city within one year of the sale; and to grant to the Levites cities in which to dwell together with the open spaces surrounding the cities. The negative commandments are as follows: not to till the soil in the *shemitah* year; not to work on any tree in the *shemitah* year; not to reap the aftergrowth of the *shemitah* year in the manner in which it is done in other years; not to gather the fruit of the trees in the *shemitah* year in the manner in which it is done in other years; not to demand the return of a loan after the *shemitah* year; not to refuse to make a loan to a poor person because of the approach of the *shemitah* year; not to work the soil or work on any tree in the jubilee year; not to gather the fruit of the tree in the jubilee year in the manner in which it is done in other years; not to harvest the aftergrowth of the jubilee year in the manner in which it is done in other years; not to sell a field in the Land of Israel forever; not to allow the members of the tribe of Levi to have a portion of territory in the Land of Israel; not to allow the members of the tribe of Levi to participate in the spoils of war in the conquest of the

the agricultural laws of the *shemitah,* or seventh year; the laws of the jubilee year; and the laws of remission of debts.

This chapter discusses only the cancellation of debts arising from loans or other forms of credit that have been transformed into loans. The term *loans* in this context refers to all credit reduced to an obligation, as shown in the text.

# TEXT

## Cancellation of debts

The cancellation of debts at the end of the *shemitah* year in modern times is of Rabbinic origin and is applicable in all places.[11] When jubilee years were in effect, the cancellation of debts was of Torah origin.

Debts are cancelled on the last moment of the *shemitah* year—that is, on the last day of the year in the month of Elul, moments before Rosh haShana (New Year) of the first year after the prior *shemitah* year. (See Volume I, page 39) Thus if a loan is made during the *shemitah* year, it may be collected or a *prosbul* written until the last moment of that year.

## Cancellable debts

*Shemitah* cancels all loans, whether oral or evidenced by a writing, even if the writing contains a clause placing a lien on the borrower's real estate as security for the loan.[12]

If the borrower gives the lender a general mortgage on the

---

Land of Israel; and not to change the character of the open spaces surrounding the cities of the Levites or their fields.

11. There are also opinions that even at the present time the cancellation of debts is of Torah origin. Other opinions hold that the laws of cancellation of debts are not in effect at the present time.

12. See the Glossary regarding categories of loans. Secured loans are cancellable because even if they are secured by a general lien on the borrower's real estate, they are still not deemed to have been collected.

borrower's real estate, and the lender has the use of the real estate until the loan is repaid, then if the borrower may at any time pay off the loan and have the real estate released from the lender's lien, the loan is cancelled by *shemitah*.[13] However, if the borrower does not have the right to pay off the loan until the due date, then the loan is not cancelled by *shemitah*.[14] There are those who hold if the borrower designated a specific piece of real estate as security for the loan, then it is not cancellable, even if the lender did not have the right to use the real estate. A dissenting opinion holds that even such a loan is cancellable if the borrower may pay off the loan at any time without any restriction and have the security removed from the real estate.[15]

In order to comply with the laws of usury, which do not permit loans on interest, the halachah suggests that the amount advanced be divided into two parts. The first part is deemed an investment in the business of the borrower, and the second half is considered a noninterest loan. *Shemitah* cancels the half that is considered a loan.[16]

If a surety or guarantor pays the lender and before the surety or guarantor has time to be reimbursed by the borrower, *shemitah* intervenes, the borrower's debt to the surety is cancelled.[17]

---

13. It is the same as any other loan secured by a written note with security. The lender has nothing tangible in his hands; he has only the right to foreclose on the land, and until he does so, the land is not his. In the case of personal property, however, the personalty given as pledge belongs to the lender, with the right of the borrower to retrieve the object when he pays off the loan. Thus, in the latter case, as will be noted in the text, the loan is not cancelled, since the lender who holds the object is deemed to have enforced collection of the amount due.

14. If the borrower does not have the right to pay off the loan and demand return of the mortgaged property, then the lender/mortgagee is deemed to have purchased the land for the period of the loan, and then *shemitah* does not cancel the loan.

15. If the borrower is in any manner restricted from paying off the loan, even for a day, then the loan is not cancelled by *shemitah*; but if the the loan can be repaid at any time without any restrictions whatsoever, then the loan is cancelled by *shemitah* according to the latter opinion.

16. The laws of usury are not covered in the civil code but rather appear in the *Shulhan Aruch, Yoreh De'ah*, which deals with ritual laws and prohibitions. Violation of the laws of usury entails a violation of the obligations that a person owes to his Maker.

17. For example, B borrows $100 from L, and G guarantess to L that B will repay the loan and that if B does not repay the loan, then G will repay to L. When B fails to repay, L demands that G repay, and G does so. G could then sue B to reimburse him.

Often a litigant—sometimes the plaintiff and sometimes the defendant—is required to take an oath to bolster his position in the litigation. If the oath is required because it bolsters the position of a borrower, and *shemitah* cancels the underlying debt, then the borrower need not take the otherwise required oath.[18] This applies only to oaths required with respect to debts that arise from loans. But if the oath to be taken arises from a pledge or from a partnership or similar matters that are not related to or reduced to borrowings, then the oath has to be taken, since an underlying indebtedness that does not arise from or is not reduced to a borrowing is not cancelled by *shemitah*. If the borrower takes an oath to the lender that he will repay the loan by a certain date and *shemitah* intervenes before he repays, then the debt is cancelled because the oath is only in furtherance of the underlying debt (and since the debt is cancelled, the oath is not enforceable). However, if the oath is to pay off the debt after *shemitah*, then the intervening of *shemitah* does not cancel the debt because the debt is in the same category as an original loan that is to be repaid after *shemitah*.

A lender loans money to a borrower and demands payment. The borrower denies the loan and swears that he does not owe the money. Thereafter the borrower admits the loan or else witnesses are produced who testify to the loan.[19] Thereafter *shemitah* intervenes and there is as yet no written judgment rendered by the beth din. The debt is cancelled. But if *shemitah* had intervened before the borrower admits the loan or before the witnesses were produced, the loan would not have been cancelled.[20]

If beth din renders a written judgment in favor of the lender prior to the intervention of *shemitah*, then the debt is not cancelled, since it is

---

However, if *shemitah* intervenes before G is reimbursed, then the obligation of B to G is cancelled, since G is now in the place of L as a lender to B whose debt has not been paid and is therefore cancelled by *shemitah*. For the purpose of this rule, a surety is in the same position as a guarantor. The difference between a surety and a guarantor is that the lender may, in the first instance, proceed against either the borrower or the surety. In the case of a guarantee, the lender must first sue the borrower, and if he cannot collect from the borrower, then he may sue the guarantor.

18. Oaths are discussed in Volume III, Chapter 87.

19. But beth din did not yet render a judgment in favor of the lender.

20. Since the borrower denied the loan and swore that he was not indebted, the lender did not at that time have a loan outstanding to be cancelled by *shemitah*. When, after *shemitah*, the borrower admits the loan, it is as if a new loan has then been made.

no longer a debt; rather, it is a judgment of the beth din that is tantamount to collection of the debt.

If a lender loans money to a borrower on condition that *shemitah* shall not cancel the debt, the debt is nonetheless cancelled because the lender cannot cancel a law of the Torah. However, if the parties stipulate that the borrower will not raise the passing of the *shemitah* year as a defense to the lawsuit brought by the lender on the loan, the stipulation is valid and the loan is not cancelled.[21]

## Debts that are not cancellable

In addition to the cases just described, there are other cases of debts not being cancellable.

If partners divide up their property or their profits and one of the partners receives more than his share, *shemitah* does not cancel his obligation to make an even division, since *shemitah* cancels only loans, and not investments or property deposited with another person.

If the writing made by the parties refers to the loan as a deposit, the loan is not cancelled.[22] If the general practice of the community is to refer to loans as deposits so as not to have the loans cancelled by *shemitah*, and an instrument entered into between the parties does not so characterize the loan, then *shemitah* will cancel the loan.[23]

If a loan was made for a term that would run beyond the *shemitah* year, *shemitah* does not cancel the loan, since the lender could not have sued for the repayment during the *shemitah* year.[24]

---

21. Stipulations regarding money are generally valid. The borrower had the right to obligate himself to a debt for which the Torah has stated that he is not liable. In the first sentence in this paragraph, *shemitah* is the subject—that is, "*shemitah* shall not cancel the debt." In the next sentence, the borrower is the subject, and he can accept any condition upon himself.

22. Stipulations regarding money are generally valid, and the borrower had the right to frame the note of indebtedness in a manner that would not be cancelled by *shemitah*.

23. Ordinarily, if there is a practice in a community to write notes in a certain manner and a note does not conform, then it is held that there was an error on the part of the scribe who drafted the note. In this case, however, the omission can be attributed to the lender's wanting to comply with the laws of *shemitah*.

24. Since the lender could not have demanded payment during the *shemitah* year,

If the lender delivers his notes of indebtedness to beth din and requests that they be collected upon, the loans evidenced by these notes are not cancelled.[25]

Loans that are collateralized by the lender's taking personal property into his possession as security are not cancelled by *shemitah*. There is an opinion that the amount of the loan not cancelled is only up to the value of the security, and the balance is cancelled.[26] The other opinion holds that if collateral security has been taken, even the amount of the loan that exceeds the value of the security is not cancelled.[27]

*Shemitah* does not cancel the amount owed for merchandise purchased on credit, unless the credit has been converted into a loan.[28] A credit is considered converted into a loan from the time payment is due. A contrary opinion holds that credit is converted into a loan from the time the total running account due from the customer is entered upon the merchant's account books as one total sum.

Wages earned by a worker are not cancelled by *shemitah* unless the moneys due were converted into a loan.

Penalties are not cancelled by *shemitah*.[29] However, if they were

---

he is not in violation of the verse that states "he shall not exact payment during the *shemitah* year" (Deuteronomy 15:2).

25. The prohibition of the Torah is against the individual collecting on a loan after the *shemitah* year; therefore, the prohibition does not apply to the beth din. See Deuteronomy 15:3.

26. While the security is held by the lender, it belongs to him. The reason is that since the lender holds security, he does not have to "exact payment" in violation of Deuteronomy 15:2.

27. The reasoning of this opinion is that since the lender originally took the lesser collateral as security for the entire loan, it is the equivalent of having collateral for the entire loan.

28. This applies to merchandise purchased from a store, since stores extend credit for long periods of time that may run beyond the termination of the *shemitah* year. Such credit is thus analogous to a loan made for a period that will terminate after the *shemitah* year. But if merchandise is sold on credit by an individual, *shemitah* will cancel the amount owed because such credit amounts to a loan (since individual sellers are not in the business of making sales on credit).

29. One example of a penalty is the amount of money required to be paid by a person who seduces or rapes a virgin. (See Deuteronomy 22:29 and Exodus 22:16, respectively.) Another example is the amount to be paid by the person who wrongfully defames his bride. (See Deuteronomy 22:19.) The Torah prescribes the penalties in these instances, and they are not loans that are cancelled by *shemitah*.

sued upon and were thus converted into loans, they are cancelled by *shemitah*. Such penalties are considered loans from the time the plaintiff brings the lawsuit.[30]

If a man divorces his wife prior to the *shemitah* year, her *kethubah* is not cancelled, since *kethubah* is not a loan.[31] However, if it had been converted into a loan or had been impaired, it is cancelled by *shemitah*.[32]

If a Jew purchases an instrument of indebtedness from a Gentile, he stands in the same position as the Gentile and the indebtedness is not cancelled by *shemitah*.[33] Similarly, if a Jew was a guarantor for another Jew who owed money to a Gentile, and the guarantor paid the Gentile, the guarantor would stand in the postion of the Gentile and he would be able to enforce reimbursement from the Jewish debtor even if *shemitah* had intervened.[34]

## *Prosbul*

Hillel the Elder observed that people were not lending money to one another and were thereby transgressing the Torah injunction "Beware

---

30. The penalties are not cancelled because there is no indebtedness until there is a lawsuit, at which time there is manifested an intent that there is a debt due to the plaintiff from the defendant. They are converted into loans from the time that the lawsuit is brought until the written judgment is rendered, from which time they are no longer cancellable by *shemitah* (like any judgment of the beth din that is not cancellable by *shemitah*).

31. A *kethubah* is a document executed at the time of marriage which stipulates that the husband will pay a sum certain to his wife in the event that he divorces her. In the event of his death, she will receive that sum from his estate. The document also provides for other obligations that the husband undertakes for the benefit of his wife.

32. The *kethubah* falls under the laws of *shemitah* from the moment that the wife takes part payment or converts the *kethubah* into a loan. (After she takes part payment, she has the balance drawn into a note of indebtedness.)

33. The Gentile loaned the money to the Jewish borrower according to the laws of the land, and the laws of the land do not provide for cancellation of debts in the *shemitah* year. Thus the Jewish purchaser of the indebtedness takes with the benefit the fact that the loans will not be cancelled by *shemitah*. On the other hand he also takes the liabilities such as defenses that would not be available in halachah, such as the laws of bankruptcy.

34. This is true only if the guarantor took an assignment of the note from the Gentile and sued the Jewish debtor on the note. If, however, he sued on the guarantee, *shemitah* would cancel the debt owed by the debtor to his guarantor.

that there should not be a base thought in thy heart, saying: 'The seventh year, the year of release, is at hand'; and thy eye be evil against thy brother, and thou give him nought; and he cry unto the Lord against thee, and it be sin in thee" (Deuteronomy 15:9). Hillel instituted the *prosbul* so that debts would not be cancelled and therefore people would not be reluctant to loan money to one another. Debts delivered to beth din are deemed collected by the beth din and thus they are not cancellable by *shemitah*.[35]

The *prosbul* may be written at any time prior to the termination of the *shemitah* year, up until the last moment. If they are written at an earlier time they will not cover loans made after the *prosbul* was written. Some authorities hold that a *prosbul* should be written twice—once at the end of the sixth year, just before the *shemitah* year, and once at the end of the *shemitah* year. However, the latter opinion is not generally followed.

A predated *prosbul* is valid, since the lender has harmed only his own position.[36] A postdated *prosbul*, on the other hand, is not valid, since it perpetrates a fraud on the debtors of the lender.[37]

There are opinions that the *prosbul* can be written only by a very distinguished beth din, which would preclude its universal use. The preferred opinion is that it may be written by any beth din.[38]

Minor orphans who are creditors do not require a *prosbul*, since beth din is deemed to be their protector and thus beth din already holds the debts.[39] Beth din pleads on behalf of inheritors who are not

---

35. It was stated earlier that if notes of indebtedness are delivered to beth din, they are not cancelled by *shemitah*. Similarly, delivering the claims to beth din prevents their cancellation. There is an opinion that the *prosbul* and the delivery of the notes to beth din are the same thing, but most authorities disagree and hold that they are two distinct things.

36. If a *prosbul* is written on February 1 and is predated to January 1, and if the lender made a loan on January 15, the *prosbul* does not cover the loan, but if it was properly dated, then the *prosbul* would cover the loan.

37. If a *prosbul* is written on February 1 and is postdated to March 1, and if the lender made a loan on February 15, the *prosbul* would cover the loan; if it were properly dated, however, it would not cover the loan.

38. This is the preferred opinion, especially since there are those who hold that the law of cancellation of loan is not in effect in modern times outside the Land of Israel.

39. The law is the same whether the loans were made for the orphans as lenders or by their father as lender and the orphans are now the creditors, having inherited the loans.

minors that perhaps the decedent had a *prosbul* written on the loan.[40]
Loans made by charity as the lender are not cancelled by *shemitah*
and do not require a *prosbul*.

The form of the *prosbul* is as follows: The lender writes to the
judges of the beth din, "I hereby transmit to you, Judge A, Judge B,
and Judge C, in place D, all debts that are due to me may be collected
by me at any time as I please." One opinion holds that if the lender is
a very learned person, he may make the declaration before other
scholars and there is no necessity for a writing. The prevailing opinion
states that any person, even if he is not learned, may make the
declaration orally before a beth din. The declaration may be written
outside the presence of the beth din and then delivered to them, and
they will then sign the written declaration. The three judges write that
they sat together and that Mr. E, the lender, appeared before them and
transmitted to them all debts that may be due to him. The judges then
sign at the bottom as judges or in the role of witnesses.

The lender need not deliver the notes to the beth din if the loans
are secured by notes. The declaration of transmission of the notes is
sufficient.

If one borrower borrows money from five lenders, then each
lender needs his own *prosbul*. If five borrowers borrow from the same
lender, one *prosbul* is sufficient.

## Necessity for the debtor to own land

A *prosbul* may be written only if the debtor owns real estate.[41] The
amount of real estate is not important; even a very small piece of real
estate is sufficient. Even a flowerpot that has a hole in the bottom and
that stands on sticks on land that does not belong to the debtor is
sufficient to satisfy the requirement.[42] If the lender loaned or rented

---

40. Or, beth din may plead that perhaps there was a stipulation between their
decedent (the lender) and the borrower that the borrower would not raise the
defense of *shemitah*.

41. If the debtor owns real estate, then the loan created a lien on the real estate and
thus is closer to having been collected, and the *prosbul* enforces only this "almost
collected" loan. Alternatively, as has been suggested, the *prosbul* was meant to deal
with the ordinary situation, and in most instances loans were not made unless the
borrower owned land on which a lien could be placed to secure the debt.

42. In halachah, a flowerpot that has a hole in the bottom is deemed to be standing
on the ground beneath it and therefore has some of the characteristics of real estate.

to the debtor a piece of land sufficient to hold a stove or an oven, or if he sold to him a piece of land enough to hold a cabbage stalk, in all of these cases it is sufficient. If the debtor held land as a mortgagee, it is sufficient. A *prosbul* may be written for a husband if his wife has real estate, or for orphans if their guardian has real estate. It is sufficient if the debtor's debtor has real estate, since the creditor may look to the debtor's debtor to collect his debt. Similarly, if the guarantor or the guarantor's debtor has real estate, it is sufficient. Even if none of these has real estate, if the lender's other debtor owns real estate, then the lender may give some of this land to the debtor to satisfy the requirement of land ownership. This transfer of land may be made without the debtor's consent, unless the debtor objects and declares that he does not want to take title to the land from the other debtor.

## Credibility of the lender

If the lender makes certain pleas regarding the loan, then the beth din will believe these pleas.[43] The lender in his claim against the debtor may plead that he had a *prosbul* but it was lost. If the creditor does not so plead, the beth din may ask him if he wishes to enter such a plea, and if he answers in the affirmative, the plea will be entered.[44] In fact, the creditor may, at any time before beth din renders its judgment, plead that he had a *prosbul* and it was lost.[45]

The lender may plead that there was a stipulation between himself and the borrower that the borrower would not raise the defense of *shemitah* to cancel the debt.[46]

If the debtor pleads that the *prosbul* was written before the loan and thus does not affect the cancellation of the loan, and the lender pleads that it was written after the loan and thus the loan is not cancelled, the lender's plea is believed.

---

43. If there are witnesses to refute the lender, then the testimony of the witnesses is believed.

44. The creditor is believed in these cases, since the *prosbul* procedure is so simple that there is no reason for a person to transgress and collect after the *shemitah* year when he could simply comply with the procedure.

45. If the judgment is rendered by the beth din and the lender never raised the claim that he had a *prosbul* and lost it, then it is presumed that he never had a *prosbul*.

46. The lender is believed because he could just as easily have pleaded that he had a *prosbul* and lost it.

If the lender pleads that the money due arose from a sale and the debtor alleges that it arose from a loan, then the lender is believed.

## Status of the loan after *shemitah*

If the loan has been cancelled by *shemitah* because there was no *prosbul* and because the loan did not come under any of the categories just described that are not affected by *shemitah*, then the borrower, if he insists, is entitled to have the note of indebtedness returned to him.

The Rabbis have declared that they are pleased with debtors who do not avail themselves of the defense of *shemitah* but instead seek to repay their loans despite the fact that they are cancelled by *shemitah*. The creditor should tell the debtor that the debt is cancelled and that he has no further liability thereunder. The debtor should then state that it is his wish that the creditor accept the money as a gift.[47]

If a note of indebtedness was purchased before *shemitah* and then *shemitah* intervened, the purchaser has no recourse against the debtor because *shemitah* has intervened. He also has no recourse against the seller of the note, since the purchaser should have written a *prosbul*. The purchaser has brought the loss upon himself. If the note was purchased after *shemitah* intervened, then beth din will raise the plea on behalf of the purchaser that there was a *prosbul* written and thus the loan was not cancelled. If in this latter case the seller testifies that he did not write a *prosbul* before the end of the *shemitah* year, then the seller is liable to the purchaser if he has assets to pay. If he has no assets with which to compensate the purchaser, then the debtor under the note will be liable to the purchaser.[48]

---

47. If the debtor returns the money without stating that it is a gift, then the creditor should attempt to make the debtor understand that he must tell the creditor that the money is a gift. If the debtor does not do so, the creditor cannot keep the money.

48. If the seller has no assets from which to pay the purchaser, then the seller's testimony is not believed, since a person may not make an admission that will cause loss to another party. And if the seller is not believed and has no assets, then the debtor is liable, since it is assumed that a *prosbul* was written.

# Chapter 68

# DOCUMENTS EMANATING FROM GENTILE COURTS

## INTRODUCTION

There is a general principle in halachah that a Gentile may not serve as a witness in a halachic proceeding. This exclusion also prohibits a Gentile from serving as a witness to events or documents, including instruments of indebtedness, promissory notes, or other documents that establish legal relationships.

There is also a general principle in halachah that the Gentile courts are trustworthy. The rationale for this principle is that the Gentile courts would not want to tarnish their image by falsely stating that an act took place when it could later be ascertained that their statement was false. By Gentile courts we mean the courts of all countries including the State of Israel. (Jewish religious courts are the only non-secular courts.) Thus the civil courts of the United States would be considered Gentile courts. The fact that the judge of a Gentile court happens to be Jewish does not make the court a beth din; it is still classified as a Gentile court. Because Gentile courts have credibility, documents emanating from them are considered credible.

This chapter discusses the extent of the credibility within the framework of individual cases.

Beginning with Chapter 39, reference has been made to the difference between instruments of indebtedness and other writings.

What status should be given to these and other documents emanating
from Gentile courts? When such documents are introduced into beth
din, what proof is required that the documents are genuine? What
proof is required of the identities of the witnesses and the judges, and
of the contents of the documents, since they are not written in
Hebrew? A document is valid regardless of the language in which it
is written, provided that the subscribing witnesses were able to read
and understand it.

There are two sets of witnesses to a document—the subscribing
witnesses and the delivery witnesses. The subscribing witnesses are
usually also the delivery witnesses. What if one set of witnesses or
both are Jewish?

Halachah deals with four matters regarding documents emanating
from Gentile courts. There are two distinct opinions regarding these
matters.[1] There is also the question of which type of documents these
four matters apply, and of the status of all other documents.


## TEXT


## Documents from Gentile courts


If the subscribing witnesses to a document are Jewish, then the
document is valid if it complies with all of the criteria necessary to
validate a document.[2] The language of the document does not matter
so long as the subscribing witnesses were able to read and understand
it. If the document is a note of indebtedness, then it will effect a lien
on the debtor's realty.

If the subscribing witnesses are Gentiles but the document does not
emanate from a Gentile court, the document has no legal effect.

According to one view, (1) the document was drawn and the
Gentile subscribing witnesses signed it, and (2) the parties then
appeared in the Gentile court together with the signed document, and

---

1. There is the view of Maimonides, set forth in Chapter 27 of *Laws Concerning
Creditor and Debtor*, and the view of Asheri, set forth in his compendium on tractate
*Gittin*, Chapter 1, Law 10.

2. For example, the paper must be nonerasable, and the words must be written on
the page so that nothing can be added or deleted. These criteria are set forth in
Chapters 42–45.

the Gentile court witnessed the transaction.[3] For example, if the transaction was a loan, they would watch as the lender passed the money to the borrower. The Gentile court would state in the document that they witnessed the money being passed from the lender to the borrower. (3) When such a document is presented to beth din, there must be Jewish witnesses who testify that they know the Gentile subscribing witnesses to be honest people who would not accept a bribe to testify falsely to the document, and that they know that the Gentile court judges are not reputed to accept bribes. (4) If beth din accepts the document, its effect is to permit the lender to levy on the property in the hands of the borrower. The lender may not trace the borrower's property to purchasers.[4]

The other view holds that (1) the entire transaction must take place in the Gentile court. The loan or other transaction must take place there, and the document must be written there and signed there by the Gentile witnesses.[5] The document need not state that the judges witnessed the transaction. Thus, item 2 in the foregoing view is not relevant, since it is now part of item 1 in this view, and the balance is dispensed with. There is also no necessity for Jewish witnesses to testify as to the integrity of the Gentile subscribing witnesses and of the judges, since it is presumed that the judges of the Gentile courts are honest. (4) If the document complies with the foregoing, then it will effect a lien on the borrower's realty and it may be traced to a purchaser. It will also prevent the borrower from alleging that he paid the note, as he could do with a promissory note.

The two views differ on the question of how the document comes into being and on its legal effect. According to both views, the document must comply with all of the halachic requirements as discussed in Chapters 39 through 45. For example, it must be written on nonerasable paper and positioned on the paper so that nothing can be added or deleted.

The validity of documents emanating from a Gentile court is limited to official Gentile courts; it does not include nonofficial bodies, unless the law of the land provides that the clerk of the court may sign documents.

---

3. Maimonides' view is set forth first, followed by Asheri's view.
4. See the Glossary regarding tracing of realty of the debtor.
5. Contrary to the first view, this view holds that if the document was prepared and signed before the parties came to the Gentile court, then it is worthless.

## In which matters are such documents effective?

Whether one accepts the first view or the second view to give effect to the document, the question arises as to which type of documents are effective.

Documents are of two types. They either give legal effect to an event or else are just evidence of the event. If a person gives his friend a gift of real estate, the deed is the document that makes the transfer. This deed provides the legal effect. On the other hand, if a lender loans money to a borrower, the giving of the money is the legal act, and the note of indebtedness is only evidence that the loan took place. If it is the document that makes the act effective, it is not valid if the subscribing witnesses were Gentile. In the case of a loan, where the document is to be used only for evidence, the document is valid if it emanated from the Gentile court, even if the witnesses were Gentile. In the case of a deed, the transfer is not effective because the parties relied on the deed to transfer the property.[6]

Among the documents that are considered valid are promissory notes, instruments of indebtedness, and bills of sale and deeds in those cases where title passes independent of the documents and the documents are offered only to prove that title had passed by another method. This latter concept would also permit notes of admission to qualify if the note was only to prove that the admission was made and the admission was made before the Gentile court and thus became effective. Similarly, releases of claims and agreements to arbitrate are valid if the release or the agreement was effective by the statements made in the Gentile court and the writing serves only as evidence of the occurrence. However, if the document gives effect to the note of admission, or to the release or the agreement to arbitrate, then the document emanating from the Gentile court with Gentile subscribing witnesses is worthless. A gift *causa mortis* declared by the donor in the Gentile court would be valid.[7]

---

6. If the parties intended that title to the property pass when the money was paid, and that the deed is only evidence that title had passed, then this document would also be valid, since the deed does not give effect to the act.

7. A gift made in contemplation of death has a special status in halachah. The declaration by the donor is equivalent to the document's having been reduced to writing and delivered to the donor's beneficiaries. Thus if the donor makes the declaration to the Gentile court before he dies, it is as if the gift has been completed.

## Proving the documents

If the judges of the beth din do not know how to read the document emanating from the Gentile court, they call in two Gentiles who are familiar with the language of the document and each, not in the presence of the other, informs the beth din as to the contents of the document. The Gentiles are not told the importance of the document.

There is an opinion that holds that if there is a document that the borrower delivered to the lender, or the seller to the purchaser in the presence of two Jewish witnesses who read the document, then a judgment may be entered on the strength of the document and may be used to levy on the defendant's property, even if it did not emanate from a Gentile court and the subscribing witnesses are Gentiles.[8] According to this view, the document will be valid only if the names of the Gentile subscribing witnesses are obviously not Jewish names.[9] A contrary view holds that no document that is subscribed by Gentiles is valid.

If the borrower alleges that the document emanating from the Gentile court is not valid, the scribe of the Gentile court is believed when he states that he wrote it.

If the document was made in the presence of Gentiles, but not in a Gentile court, and is signed by the borrower, then he is bound by it, even if he did not know how to read it.[10]

## Following the law of the land

The laws of following the law of the land are treated in Chapter 369. Regarding documents emanating from the Gentile courts, if the

---

The fact that the Gentile court made a writing out of the donor's declaration does not mean that the gift has been conveyed by writing. (See Chapters 250 through 258.)

8. This assumes that the document met all of the necessary requirements (such as being written on nonerasable paper, with the amounts noted not being susceptible to change).

9. If the names are obviously Gentile, then the beth din relies not on the subscribing witnesses but rather on the Jewish witnesses who read the document and witnessed the delivery thereof. This will be obvious to observers, and they will not make the mistake of relying on these witnesses another time. If their names are not distinctively Gentile, then reliance may be mistakenly placed on them without requiring delivery in the presence of Jewish witnesses.

10. The fact that he signed it proves that he intended to be bound by it. It is presumed that he would not have signed it if it had not been read to him.

government has enacted laws that fulfill the requirements set forth in Chapter 369, then the beth din will give effect to such documents even if the documents give effect to the act, such as in the case of deeds of gift. This also holds true if the community's custom is to give effect to such documents.

In order for beth din to recognize such documents, they must comply with both the law of the land and the halachah. If they fail to comply with either, they will not be given effect in beth din.

## Document signed by the debtor

A promissory note signed by the debtor will be given effect in beth din even if the witnesses thereon were Gentiles, and even if the debtor could neither read nor understand the language of the note. Since the debtor signed the note, the beth din can presume that he had it read to him by a reader whom he trusted to read accurately, or that he was satisfied enough to sign the obligation even though it had not been read to him. If he can prove with competent testimony of witnesses that he was misled, and that he signed the note without knowing its contents, then the note would be set aside.

# Chapter 69

# WRITTEN EVIDENCE OF LOANS

## INTRODUCTION

As already stated in Chapter 39, there is a difference between an instrument of indebtedness and other writings that evidence a loan. An instrument of indebtedness, in addition to stating the pertinent facts of the loan, must have subscribed thereto the signatures of two witnesses and must be delivered to the lender. There can be other writings that evidence loans; these will be referred to as "other writings" in this chapter. Such writings include the promissory note, which is a writing signed by the borrower attesting to the fact that he borrowed money from the lender, but this writing does not contain the signatures of two subscribing witnesses. A promissory note may or may not be written by the debtor, and the debtor's name may be signed somewhere other than at the bottom of the instrument.

An instrument of indebtedness effects a lien on all of the real estate that the borrower owned when the loan was made. If he thereafter sold any of such real estate and does not have the money to repay the debt when it is due, then the creditor may trace the real estate to the purchaser to make his levy. Other writings of the indebtedness do not create a lien on the debtor's real estate, and thus a purchaser for value need not fear that the creditor will levy against the purchased realty.[1]

Generally, the debtor's heirs are responsible for paying the decedent's debts out of the estate. What is the effect of other writings on the debtor's heirs?

Merchants, whether in large manufacturing corporations or small grocery stores, often extend credit to customers. The merchant enters each credit transaction in a book and then asks the debtor to sign the book; there may or may not be a witness (or witnesses) who also signed. A writing evidencing indebtedness need not always be in the form of an instrument of indebtedness or a promissory note. It may arise from a normal sale. This writing, called a shopbook entry, is discussed with regard to the possibility of disputed veracity. (See Volume III, Chapter 91.)

# TEXT

## Instruments of indebtedness

As was stated in Chapter 39, an instrument of indebtedness, in addition to containing all of the relevant facts of a transaction, must be subscribed by two witnesses.

If a writing is signed by the debtor and also by two witnesses who attest to the debtor's signature but not to the transaction, then the document does not rise to the status of an instrument of indebtedness, but rather remains in the category of "other writings."

## Other writings

All instruments that are not instruments of indebtedness are in the category of other writings. Other writings reciting a debt may be in the handwriting of the debtor and may or may not be signed by him; or,

---

1. The subscribing of the instrument by the witnesses and the delivery to the creditor in the presence of two witnesses is presumed to publicize the loan so that a purchaser of the debtor's real estate has constructive notice of the lien on the realty. In the case of other writings or an oral loan (where there is no writing whatsoever of the loan), there is no attendant publicity and thus no constructive notice to the purchaser of the realty. There is therefore no lien created in such other cases.

they may be written by other persons and signed by the debtor. The debtor's signature may or may not have been authenticated by beth din. The entire other writing may consist of one line wherein the debtor recites that he owes money to the lender and affixes his signature. If the debtor signed on the top, then the rest of the other writing must be in the handwriting of the borrower in order for it to be authenticated. Even if the debtor's name does not appear in the other writing, if the document is entirely in the debtor's handwriting, then it will be held valid, even though some authorities hold that this type of other writing is not valid.

## Effect of other writings

If the creditor does not have an instrument of indebtedness, he may levy only on the property, real or personal, in the hands of the debtor; he may not trace the debtor's property to innocent purchasers.[2] Other writings also do not afford the creditor any priority over later creditors of the debtor in levying on the debtor's property.

If the creditor holds other writings of the debt, and if the debtor admits that he has not yet repaid the loan then the creditor may levy only on property in the hands of the debtor. But if the debtor alleges that he repaid the loan, then he swears a *hesseth* oath and is free, despite the fact that the other writing is still in the hands of the creditor.[3] However, beth din may decide that the other writings are in the hands of the creditor because the debt was not paid.[4] In such a situation, the beth din, upon the debtor's application for valid cause,

---

2. This holds true even if the promissory note in the handwriting of the debtor stated that it should be given the effect of an instrument signed by two witnesses.

3. The creditor may not plead that the fact that the instrument is still in his hands proves that the debtor has not repaid the debt. The debtor can respond that since the writing was not subscribed by witnesses, he had no concern about permitting it to remain in the creditor's hands. A minority opinion holds that the debtor may not, in the face of the writing in the hands of the creditor, plead payment.

4. For example, if the note was a bearer instrument, beth din may well feel that if the debtor had paid the instrument, he would not have permitted such an instrument to be in the hands of the creditor. Or, if beth din sees that the creditor may use the instrument to sue in the civil courts of the country, and if the debtor knew that the creditor might avail himself of such opportunity but nevertheless left the instrument with the creditor, then this negates the debtor's plea of payment.

may require the creditor to take an oath that he was not paid. If the other writing contains a credence clause stating that the creditor would be believed upon presentation of the other writing, then the debtor's plea of payment is dismissed.[5] If payment of the loan is not yet due, then the debtor's plea that he repaid it is not believed.[6]

If the custom of the community or of a trade is for the customer or debtor to give a blank writing or check and to have the amount filled in by the creditor, such writing is in the category of other writings.

## Denying the authenticity of other writings

The creditor produces an other writing signed by the decedent and wishes to collect the debt from the estate, the validity of the decedent's signature having been admitted or authenticated in beth din. If the decedent could have pleaded payment, and if the heirs do not raise the plea of payment, then beth din will raise the plea for them, and the estate will be free of liability without the heirs having to take the oath of heirs. Beth din may proclaim a ban in the presence of the heirs by calling upon all those who have any information about whether the decedent still owed the debt. If the other writing contains a credence clause, then the heirs cannot raise the defense of payment even if the credence clause did not state that it would be binding on the debtor's estate. If the signature on the other writing has not been proven to be that of the decedent, then the creditor may not sue on the writing. Beth din will, in the presence of the heirs, proclaim a ban on those who kept silent even though they knew whether the signature was that of the decedent, or whether the decedent advised them that he owed the money to the creditor, or whether an examination of the decedent's books and records revealed that the money is due. If the creditor produces a judgment of the beth din against the decedent that would be valid unless the decedent had taken an oath and demands payment from the estate, then the heirs can allege that perhaps the decedent had indeed taken the oath, or paid the judgment, and thus there is no liability. Here, too, the beth din will proclaim a ban in the presence of the heirs against those who

---

5. See Chapter 71 regarding credence agreements.

6. See Volume III, Chapter 78, regarding pleas of payment prior to the due date of repayment.

know whether the decedent had admitted the debt to be still outstanding or who have any other information regarding the debt.

If the alleged debtor denies that the signature on the other writing is his, then the holder of the other writing must bring two witnesses to beth din to prove that the signature is that of the debtor.[7] If the signature is authenticated after the debtor denies that it is his, then he is no longer believed when he states that he paid the debt.[8] If the signature is not proved in beth din, then the other writing is valueless, even if it contains a credence agreement.

If the debtor admits that it is his signature on the other writing but denies that it was for an actual loan, then he is believed if he takes a *hesseth* oath. For example, he may plead that he never borrowed money from the lender, but that he did at one time sign his name at the end of a blank piece of paper, which he then lost. Perhaps the lender found the blank signed paper and wrote the other writing of debt on top of the signature.[9]

The debtor named in the other writing is also believed if he states that the other writing is an instrument of trust. He may claim that the instrument was given to the lender named therein to hold in case the lender actually did lend money to the borrower, but that the money was never loaned. The borrower named therein is believed, since he would have been believed if he pleaded that he paid the loan.[10]

## Book entries

If the debtor signed a book entry that was also subscribed by a witness, then the debtor may not plead that he made payment, so long

---

7. Opinions differ as to whether the signature may be authenticated in any other manner, such as comparison with signatures on writings that have already been authenticated. (See Chapter 46.)

8. The debtor is presumed to be nonbelievable, even if he does not deny the loan but denies only that the other writing is genuine, and witnesses proved that it is genuine.

9. The debtor is believed only if he is certain that he never borrowed money from the creditor. However, if he states that he has no recollection, then he is not believed if he states that the other writing is not genuine.

10. If the allegations of the borrower named in the other writing are farfetched, he will not be believed. For example, he will not be believed if he alleges that he wrote and signed the other writing and then lost it, and, by coincidence, someone with the same name as the person named as the lender in the instrument found it and is now suing on it.

as the entry remains on the creditor's book and in his possession. A conflicting opinion holds that the debtor may allege payment, since the document lacks the requisite two witness subscribers and is thus in the category of an other writing, to which a debtor may plead payment. The beth din should rely on the custom of the community regarding the particular business and the types of books that the merchant keeps in determining whether to treat the entries as book entries, so that the plea of payment will not be accepted, or as an other writing. In modern times, the practice of book entries is widely accepted.[11]

---

11. In modern times, with methods of payment that are generally easily verifiable, the question of payment is usually not raised.

# Chapter 70

# LAWS OF ORAL LOANS, AND LENDER'S INSTRUCTIONS REGARDING REPAYMENT

## INTRODUCTION

This chapter applies to oral loans—that is, any loan that is not evidenced by a note of indebtedness that sets forth the facts required for such a note, nor subscribed by at least two witnesses, nor delivered to the lender in the presence of two witnesses. A promissory note signed, and perhaps even signed *and* written, by the borrower is still an oral loan.

This chapter advises the lender on how to protect himself so that he will be able to prove his loan, and it advises the borrower on how to repay so that he will not be compelled to repay again.

The best practice is to have witnesses present when the loan is made, and, better still, to have the borrower give the witnesses authority to reduce the loan to writing—that is, to a note of indebtedness. Alternatively, if a *kinyan* is made, the witnesses have the authority to reduce the loan to writing and then to sign as subscribing witnesses so that the writing will be a note of indebtedness. This way, both the lender and the borrower are protected—the lender by having a writing of the loan from which he can sue if necessary, and the borrower by having a note that can be returned to him when he repays the loan.

However, some loans are not reduced to notes of indebtedness and will therefore retain the status of oral loans. Several questions are covered in this chapter regarding the repayment of the oral loan. Must such a loan be repaid in the presence of witnesses, or may the borrower repay the loan directly to the lender without witnesses being present? In the latter case, who is believed if the lender says the loan was not repaid and the borrower alleges that it was repaid? What if the lender designates the witnesses before whom the loan must be repaid? These questions go to the essence of the lender's claim that he intentionally gave instructions so that he would not be left to the allegations of payment by the borrower. On the other hand, how strictly must the borrower follow the lender's instructions regarding repayment?

## TEXT

### Loans should not be made unless there are witnesses present[1]

The best practice is to have the loan witnessed and to have the transaction reduced to a writing subscribed by the witnesses (a note of indebtedness).[2] If that is not feasible, or if the borrower objects to the writing of a note of indebtedness, then there should at least be some sort of writing setting forth all of the facts, handwritten and signed by the borrower (the promissory note). The written promissory note remains in the category of an oral loan.

It is prohibited to make an oral loan unless there are witnesses present.[3] An exception might be the case in which the lender took

---

1. The parties may be honest but the borrower may truly forget that he borrowed money. Even a great scholar is capable of such an oversight: he may be so busy studying Torah that he may have truly forgotten about the loan.

2. A writing contains all of the pertinent details so that the parties and the witnesses need remember nothing. The writing should contain the names of the parties, their capacity in the transaction (such as lender and borrower), the time and place of the making of the loan, the amount loaned, the time of repayment, any other terms that have been agreed upon by the parties, the names of the witnesses, and the witnesses' signatures.

3. Such a transaction is not actually prohibited. Rather, this statement is intended as an admonition to the parties to have witnesses present when making a loan.

collateral security for the repayment of the loan.[4]

If the loan was evidenced by a writing, whether by a note of indebtedness or a promissory note, then the borrower should receive it when he repays. If the note is not available, he should obtain a receipt of repayment from the lender.[5] If the lender's note was obliterated and beth din wrote a substitute note for him, it is the same as any other written note of indebtedness.[6] There is also an opinion that if the lender obtains a judgment in beth din even on an oral loan, the judgment has the same force and effect as a written note of indebtedness and should be repaid only in the presence of witnesses.

## When it is not necessary to repay in the presence of witnesses

If the loan is not evidenced by a note of indebtedness, and was made without a *kinyan*, the borrower is permitted to repay the loan even though there are no witnesses present to the repayment. Thus the borrower may allege that he has repaid the loan directly to the lender, or that the lender released the loan, and the borrower must take a *hesseth* oath and is believed.[7]

If a *kinyan* is made whereby the borrower obligates himself to

---

Furthermore, the lender may actually be violating the law against putting a stumbling block in the path of the blind. If there were no witnesses present when the loan was made, then when the lender makes a demand for repayment of the loan, the borrower may, with or without intent to cheat the lender, deny the making of the loan. The borrower is guilty of lying when he denies the loan, and the lender is guilty for placing the borrower in a position in which he can tell a lie. Furthermore, the lender puts himself in a position to be thought a liar when he alleges that the borrower owes him money despite the borrower's denial of the loan, and he cannot prove the loan.

4. If the lender holds the borrower's collateral, the borrower is not tempted to deny the making of the loan.

5. The return of the note is more favorable to the borrower, since he can then destroy or mutilate the note and is then in no danger of having to pay the note a second time. If the borrower obtains a receipt of repayment, he must take care of the receipt, for if he loses it, he will have no proof of repayment in the event that the lender sues him on the note.

6. See Chapter 41.

7. This holds true only if the time for repayment has arrived. If the time for payment has not yet arrived, then the borrower is not believed if he alleges that he has repaid the loan.

repay the lender the sum of the loan, then the witnesses to the *kinyan* may at any time reduce the transaction to writing and the lender will have a writing on which to sue. Even if the witnesses did not reduce the loan to writing, and all the more so if they did, the borrower should not then repay the loan unless there are witnesses present.[8] If he does so and the lender denies the repayment, the borrower's plea will not be believed.

In those cases in which the borrower need not repay the loan in the presence of witnesses, he need not allege that there were witnesses present when he repaid the loan. However, if the borrower alleges that he repaid the loan in the presence of witnesses, and if the lender denies the repayment, then the borrower must produce the witnesses if they are in the city. If he does not produce the witnesses, or even if he produces them and they deny having witnessed the repayment, then the borrower is free of liability if he takes a *hesseth* oath.[9] However, if the borrower alleges that he had these two persons designated as witnesses before he made the repayment, and if the witnesses now contradict the borrower, there is one opinion that the borrower will have to make repayment to the lender and another opinion that the borrower may take a *hesseth* oath and be free of liability.

## Necessity to repay oral loans in the presence of witnesses

In case of oral loans, if the borrower is instructed by the lender in the presence of witnesses, either at the time the loan is made or

---

8. The making of a *kinyan* is equivalent to instructing the witnesses who are present to reduce the loan to writing. If a *kinyan* is made, then the borrower need not be consulted before the witnesses draw up a writing of the loan transaction. If no *kinyan* is made, then the witnesses may not draw up a note of indebtedness unless the borrower authorized such a writing. (See Chapter 39.)

9. The borrower could have repaid without any witnesses. His allegation of the identity of the witnesses at the time of repayment is probably the truth, since he has no incentive to lie. The witnesses who deny the repayment may not have remembered the repayment. As a general rule, people are less apt to remember events that do not directly concern them. There is also an opinion that it is the borrower who does not remember correctly and that he somehow believes that there were witnesses present to the repayment when in actuality there were not.

thereafter, that he may repay only in the presence of witnesses, then the borrower must repay in the presence of witnesses.[10,11] If he alleges that he repaid without witnesses present, then he is not believed, and the lender will win the lawsuit without even having to take an oath.[12] If the borrower alleges that he repaid in the presence of two specific witnesses who have since died or gone overseas, the borrower is believed if he takes a *hesseth* oath. If the borrower does not specify the names of the witnesses, he is not believed.

If the lender specifies the witnesses before whom the loan should be repaid and the borrower repays before other witnesses, and if these other witnesses testify that they saw the loan repaid, then the borrower is free of liability. In this case, the lender may allege that the repayment was for another debt, and the borrower will still be liable on that debt. If the other witnesses died or went overseas, the borrower is not believed that he repaid the loan. If the borrower alleges that he repaid before the witnesses whom the lender had designated but that they thereafter died or went overseas, the borrower takes an oath and is believed.[13] If the borrower admits that he did not repay before the witnesses designated by the lender because they are not available to appear, then he is paid no heed and he must pay the moneys to beth din. Beth din will then issue a receipt.

## Repayment to the lender

The lender instructs the borrower to pay only in the presence of designated witnesses. The borrower repays the lender directly, and the moneys are lost by an act of God. The lender alleges that the moneys were given to him for safekeeping until the designated

---

10. If there are no witnesses to the instruction, the borrower can deny the instruction. He is thus believed when he alleges that he repaid without witnesses.

11. If at the time the lender gives the instruction the borrower states that he will not abide by the instruction, some say that the borrower need not repay in the presence of witnesses.

12. The borrower may not impose an oath on the lender before the repayment has been made. After the repayment, however, the borrower may insist that the lender take a *hesseth* oath that he was not repaid before.

13. He is believed when he alleges that he has fulfilled the condition.

witnesses arrived so that the payment could be made in their presence.[14] The lender's allegation is discarded, since he admits that he did receive the moneys.[15]

---

14. If the moneys are a deposit and not a repayment, then the holder of the deposit is free of liability if the moneys are lost by an act of God. Thus if the lender's claim is believed, the lender would be free of liability for the moneys and the borrower would have to repay once again.

15. If the lender can prove that he told the borrower that he was accepting the moneys only to hold until the designated witnesses appear, there is an opinion that his claim is believed. However, the majority opinion is that he is not believed.

# Chapter 71

# CREDENCE GIVEN TO THE LENDER'S ALLEGATIONS BY THE BORROWER

## INTRODUCTION

The parties to a credit transaction may agree that the creditor or lender will be believed upon his mere allegation, without further proof. We have referred to such an agreement as a *credence agreement*, and we have called the clause within the agreement that contains this statement a *credence clause*. The clause may be part of an instrument of indebtedness, or such agreement may be orally made between the parties in the presence of witnesses. Often such an agreement is set forth in a letter of credit. The seller may present the writing and receive payment from a bank, and the purchaser may not raise defenses to the writing. Terms may be attached to the writing, such as a stipulation that presentment can be made only if a third party certifies that the goods were delivered or if the seller presents an affidavit stating that the goods were delivered. Similarly, the parties to a loan transaction may agree that the instrument of indebtedness will be paid upon presentation without any defenses or offsets available to the borrower. In halachah, the testimony of two witnesses is equivalent to the testimony of one hundred witnesses. The parties may provide that the lender or the borrower will be believed as though they were two witnesses; such a provision is called a *witness agreement*. The parties may also agree that the borrower will not assert any defense if the lender brings a lawsuit to collect the loan. This chapter also discusses the converse—circumstances under which the debtor may assert defenses that will be believed without question by the lender.

One of the major reasons for such agreements is that the witnesses to a credit transaction may not be available to testify in beth din as to whether the payment was made. The party who is to extend credit may hesitate to do so if he knows that he will have to present proof regarding all of the facets of the transaction. Nowadays, with modern methods of tracking payments, many of the agreements described herein may not be necessary. However, regarding letters of credit, negotiable instruments, bills of lading, and warehouse receipts, to name just a few, the person who holds the document wants to feel secure that no defenses will be asserted.

Chapter 16 in Volume I discussed the proclaiming of a ban by a litigating party who is seeking witnesses. It was stated that all those who knew of testimony in favor of the party and did not come forward to testify would be placed under a ban. This chapter elaborates further on the procedure for proclaiming a ban.

# TEXT

## Creation of credence agreements

Whether the agreement is intended to give credence to the lender or to the borrower, it may be created by mere verbal or written agreement, if made prior to or at the time the credit is extended. In such a case, no *kinyan* is necessary. However, subsequent to the advancement of the loan or credit, the credence agreements must be formalized with a *kinyan*.[1]

## Agreement to give credence to the lender's allegations

All that is said herein regarding the lender applies equally to any creditor or plaintiff who is suing on moneys due to him; that which is

---

1. The topic of *kinyan* is discussed in Chapter 195 and in the Glossary.

said regarding the borrower applies equally to any debtor or defendant in a lawsuit; and that which is said regarding the loan transaction applies equally to any credit transaction.

The parties to a loan transaction may make certain agreements regarding the repayment of the loan, and they may assert those agreements in beth din. The agreement may be in writing, and may be either a portion of an instrument of indebtedness or a separate writing. If the agreement is oral, it should be witnessed by two witnesses to support the allegation of the party who asserts the agreement of credence. If the agreement is oral, and if the proof of the agreement rests on the admission of the borrower because there are no witnesses to the agreement, then the borrower is believed if he says that he paid the indebtedness.[2] The agreement applies to loans evidenced by an instrument of indebtedness or even if not evidenced by a writing.

The borrower may stipulate several things regarding the credence to be attributed to the lender when he alleges that the loan was not paid. In the case of a simple credence agreement, the lender will be believed when he alleges that the loan was not paid against the borrower's allegations that the loan was paid.

Unless the agreement states otherwise, the lender need not even take an oath to support his allegation, even if the borrower alleges that he repaid the loan.[3] The parties may limit the agreement to provide that the lender will be believed if he takes an oath that he was not repaid. Because there are situations in which revolving oaths may be placed on the lender even if this was not the original intent of the parties when drawing up the agreement, the better practice would be for the simple credence agreement to be broadly drawn to relieve the lender of having to take any kind of oath, whether of Torah or

---

2. The borrower is believed with a *migoo*, which means "since." Since the borrower could have kept silent and there would be no way for the lender to prove the agreement, then if the agreement rests on the borrower's admission, he is also believed when he states that he made the repayment.

3. The lender need not take an oath, even if the agreement did not state that he was relieved of the obligation to do so. The agreement merely said that the lender is to be believed when he states that the loan was not repaid. The reason is that a simple agreement of credence implies that there is no need for the person who is believed to take an oath.

Rabbinic origin, and whether direct or revolving.[4] The agreement can further provide, if the parties so agree, that it shall be effective forever.[5] The simple credence agreement may also provide that the lender is relieved of the obligations of a general ban which may be proclaimed as described in the last section of this chapter.

A general statement that under the simple credence agreement the lender is given the broadest credence that the Torah provides will result in the lender's being relieved of all conceivable requirements of the borrower, whether in the form of an oath or in the form of a specific ban regarding this transaction.[6]

Instead of a simple credence agreement, which is effective only against the allegation of payment made by the borrower, there may be a two-witness agreement—that is, an agreement that states that the lender's allegations of nonpayment shall be given the credence of two witnesses.[7]

The credence agreement may provide that the only defense to the demand for payment is a written receipt. It may further provide that the receipt be in the lender's handwriting, and that it be endorsed on the original instrument.

An instrument of indebtedness named the lender as "Mr. A and Mr. B" or "Mr. A or Mr. B," and the instrument contained a credence clause to the bearer thereof. Under the practice of the community, it was not clear whether Mr. A and Mr. B were partners or whether each owned part of the debt. Mr. A produced the instrument and demanded complete payment, alleging that Mr. B was named in the instrument only to serve the purpose of Mr. A. The borrower produces Mr. B in beth din, and Mr. B admits that he collected the loan. The law is that Mr. A will collect from the borrower, since he holds an instrument that

---

4. The various types of oaths are discussed in Volume III, Chapter 87.

5. This will protect the lender if he is being sued by the borrower for repayment as provided in the text that follows.

6. A general ban cannot be waived, since it applies to all those who are in violation of the law. A specific ban relates to the transaction, while a general ban applies to anyone who may have stolen something from the borrower.

7. In halachah, the testimony of two witnesses is equivalent to the testimony of one hundred witnesses. Thus, if the lender adduces two witnesses who state that the loan was not repaid, even if the borrower produced one hundred witnesses that it was repaid, the lender's allegations will be believed, since he has witnesses to the loan or a writing regarding the loan.

contains a credence clause in favor of the bearer.[8] However, if it can be proved with competent testimony or by the admission of Mr. B that Mr. A and Mr. B were partners, then if Mr. B admits that the borrower repaid the loan to him on behalf of the partnership, Mr. A has recourse against Mr. B for his half of the repayment. If Mr. B does not have assets from which to pay Mr. A, then the borrower will have to pay Mr. A only his half repayment, since Mr. A does have the instrument of indebtedness that includes a credence clause in his possession.[9]

## Effect of the credence agreement

A simple credence agreement that the lender's allegation of nonpayment is to be believed is effective against the borrower's allegation that he has repaid the loan, even if there is one witness who substantiates his allegation of repayment.[10] However, it is not effective against two witnesses who state that the loan was repaid.[11]

A two-witness credence agreement is effective even against any number of witnesses who state that the loan was repaid.[12] If the agreement provides that the lender is to be believed as though he were three witnesses or any other number greater than two, then if the borrower produces a number of witnesses greater than that number in the agreement who testify that the loan was repaid, the borrower's witnesses will be believed.[13]

---

8. The borrower should not have paid the loan without obtaining the return of the instrument that contained a credence clause.

9. Mr. A is not believed when he states that he purchased Mr. B's interest in the instrument, since the credence clause does not cover this allegation.

10. There is an opinion that if there is one witness who testifies that the borrower repaid the loan, then the lender must take a *hesseth* oath to collect the amount that he claims is due him.

11. The agreement that the lender is to be believed is only applicable against defense of repayment raised by the borrower without any witnesses to the repayment. However, if there are witnesses to the repayment, this is outside the scope of the agreement. The agreement waiving the borrower's right to raise the defense of payment is to be strictly construed.

12. Under a two-witness agreement, the lender may collect his debt without taking an oath. When the borrower agreed to believe the lender as two witnesses, he implied that no other witnesses would be given credence regarding the transaction.

13. By stating a number of witnesses larger than the Torah number of two

In all cases where the credence agreement is effective, it survives the date set for repayment of the loan unless the agreement stipulates that it shall terminate on a certain date, which may be the date for repayment.[14]

The credence agreement is limited in scope and is to be strictly construed. If the credence agreement applies to the credence to be given to the lender regarding his allegations of nonrepayment, it will not be given scope regarding the release of the loan. Thus if the borrower alleges that the lender released the loan, the lender will have to take an oath that the loan was not released; he cannot rely on the agreement of credence.[15] Similarly, if the borrower produces two witnesses who testify that the loan was released, the two-witness credence agreement will not affect the witnesses, since they are testifying to something outside the scope of the credence agreement.[16]

Investment agreements may contain credence clauses that permit the investor to state that the active partner in the business did not lose money, and in fact made a specified profit.[17] The active partner is bound by such an agreement, but the credence agreement does not give the investor the right to state that moneys being held by the active partner's heirs or by a third party with whom the active party deposited moneys are the moneys of the business. The credence

---

witnesses, the borrower indicated that he wanted to specify an exact number. (The two witnesses of the Torah implies an indefinite number.)

14. Letters of credit often provide for termination on a certain date, which is usually the date for performance, but for the creditor to extend the date if payment is not made before the expiration.

15. See Chapter 241 regarding release of debts.

16. One opinion holds that if the borrower produces two witnesses who testify that the lender admitted to them that he received repayment of the loan, then they may testify even if there is a two-witness credence agreement. However, the majority of authorities do not rely on this opinion. They reason that the admission goes to the question of indebtedness, and the agreement refers to the same; thus the agreement is controlling.

17. Such an agreement is often used if the borrower wishes to pay interest to the lender. The loan was couched in the language of investment, with the lender being the silent-partner investor and the borrower being the active partner. The silent partner, after examining the records of the partnership, would determine how much profit was made and would thus be able to determine how much should be paid to him as his share of the business. If the business were to fail, the silent investor would lose his investment rather than having a loan outstanding against the other "partner."

agreement will not be given effect outside the scope of the agreement.[18]

If the credence agreement states that the lender is to be believed unless there is a written receipt of payment, and the borrower produces two witnesses who state that they witnessed the repayment, then they are believed against the credence agreement.[19] In a two-witness credence agreement, however, the witnesses to repayment have no standing against the agreement.

If the agreement of credence relieves the lender from the requirement of taking an oath, it does not relieve him of falling under a ban proclaimed against all those who hold the borrower's property and do not return it. Even if the agreement included such exemption, the ban would be effective against the lender.

The credence agreement is available only against the borrower, and not against the heirs of the borrower after his death.[20] If the instrument stated that the agreement of credence is to be binding on the heirs, then it is so binding.[21] The credence agreement in favor of the lender does not apply to the lender's heirs, and they must take the oath of heirs.[22]

A credence agreement is not binding on the purchasers of the borrower's realty if the lender traces it, nor is it binding on the recipients of gifts of real estate from the borrower.[23] In all cases in

---

18. Tracing of moneys is not included in the scope of determination of profit or loss.

19. Unless otherwise provided, the credence agreement requiring the borrower to produce a receipt as a defense is intended to stop the lender if he alleges that he did not receive payment. It is not intended to be effective against witnesses of repayment.

20. Beth din may plead on behalf of the heirs that perhaps the debt was paid, but the borrower trusted the lender enough to permit him to keep the instrument of indebtedness, knowing that the lender would not be so audacious as to present the instrument to him after it had been paid. The lender may not feel as reluctant to present the instrument to the borrower's heirs even if it was already paid.

21. The instrument is also binding if the agreement of credence states that it will be binding on all those who stand in the position of the borrower.

22. The heirs take an oath that they have no knowledge that the loan has been repaid and that they have found no documents among their father's effects to indicate that the loan was paid. The borrower trusted the lender not to present the instrument after it was paid, but such trust does not apply to the lender's heirs. (See Chapter 108, Volume IV, regarding the oath of the heirs.)

23. For example, the borrower borrowed money on January 1 and on that date he

which the credence clause is not binding, the lender will have to prove his case as if the credence clause were not present.

There are certain situations (as described in Volume IV, Chapter 106) in which the lender may collect on the debt even if the borrower is not present in the beth din. Credence agreements will not be given effect in such situations.[24]

## Defenses to the agreement

The borrower may defend against the effect of a credence agreement by making payment to beth din or by obtaining a receipt in the lender's handwriting.[25] The receipt must be specific and must refer to the loan for which the lender holds a credence agreement. Whether endorsed on the instrument of indebtedness or separate therefrom, the written receipt in the handwriting of the lender vitiates the credence agreement that the lender holds.[26] If the credence agreement provided that it must be endorsed on the instrument of indebtedness, a receipt not so endorsed is of no effect.

If the agreement containing a credence statement is in the hands of a third party who does not know whether the debt has been paid, the

---

owned real estate. If the loan was evidenced by a writing signed by at least two witnesses, the debt became a lien on all of the borrower's real estate. On February 1, the borrower sold his real estate to Mr. Purchaser. On March 1, the date for repayment of the loan, the borrower has no money or assets to repay the loan. The lender may trace the real estate that Mr. Purchaser purchased, and Mr. Purchaser may repay the loan to the lender or else the real estate will be taken from Mr. Purchaser to be sold to pay off the borrower's loan. The result would be the same if instead of purchasing the realty from the borrower, Mr. Purchaser received it as a gift.

24. Beth din may determine that perhaps the credence agreement was entered into by the borrower because he believed that if he repaid the loan, the lender would not be so audacious as to sue on a paid note of indebtedness in the presence of the borrower. But now that the borrower is no longer present such reasoning does not apply.

25. The receipt given to the borrower by the beth din is valid even against any credence agreement. Even if the credence agreement states that is is effective against a receipt of beth din, the receipt of beth din will override such credence agreement.

26. Sometimes the loan will call for a series of partial repayments. In such event there may be a series of receipts in the handwriting of the lender, all of which will be applied toward the loan. The lender may not assert that these receipts apply to another loan.

lender will be given the opportunity to take an oath that the debt has not been paid, and if he does so, he will prevail. If the lender refuses to take such an oath, the agreement will be given to the borrower.

If the borrower can, by the testimony of two witnesses, prove that the lender has sworn falsely in any matter, even if unrelated to the debt between the parties, then the agreement of credence will be disregarded, and the parties will be in the same position as if an agreement had never been made.[27]

If the custom of the community is to include some type of credence agreement, then it will be assumed that the transaction was to have included a credence agreement, even if the borrower alleges that the credence agreement was written without his knowledge, unless it can be shown that the borrower was not aware of the custom.[28] If the community has no such custom, then the witnesses to the agreement should be asked what the agreement was. If such witnesses are not available, and if the final clause of the agreement states that the borrower accepted the agreement by *kinyan*, then the clause will be given full force and effect.[29] If the agreement is signed by the borrower himself, he will not be believed that he was not aware of the custom, and his allegation to that effect is of no avail.

## Agreement to give credence
## to the borrower's allegations

Just as the parties may make credence agreements regarding the lender, so may they make credence agreements regarding the

---

27. The reason for the agreement of credence is that the borrower has confidence that the lender will not falsely take advantage of the agreement. Once the lender has been proven to be untruthful, however, the credence agreement is not effective, since it was not the borrower's intent to give credence to an untruthful person. Some authorities hold that if the lender has been proven to be a transgressor of the law, he will lose his credence even if the transgression does not involve truthfulness. If the lender's transgression and/or untruthfulness was known to the borrower before he entered into the credence agreement, then it is presumed that he assumed the agreement with the knowledge of the lender's shortcomings and nevertheless agreed to its terms.

28. It is assumed that consent to reduce any agreement to writing includes consent to include the clauses that are customary in the community.

29. This assumes that the note of indebtedness was authenticated without the testimony of the subscribing witnesses. (See Chapter 46.)

borrower. The agreement may state that if the borrower alleges that the loan was repaid, he shall be believed. If the loan was evidenced by a witnessed writing, then the borrower will still have to take an oath that he repaid the loan unless the credence agreement specifically states that he shall be believed without the necessity of taking an oath. If the loan was an oral one, then the credence agreement will be given full effect.[30]

The credence agreement in favor of the borrower is effective not only against the lender but also against his heirs. If the loan is an oral one, then the borrower is believed even if he does not take an oath; if the loan is evidenced by a witnessed writing, then the borrower will be believed if he takes an oath.

One opinion holds that if the borrower dies, then the lender must prove the nonrepayment of the loan even if the time for payment had not yet arrived. A conflicting opinion holds that the lender is to believe only the borrower; such credence does not transfer to the borrower's heirs.

The credence agreement in favor of the borrower permits him to allege payment even before the due date of the repayment of the loan. If the borrower alleges that he made a partial payment and the lender alleges that none of the loan was repaid, then the borrower pays the difference according to his own allegations, takes a *hesseth* oath on the balance, and is free of further obligation.

An instrument that contains a credence agreement in favor of the borrower may not be used by the lender to trace assets that the borrower has sold to third parties.[31]

## Proclaiming a ban

A party may make an application to beth din to proclaim a ban or to enable the party himself to proclaim a ban. If the beth din deems it

---

30. If there are witnesses that the lender agreed to give credence to the borrower, and the lender admits that there was such a credence agreement, then even if they did not discuss the waiver of the borrower to take an oath, he will not have to take an oath.

31. The reason is that there may be a fraudulent conspiracy between the lender and the borrower to deprive the purchaser of the borrower's real estate. The fact that the instrument contains a credence clause in favor of the borrower is unusual and therefore renders the instrument suspect. (See note 23.)

appropriate, it will issue a *pithka d'latotah*, "an authorization to curse" anyone who violates the ban to be pronounced. In the ordinary course of events, beth din will not authorize a party to proclaim a general ban, since that would be an insult to the community. Rather, it will instruct the party to bring the person whom he wants to perform the act to come to beth din; if such person refuses to do so, then the requesting party will be authorized to proclaim the ban.

If a party wishes to proclaim a ban against all those who know the facts of a case but nevertheless fail to come forward to testify, he may be given permission to proclaim a general ban.[32] Another exception is made when minor orphans request that beth din proclaim a ban against all persons who hold their father's property but fail to come forward and deliver it.

The public ban is generally made in the synagogue. The persons in the synagogue answer "amen" when the statement is over. The beth din should endeavor to persuade all those who are present to remain in the synagogue while the ban is being pronounced. Nevertheless, should a person leave the synagogue, the ban is effective even against him.

A ban does not refer to past conduct. A proclaimer cannot, for example, place under a ban all those who stole from him. Rather, the proclamation would state that all those who hold property of the proclaimer are under a ban unless they return the property.[33]

---

32. See Volume I, Chapter 16.

33. The ban provides a psychological impetus for a person to come forward who might not otherwise do so. The ban includes a curse that the Rabbis instituted to take effect on those who knowingly violate the ban. (See Volume I, Chapter 16.)

# Chapter 72

# COLLATERALIZED LOANS

## INTRODUCTION

As was stated in Chapter 39, there is a Torah commandment that one Jew must lend money to another Jew who needs it; however, the lender is permitted to secure himself. He may attempt to do so by seeking a guarantor, or a mortgage on the property of the borrower, or collateral for the loan. This chapter discusses the collateralized loan. May the lender use the collateral? May he lease it to others? What are his responsibilities and liabilities while he holds the collateral? What if the collateral is lost? What if there is a dispute as to the value of the collateral? What if the holder of the collateral is a Gentile or convert who dies without legal heirs? This chapter discusses these and many other questions regarding the holding of collateral by a lender. Chapter 73 discusses some of the laws of the application which may be made by the lender to obtain collateral from the borrower after the loan has been made. The lender senses that he will not be paid and the borrower will on the due date not have any assets left to pay the debt. The lender wishes to have beth din issue an order to attach the assets of the borrower. Chapter 73 also discusses the selling of the collateral security to repay the loan.

Chapter 97 in Volume IV discusses taking collateral after the due date of the loan repayment but before the creditor has commenced proceedings to enforce payment. It also discusses which things may not be taken as collateral security.

The person who borrows an object without fee or charge will be designated as a "commodatary" to distinguish him from the "borrower," who has borrowed money from the lender.

## TEXT

## The lender may not make use of the collateral

The lender may ask that collateral be posted by the borrower before the loan is made and that the collateral stand as security from which the lender may exact payment if the loan is not repaid according to its terms. The lender may assume that the collateral deposited with him by the borrower may legally be deposited by the borrower. A husband may give his wife's clothing or jewelry as collateral without her permission, unless he made them for her.[1]

If parties agree that the lender may use the collateral in consideration for reducing the indebtedness by a stipulated sum, their agreement is binding.[2]

Unless so agreed upon between the parties, and except as hereinafter stated, the lender may not make use of the collateral. If the lender did use the collateral, then it is as if he has transgressed the

---

1. Except for the last-mentioned case, the husband does not require his wife's permission. In all events, the lender is not required to ask the husband whether he has his wife's permission; he may assume that the husband has permission. If the wife uses self-help and seizes from the lender the clothing or jewelry that the husband gave as collateral without her permission, she may take an oath that her husband did not receive her permission. If she does so, collateral will remain with her in those cases in which her permission is required.

2. If the indebtedness is not reduced, the arrangement is not legal even if the borrower agrees that the lender may use the collateral, since the collateral is in the nature of interest and the borrower may not waive the prohibition against taking or giving interest. This prohibition would apply even if the collateral is a Torah book and the lender can claim that he is performing a great good deed with the collateral by studying Torah. There is an opinion that even if there is an agreement between the lender and the borrower regarding the lender's use of the collateral, he nevertheless should not use it, since people will not realize that the loan will be reduced by the value of the use of the collateral.

Torah commandment against taking interest.[3] If the collateral is of the type that is not kept for hire, then the lender is guilty of the interest transgression; he has also made himself ineligible to take oaths at any time.[4] Furthermore, he has illegally used someone else's property and is now liable if anything happens to the collateral, even if caused by *force majeure.*[5] Also, if the borrower alleges that the value of the used collateral has diminished, then he must take an oath as to the amount of the decrease in value, or else beth din will determine the amount of the decrease, and that amount will be deducted from the loan.[6]

Even absent an agreement, if the collateral is of a type that is usually leased to others, then the lender may use the collateral and

---

3. To use the collateral would in essence be giving the lender more than he loaned and would be akin to interest on the loan. However, the use does not amount to actual interest because it was not agreed upon when the loan was made that the lender would be permitted to use the collateral and that the loan would not be reduced by the value of the use of the collateral. Had such an agreement been made, it would be actual interest. Furthermore, it is almost like robbery because the lender would be using the borrower's property without his permission.

4. He becomes ineligible to take oaths only if there were two witnesses who testify that they saw him use the collateral. The lender may, however, allege and take an oath to the effect that he reduced the indebtedness because he used the collateral; he then must tell the beth din the extent to which he reduced the debt. Beth din can then determine whether he reduced the debt by a sufficient amount; otherwise, they will determine the amount of the reduction. There is also an opinion that if the collateral used is a book of Torah subjects, then the lender is not ineligible to take oaths. Even in such an instance, however, he should pay for the use of the book. The prohibition against stealing applies to the use of someone's books without his knowledge. Any person who uses someone else's property without permission is liable if that property is damaged or lost, even if such damage or loss was occasioned by *force majeure.* The occasional use of someone's *tallit* or *tefillin* without his knowledge is an exception. The exception is based on the thought that the owner would be pleased that his religious articles are being used to perform a commandment from God. One opinion holds that in modern times the rule that applies to *tallit* and *tefillin* also applies in most instances to printed books.

5. As will be noted, if the lender has permission to use the collateral, then he is generally not liable if the collateral is lost or destroyed by *force majeure,* such as a fire or storm.

6. If the collateral is of a type that is not usually leased and the lender does use it, then he may not be sued to make payment to the borrower even though he has transgressed the law. However, if he wishes to free himself of obligations to Heaven, then he will have to make a payment to the borrower equal to what a rental payment would have been for that item.

give the rental value to the borrower,[7] or the lender may lease the collateral to others without obtaining the borrower's consent and reduce the debt by the amount of the rental income.[8] There is an opinion that absent an agreement, the lender may not himself use the collateral.[9]

If the lender pressures the borrower to repay the loan and to retake his collateral, and the borrower tells the lender to retain the collateral and thereafter changes his mind, then the lender has not acquired the collateral, since the beth din accepts the view that the borrower was merely fending off the lender. If there is an actual *kinyan* made, then the lender will acquire title.[10] No *kinyan* is necessary for the lender to acquire title to the collateral in case of default of repayment of the loan because the collateral was given to the lender for that purpose. But in the case where the borrower is merely putting the lender off, he does not intend the title to actually transfer.[11] If a *kinyan* is made, as distinguished from mere words of transfer, then title transfers.

The borrower cannot require the lender to accept the collateral in payment of the loan. The borrower must repay the loan even if there

---

7. The lender may not plead that he intended to use the collateral without permission and that he acted like a thief and is therefore free of making the equivalent of a rental payment. He will be deemed to have acted not as a thief but in accordance with the law, and he will have to reduce the loan by the value of the use of the collateral.

8. If the value of the collateral will depreciate greatly, then it may not be leased by the lender to others even if the proceeds of the lease will be applied to reduce the loan.

9. People who see the lender use the collateral may assume that he does not intend to reduce the amount of the loan by the value of the use of the collateral. However, if the people around the lender know of the agreement between the lender and the borrower, then the lender may use the collateral.

10. *Kinyan* is a method of acquisition of both realty and personalty. (See Chapter 195.) The purchaser gives his handkerchief, or almost any other personalty, to the seller. In exchange for the seller's taking hold of the handkerchief, the purchaser obtains title to the property being sold. In the case in the text, the lender will give his handkerchief to the borrower, who will thereby transfer title to the lender in exchange for the handkerchief.

11. If after being told to take title to the collateral without an actual *kinyan*, the lender sold the collateral to a third party in the presence of the borrower, then it can be said that the borrower intended to transfer title to the lender without the necessity of a *kinyan*.

was no written instrument of indebtedness. It does not matter whether the collateral was worth more or less than the collateral being held or was equal in value thereto. The borrower borrowed money, and the collateral is only security for the lender. In the event that the borrower does not have money or assets with which to repay the loan, then the lender will collect out of the collateral.

If the lender accepts the collateral because it is worth the amount of the loan or represents a proportion of the loan (whether more or less), and the value of the collateral then falls (not through deterioration), the lender may insist that the loan be paid, or that the borrower increase the collateral to maintain the same ratio as was present when the collateral was given.

## The degree of care required of the lender in holding the collateral

The halachah recognizes four types of bailees: (1) the unpaid bailee, (2) the paid bailee, (3) the hirer, and (4) the commodatary.[12] The *unpaid bailee* receives no compensation for watching the object entrusted to him for safekeeping, and the entire benefit of the relationship flows to the bailor. In the absence of negligence, the unpaid bailee has no liability if the object is lost or stolen, and certainly no liability if the object is lost through *force majeure*, such as to armed robbers or to natural calamities such as fire or flood. He is liable only if the object is lost through his negligence. In the case of the *paid bailee*, benefit flows to both the bailor and the bailee. The bailor's object is being watched and the bailee benefits in that he is paid for watching the object. In this situation the bailee is liable not only if the object is lost through his negligence, but also if the object is lost or stolen from the bailee. However, the paid bailee is not liable if the object is lost through *force majeure*. This situation of *the hirer* is similar to that of the paid bailee,

---

12. The person who deposits the collateral or other object is the bailor, and the person who holds someone else's property is the bailee. When an owner places furniture in a warehouse, the owner of the furniture is the bailor, and the warehouse operator is the bailee. In the case of car rental, the person who has rented the car is the bailee, and the car rental agency is the bailor. When someone borrows an object, the commodatary is the bailee, and the lender is the bailor. The laws of bailments are discussed in Chapters 291 through 347.

for here, too, there is benefit flowing to both parties. The bailor receives payment for leasing the object, and the lessee/bailee receives benefit in that he has the use of the object. Here, too, the bailee is liable if the object is stolen or lost through his negligence. However, the hirer is not liable if the object is lost through *force majeure*. In the case of *the commodatary*, one who borrows an object without paying any fee or charge, the entire benefit flows to him. He is generally liable in all events, whether the object is lost through his negligence, stolen from him, or even lost through *force majeure*. One of the exceptions to his liability is if the object is destroyed or damaged merely as a result of its being used for the purpose for which he borrowed it.

The parties may stipulate that the lender who is holding collateral is under no liability whatsoever for the collateral and is free of any liability even if he was negligent in the care of the collateral. Even under such a stipulation, however, he would be liable if he intentionally damaged the collateral.[13]

Absent any agreement the following laws apply: If the lender took collateral security, whether money and/or personalty, he has the legal status of a paid bailee. He has this status because he receives benefit from holding the collateral. During the time of the making of the loan, and also during the time that he is engaged in taking care of the collateral, he is performing a good deed (commandment) and while a person is performing one good deed, he is absolved from having to perform another good one. Thus while the lender is taking care of the collateral, he does not have to respond to the poor person's plea for

---

13. Shimon held a very expensive sword as collateral from a Gentile borrower. Ruven borrowed the sword, but Shimon neglected to tell him that the sword was valuable. Ruven lost the sword, and Shimon sued Ruven for the value of the sword according to the value claimed by the Gentile. The beth din decided that Ruven need pay only the value of an ordinary sword that is readily available for sale. Since Ruven was not told the value of the sword and since he did not lose the sword or destroy it intentionally but rather was merely negligent in taking care of it, he must pay only according to the degree of liability he accepted when he borrowed the sword. However, if he had intentionally lost or destroyed the sword, he would have to pay the full value, since he had no right to intentionally destroy it. Even if the Gentile sued Shimon for more than the value of the sword and collected more than its value, Ruven would be limited in his liability according to the law herein stated—namely, if he did not know its value and had not intentionally destroyed it, he would pay its actual value, whereas if he had intentionally destroyed it, he would pay its full value even if he had not known its value when he destroyed it.

charity. Since the lender is deemed to have the status of paid bailee, he is liable if the object is lost, destroyed, or damaged either through or without his negligence. Most authorities agree that he has the status of a paid bailee whether the collateral was delivered to him when the loan was made, or was delivered to him later voluntarily by the borrower, or was delivered pursuant to the order of a beth din because the time for payment of the loan had passed or because it was found that the borrower was dissipating his assets. Some authorities hold, however, that if the collateral is delivered to the lender after the loan is made, then the lender has the status of a commodatary and is liable to the borrower for loss of the object regardless of the cause.

There are those who hold that the lender who holds collateral has the status of both an unpaid bailee and a paid bailee.[14] He has the status of a paid bailee in that he is liable if the object is lost or stolen and certainly if it is lost through his negligence. He has the status of an unpaid bailee in that if the object is lost or stolen he is not liable to the borrower if the value of the collateral exceeds the amount of the loan.[15]

If the collateral is given after the loan is made and the borrower tells the lender that he may use the collateral, and the collateral is lost through *force majeure*, the lender may be liable in the same way that a commodatary is liable.[16] If the lender states that he will not use the collateral, then he has the same status as was just stated, either as a paid bailee or as both a paid bailee and an unpaid bailee. If he agrees that he will use the collateral, then all agree that he has the status of a commodatary and is responsible even if the collateral is lost through *force majeure*.

---

14. This opinion holds that the coincidence of the lender's being asked to donate to charity while he is taking care of the collateral is remote. Thus there is no actual monetary benefit to the lender.

15. It may be that the lender is a paid bailee because he now has the psychological and economic consideration that he has something on which to levy in the event that the loan is not repaid. There is no benefit to him as to the excess, since the excess will be paid to the borrower; thus as to the excess, he is an unpaid bailee.

16. The word *may* is used because it is not entirely clear that his status should be that of a paid bailee, since the permission is granted to use the collateral in consideration of having made the loan and thus the lender has the status of a paid bailee. The borrower will receive credit for the lender's use of the collateral.

In those situations in which the lender is liable for the loss of the collateral and the collateral is lost, if the collateral is equal to the amount of the loan, then the loan is cancelled and the lender is free of liability for the loss. If the loan exceeds the value of the collateral, then the borrower pays the difference to the lender.[17] If the collateral exceeds the amount of the loan, then the lender pays to the borrower the difference between the values.

In those situations in which the lender is not liable for the loss of the collateral and the collateral is lost, and if there are witnesses that the collateral was lost through *force majeure*, then the lender is free of liability, and the borrower must still repay the loan.[18] If there are no witnesses regarding the *force majeure*, then the lender must take a Torah oath that the loss was caused by *force majeure* and the borrower will have to repay the loan.[19] If there are no witnesses regarding the *force majeure*, and if the lender alleges that the collateral was lost through *force majeure* and the borrower alleges with certainty that the lender sold the collateral and took the money, then the borrower takes an oath and is believed and the lender is responsible for the value of the collateral to the extent of the loan. In the latter case, if the collateral is equal to the amount of the loan or is worth more than the loan, then the parties have no further liability to each other.[20] If the collateral was worth less than the loan, then the

---

17. The parties may agree when the collateral is given that it shall be in lieu of payment of the whole loan if the borrower does not repay the loan. In such event, if the lender loses the collateral, he cannot obtain the difference between the loan and the value of the collateral if the loan was greater. If the parties do not make any such stipulation, then the actual value of the collateral is calculated against the amount of the loan. If the borrower gives two items as collateral and one is lost then the respective values of the items are determined to calculate how much of the loan is satisfied against the loss of the item of collateral.

18. If there is only one witness to testify that the loss was due to *force majeure*, then the lender is also free of liability and need not even take an oath.

19. The lender is free of liability even if he specifically accepted responsibility for the collateral. However, if the lender says he will be liable even in the event of *force majeure*, then he will be liable.

20. If the borrower alleges that the collateral was worth more than the loan and the lender denies this, the lender is thus in a position of any bailee, either an unpaid bailee, who is liable only for negligent loss of the collateral, or a paid bailee, who is responsible even in case of loss or theft of the collateral. The lender must take a Torah oath and is absolved from liability as would be any bailee who swears that he was not negligent. (See Chapter 295.)

value of the collateral is deducted from the loan, and the borrower pays the difference to the lender.[21]

A situation may arise in which the lender deposits the collateral with a third party to watch or even returns it to the borrower to hold. If the collateral is then lost or stolen while in the possession of the third party or the borrower, the lender still remains liable to the borrower for the collateral to the extent previously stated.[22] There are those who dispute this opinion and hold that the lender is not liable if the borrower is holding the collateral. Even according to the first opinion, if the borrower receives the collateral back so that he may use it, then the lender's liability is terminated. The example given in the *Shulhan Aruch* is as follows: Ruven borrowed money from Shimon and deposited his wife's clothing as collateral. Ruven later borrowed the clothing for a coming festival, but then died. His wife, out of fear, delivered all of the possessions in the house to Shimon, including the aforementioned clothing. Thereupon Shimon returned to Ruven's wife all of the things that she had delivered to him except for the clothing that had originally been deposited with him as collateral for Ruven's loan. When the widow sued Shimon to recover the clothing that she had redelivered to him, and that she now claimed was part of her inheritance, it was held that Shimon was entitled to

---

21. The case in which a lender is holding collateral differs from the ordinary case of a bailee holding the bailment. In the case of a bailment, even if the bailor says that he is certain that the bailee did not lose the object through *force majeure*, the bailee may take a Torah oath that it was lost through *force majeure* and thus be freed of any liability. This is because the bailee is the defendant. In the case of the loan, however, the lender is the plaintiff, who tries to collect the loan after he alleges that the collateral was lost through *force majeure*. Therefore, the borrower, who is the defendant, takes the oath and is free from paying the loan. But the borrower's oath cannot impose liability on the lender as to the alleged overage in value of the collateral over the loan. There are some authorities who hold that the borrower is given the right to take this oath only if he could have pleaded that he had repaid the loan. But if he does not have the availability of such a claim (that is, that the loan was made in the presence of two witnesses and was reduced to writing in the form of an instrument of indebtedness), then the borrower loses his right to take the oath that there was no *force majeure*. In such a case, the lender takes the oath of *force majeure* and collects the loan.

22. The lender is still liable because he is in the status of a paid bailee in relationship to the borrower, while the borrower, or third party, is an unpaid bailee, and a bailee cannot escape his responsibility by transferring the bailment to a person who has a lesser degree of responsibility.

retain the clothing as collateral on the loan. When Shimon permitted Ruven to take the clothing for his wife to use during the festival it was a loan to Ruven, but possession was rightfully Shimon's.

The ruler of a country imposes a tax on the Jewish community. The trustees of the community apportion the tax on the community members. A taxpayer questions his assessment. If collateral is given by the taxpayer to the trustees of the community for them to hold pending the outcome of the lawsuit regarding the taxpayer's obligation for taxes, and if the collateral is then lost or stolen, neither the community nor the trustees have the status of a paid bailee.[23]

In those situations in which the lender must pay for the loss of the collateral and the lender is ready to pay, the borrower may insist that the lender take a "lender's oath"[24] that the collateral is not under his control.[25] The borrower may also insist that the lender take such an oath in those situations in which the lender is free of responsibility because of *force majeure*, and if he does so, the borrower must still repay the loan.

The borrower demands from the lender the collateral that he deposited with him. The lender responds to the borrower that the borrower's son came to the lender and told the lender that the borrower wished the return of the collateral, and the lender alleges that he turned the collateral over to the lender's son. The borrower alleges that he did not send his son to retrieve the collateral nor did it

---

23. The reason that neither the community nor the trustees have any obligation to the taxpayer is that they are only collectors of taxes for the ruler of the country. A similar situation would obtain if the trustees collected taxes from members of the community and the money was stolen or lost before they turned it over to the ruler. If the trustees had no right to use the collected money, then they have no liability to the taxpayers who have already paid their taxes. It may be that these taxpayers will once again have to pay the taxes.

24. This is an oath taken while holding a sacred object. (See Volume III, Chapters 87 and 97.) He must take this solemn type of oath because the borrower suspects that he desires to retain the collateral for himself and is willing to pay for it.

25. The lender will not have to take this lender's oath if there are witnesses who will state that the collateral was lost or stolen, as the lender alleges; or if the collateral is readily available in the market for sale for the price that the lender is willing to pay the borrower; or if the borrower states that he believes the lender's claim that the collateral was lost or stolen. In those situations, the lender will pay for the collateral or deduct it from the loan or pay the difference if the collateral was worth more than the loan.

ever reach him if indeed the lender gave it to the son. The aforesaid set of facts holds that the lender was negligent in turning the collateral over to the borrower's son, even if the son was not a minor. If a person holds something belonging to another, whether as a bailee or commodatary or as a lender holding collateral, he must return the object to the person who deposited it with him or to whomever the owner of the object designates. There is an exception to this general rule. The person holding the object may return it to the owner's wife if she is engaged in her husband's business, whether in her home or elsewhere.[26] The owner of the object does not even have to take an oath that he did not give his son authority to retrieve the collateral, nor an oath that the object never reached him, except if the lender alleges with certainty that the borrower sent his son or that the borrower has received the return of the collateral. In the case in which the lender makes these allegations with certainty, the borrower will have to take a *hesseth* oath, and the lender will then have to pay for the collateral or deduct it from the loan.

The lender deposits money with a third party.[27] A borrower asks the lender to lend him the money and delivers to the lender collateral to be held as security for the loan. The lender gives the borrower a writing addressed to the third party to release the money to the borrower, and the third party gives the money to the borrower. In the process, the lender loses the collateral. If the collateral is lost after delivery of the money by the third party to the borrower, then the lender is responsible for the loss of the collateral pursuant to all of the laws previously stated. However, if the collateral is lost prior to the delivery of the money by the third party to the borrower without any negligence on the lender's part, the lender is not responsible for the loss. The borrower who receives the money from the third party after the loss of the collateral, although he probably is not aware at the time that the collateral was lost, is responsible for the repayment of the loan without any reduction for the loss of the collateral. The lender, like any other bailee, must take a bailee's oath that he was not

---

26. See Chapter 62.
27. The codes speak of a third party holding the lender's money, but the word *bank* could easily be substituted for the term *third party*. Thus it can apply to many modern-day transactions in which the lender gives the borrower a check or otherwise instructs a bank to deliver money to the borrower.

negligent with the collateral.[28] In addition, as part of the oath, the lender must swear that the loss occurred prior to the transfer of the money from the third party to the borrower. If the lender does not know whether the collateral was lost prior to or after the borrower received the moneys from the third party, then the burden of proof is on the borrower to show that the lender is not entitled to be repaid without the borrower's being able to deduct the value of the collateral.

If the lender who took collateral dies, and if the heirs are aware of the loan and the taking of the collateral, they stand in the same position as the lender. This rule does not apply, however, if the heirs are minors.

The borrower repays the loan and demands that the lender return the collateral to the borrower. The lender tells the borrower to come back the next day. The collateral is then stolen. If it was stolen prior to the time that the borrower is told to retrieve it, then the lender is responsible for the loss, since he has the status of a paid bailee who is responsible for loss occasioned by theft. However, if the collateral is stolen after the appointed time for the borrower to retrieve it, then the lender has the status of an unpaid bailee and is not responsible for the loss. The lender cannot claim that he should not even have the responsibilities of an unpaid bailee because he did not have the collateral to return to the borrower when the borrower repaid the loan. If there are witnesses to attest to the fact that the borrower arrived at the place designated by the lender at the appointed time and the lender did not then and there return the collateral to him, then the lender will be deemed to have the status of a paid bailee. If there are no witnesses, and the lender takes a *hesseth* oath that the borrower did not arrive at the appointed time and place, then the lender has the status of an unpaid bailee.

## Collateral held by a third party

If the parties agree that the collateral should be held by a third party, the lender has the same liability as he would have had if he were the

---

28. The lender has the status of an unpaid bailee because the loan was not made until the money was delivered by the third party to the borrower. No benefit has yet flowed to the lender.

holder.[29] However, when the community appoints trustees to hold collateral given by a taxpayer who is contesting his assessment and the collateral is lost or stolen, neither the trustee nor the community has the liability of a paid bailee.[30]

The borrower deposits collateral with the lender, and the lender then deposits it with Levi. The borrower wishes to repay the loan and demands the return of the collateral from the lender. Levi thereafter alleges that the collateral was lost through *force majeure*. The borrower alleges that the collateral was worth $400 and that the loan was for only $200, and thus the lender owes him $200. The lender alleges that the collateral was worth only $300 and thus he owes the borrower only $100. Since the lender admits part of the borrower's claim, he must take a Torah oath that he owes no more than the $100. He must also take both the lender's oath that the collateral is not in his possession or control and the oath that it was lost through *force majeure*. Since he cannot take the latter oath, he must make the payment as if the collateral was lost through his negligence, if (1) the borrower states that he does not believe Levi even if he takes an oath that the collateral was lost through *force majeure*, since the borrower has no connection with Levi, or (2) if it can be shown that the collateral would not have been lost if it had remained in the lender's possession and had not been transferred to Levi. A similar result would follow if the collateral remained in the lender's hands but

---

29. Some authorities hold that if the lender made the borrower the holder of the collateral, then the lender has the liabilities of a paid bailee and the borrower has the lesser liability of an unpaid bailee. Other authorities hold just the opposite—that if the borrower is the holder of the collateral, then the lender has no liability, and if something happened to the collateral while it was in the borrower's custody, then the borrower still has to pay the entire debt.

30. The reason that neither the community nor the trustee is liable is that this is not a dispute between two parties who each stand to benefit from the result of the lawsuit. The community is merely the collecting agent for the secular rulers who have imposed a tax on the community, and the leaders have to work out a fair distribution of the tax load on the members of the community. Similarly, if the trustees, who are unpaid by the community, lost the money that they had collected, then the people will have to pay the taxes again. If the trustees are paid, then they have the liability of paid bailees and are thus liable for loss or theft and certainly for negligence. Furthermore, if the trustees had the right to use the money collected, then they would be liable even for *force majeure*. All of the foregoing laws are subject to the practices of the community; such practices override all specific laws in this matter.

deteriorated. Regarding the aforementioned facts, if there are witnesses that the collateral was lost in Levi's hands through *force majeure*, or if the borrower believes Levi, then unless the second aforementioned condition applies, the lender is relieved of responsibility for the collateral as if it had been lost through *force majeure* while in the lender's possession.[31] Also, if it can be shown that the borrower himself had often deposited his things with Levi, and if Levi takes an oath that the collateral is not in his possession or control and that it was lost through *force majeure*, the lender will be relieved of his responsibility for the collateral and the borrower will have to repay the loan without deduction for the lost collateral, provided that the *force majeure* would have occurred even if the collateral had remained in the lender's hands.

## The lender's oath

When the borrower pays off the loan, he is entitled to receive the return of the collateral from the lender. If the lender states that he does not have the collateral to return to the borrower, then there are two possibilities. In the first case, the lender may allege that he lost the collateral through his negligence or it was lost or stolen, and thus he is responsible to the borrower. The value of the lost collateral will be deducted from the amount of the loan to be repaid, and if the value of the collateral exceeds that amount, then the lender will pay the overage to the borrower. If there is a disagreement as to the value of the lost collateral, then there are numerous possibilities, many of which will be discussed in this chapter. Even according to the opinion that the lender does not have the status of a paid bailee, but rather that of an unpaid bailee, the lender will be responsible up to the value of the collateral if he admits that it was lost through his negligence. However, the lender cannot merely admit liability and deduct the value of the collateral or pay the overage to the borrower. He must take an oath, which shall be designated the "lender's oath," that the collateral is not now in his possession or under his control. In addition thereto, if there is a dispute as to the value of the collateral, the lender

---

31. In cases of *force majeure*, the lender can plead that it makes no difference where the *force majeure* occurred while the collateral was in the hands of the lender or in the hands of Levi.

also takes an oath as to the value of the collateral. The reason is that the lender may have "set his eyes" on the collateral and is willing to deduct the value from the loan or even pay the overage so that he can possess the collateral. The oath is intended to prevent such action.

In the second case, the lender alleges that the collateral was lost through *force majeure*, and therefore he is not responsible and the loan must be repaid in full. In this situation, the lender must take not only the lender's oath, but also two other oaths: (1) that he has not used the collateral, and (2) that the loss of the collateral came through *force majeure*.

In either case, whether (1) the lender's allegation will result in deduction of the amount of the collateral from the loan or in the paying of the overage by the lender or (2) the allegation will result in the loan's not being reduced by the value of the collateral, the lender will have to take the lender's oath (and the other two oaths in case 2. The lender will not have to take the oath, however, if the borrower believes the lender that the collateral was lost or stolen in case 1, or that there was *force majeure* in case 2, or there are witnesses to that effect in both cases, or if the collateral is of a type that a duplicate can be readily purchased on the open market for the same price as the value assigned to the collateral in both cases.[32]

When the lender's allegation will relieve him of responsibility for the collateral, the value of the collateral becomes irrelevant. Witnesses are required to testify to the value of the collateral only if there is a difference of opinion regarding its value and the lender's allegation leaves him liable for the loss of the collateral.

## Dispute as to the value of lost collateral

There are situations in which the lender admits the loss but there is a dispute as to the value of the security. The following are the examples

---

32. This statement applies if it is only the lender who must take the oath. However, if it was the borrower who had to take an oath to prove the value of the collateral, then the lender will still have to take the lender's oath. The reason is that the borrower may take an oath that the value of the collateral is higher than the real value. The lender who has not taken the lender's oath might then produce the collateral and show that the borrower took a false oath. In order to prevent such pitfalls, the lender must take the lender's oath before the borrower takes his oaths even if the duplicate of the collateral is readily available in the open market.

that appear in the *Shulhan Aruch*. (All examples assume that the loan was for $400 and that the parties are disputing the value of the lost or stolen collateral for which the lender is responsible.)

1. The lender alleges that the collateral was worth $200 and thus the borrower still owes $200, and the borrower alleges that the collateral was worth $400 and thus he owes nothing more to lender. The lender has to take a lender's oath that the collateral is not in his possession or control. The borrower then takes a *hesseth* oath that the collateral was worth $400, and the borrower is free of further liability to lender.

2. The lender alleges that the collateral was worth $200 and that the borrower still owes him $200. The borrower alleges that the collateral was worth $300 and that he still owes the lender $100. The lender takes the lender's oath; the borrower takes a Torah oath that the collateral was worth $300; and beth din grants the lender a judgment for $100.[33]

3. The lender alleges that the collateral was worth $200 and thus there is still $200 due him. The borrower states that he does not know the value of the collateral. The lender takes the lender's oath along with an oath that the collateral was not worth more than $200, and the borrower must pay him $200.[34]

4. The lender alleges that the collateral was worth $400 and that the debt is therefore discharged and he owes the borrower nothing. The borrower alleges that the collateral was worth $800 and that the debt is therefore discharged and the lender still owes him $400. If the lender is not required to take the lender's oath because he has witnesses to testify to the fact that the collateral was lost or stolen, or

---

33. The reason for the Torah oath is that the borrower has admitted part of the amount claimed by lender, and if a defendant admits part of the claim and denies the balance of the claim, he must take a Torah oath and is free from paying the amount he denies.

34. The reason that the borrower must pay this amount is that he knows that he has to make some payment, but he does not know how much. The beth din may rely on the oath of the lender for this fact. If the lender has witnesses who will state that the collateral was stolen or lost, or if the borrower believes the lender's claim that it was lost or stolen, then the lender may collect the $200 without even having to take an oath. The borrower may proclaim a ban that anyone who has the collateral should return it.

because the borrower believes him that it was lost or stolen, then the lender takes a *hesseth* oath that the collateral was worth not more than $400 and he is free of payment to the borrower. If the lender did have to take the lender's oath, then he combines that oath with an oath that the value of the collateral was only $400 and he is free of further liability to the borrower.[35]

5. The lender alleges that the collateral was worth $500 and that the loan is discharged and that he still owes the borrower $100. The borrower alleges that the collateral was worth $800 and that the debt is discharged and that the lender still owes him $400. The lender must take a Torah oath that the collateral was worth not more than $500, and if he does not have witnesses that it was lost or stolen, and if the borrower does not believe that it was lost or stolen, then the lender combines with this oath the lender's oath. The lender will have to pay $100 to the borrower. If there are witnesses to testify to the fact that the collateral was lost or stolen, or if the borrower believes the lender, then the lender takes a *hesseth* oath as to value and pays $100.[36]

6. The lender alleges that he does not know the value of the collateral. The borrower alleges that it was worth $800 and thus the debt is discharged and the lender still owes him $400. If the lender does not have to take the lender's oath, he takes a *hesseth* oath that he does not know whether the value of the collateral was in excess of the loan; the loan is then discharged; and he is free of liability to the borrower. If the lender does have to take the lender's oath, he combines that oath with the oath that he does not know the value of the collateral, and he is then free of liability to the borrower and the debt is discharged.

7. The lender alleges that the collateral was worth $200 and the borrower still owes him $200. The borrower alleges that the collateral was worth $800 and that the debt is therefore discharged and the lender owes him still another $400. The lender takes a lender's oath along with an oath that the collateral was worth not more than $400; and the borrower takes a *hesseth* oath that the collateral was worth

---

35. While he takes an oath in both situations, in this example the former oath is not as solemn as the latter oath.

36. This follows the view that the lender has the status of a paid bailee for the entire collateral.

not less than $400; and the debt will be discharged and the lender is free of liability to the borrower.

8. The borrower gives the lender a ring with a precious stone as collateral for the loan, and the ring is lost was because of the lender's negligence. Both agree that the value of the ring exceeded the amount of the loan. They go to a dealer, and the borrower agrees that the ring in the dealer's shop is identical to the lost ring. The ring in the dealer's shop is appraised, and the appraisal value is assigned to the lost collateral. The lender must then pay to the borrower the overage of the loan. However, if the borrower alleges that the lost ring was more valuable than the ring in the dealer's shop, while the lender alleges that it was not worth more, then the lender must pay to the borrower the overage as admitted by the lender, and the lender takes an oath that it was not worth more and he is free of any further liability. If the borrower alleges that it was worth more than the ring in the dealer's shop and the lender does not know whether it was worth more, then the lender must pay to the borrower the value alleged by the borrower, deducting therefrom the amount of the loan.[37] The codes state that this last situation must be closely scrutinized by the beth din so that the borrower will not cheat the lender.

## Dispute as to the amount of the loan or the amount due thereon when collateral is given or allegedly given

Absent witnesses or a written instrument that can be produced in beth din, differences of opinion may arise as to the amount of the loan. Such differences may be honest ones, as when one or both of the

---

37. This example is different from example 6. In that case, the lender did not admit that the collateral exceeded the loan and took an oath that he did not know whether it exceeded the loan. In this example, however, the lender admits that the ring in the dealer's shop is similar to the collateral, and admittedly the dealer's ring exceeds the amount of the loan, although the lender does not know by how much. The lender's admission that it exceeds the amount of the loan subjects him to taking a Torah oath of denial on the part that he does not admit. Since he does not know the value, he cannot take such an oath of denial, and he loses the case by paying to the borrower the amount alleged by the borrower. In example 6 the oath was not a Torah oath.

parties actually forgets the amount of the loan. Or, one of the parties may be dishonest and may state a false amount in order to take advantage of the situation.

There are several situations in which a dispute as to the amount loaned or due may arise. Rules applicable to establishing the correct amount vary depending on the situation. Certain presumptions also affect the rules of proof. For example, absent proof or admission to the contrary, there is a presumption that if a person is possessed of a chattel that cannot walk into his premises, it is his chattel. (This presumption does not apply to an animal in his possession that is known to belong to another person.[38]) As will be seen, this presumption plays a part in the application of rules of evidence to disputes over the amount of a collateralized loan.

Regarding the collateral, three situations are discussed in this chapter. (1) There may be witnesses to testify that the borrower gave the object to the lender, whether as collateral or as a loan, and there may be witnesses (whether the same witnesses or different ones) to attest to the fact that the collateral is now in the lender's hands. In such a situation, the collateral is established as being owned by the borrower by proof independent of the lender. (2) There may be witnesses who will state that the borrower gave the lender the object, either as collateral or as a loan or hiring, but there are no witnesses to the fact that the lender now has the collateral. Since the lender can plead that he returned the object or that it is no longer in his possession. Therefore, if the lender admits that the collateral is in his possession, then it is he who has established that he holds the borrower's collateral. (3) There may be witnesses to attest to the fact that the object is now in the possession of the lender, and thus the lender cannot allege that he returned it to the borrower. If there are no witnesses that the object was given to him as a loan, then he can allege that the object came to him through purchase. Thus if he now admits that it is collateral that is in his possession, then he has established that he holds the borrower's collateral, since he could have denied that it was collateral. Situation 3 would not apply if the object is of the kind

---

38. The Talmud and the codes also speak of slaves and handmaidens who are not presumed to be owned by the person in whose possession they are found, but rather belong to the known owner.

that one would borrow or rent; in such case the holder cannot allege that he purchased it. Since he cannot allege that he purchased it, and also since there are witnesses to testify that it is in his possession, he is not the one who is establishing that the object came to him as collateral, and it is tantamount to situation 1.

The lender alleges that the loan was for $400, and the borrower alleges that the loan was for only $200, and either situation 2 or 3 obtains. In such a case the lender is believed when he alleges that the loan was for the value of the collateral, since the lender is the one who has established that the collateral that he is holding belongs to the borrower.[39] The lender must take an oath while holding a sacred object that the loan was for at least the amount of the collateral.[40]

The situation would be no different if the owner of the object denies that there was a loan and alleges that the holder of the object is holding it as a bailee. In situations 2 and 3, the holder is believed that he is a lender to the extent of the value of the collateral if he takes an oath while holding a sacred object. If the lender alleges that the loan was larger than the value of the collateral, then the borrower is freed of further liability if he takes a *hesseth* oath.

The foregoing would apply even if the collateral consisted of things that a lender is not permitted to retain as collateral, such as cooking utensils or the clothes of a widow. It would also apply if the borrower died and then the lender died. The lender's heirs would be able to collect on the debt to the extent of the value of the collateral. They would have to take an heir's oath that their decedent had not told

---

39. The lender is believed, since he could under these circumstances have denied that he was holding collateral, and thus the collateral could have been his. Thus he has a *migoo* (literally, "since"). Since he could have denied that he was holding the collateral, he is believed that the loan was equal to at least the value of the collateral. As stated, he will also have to take an oath.

40. See Volume III, Chapter 87, regarding the various types of oaths. The oath is administered to the lender because the *migoo*, which works in his favor, has nothing to do with the loan, but only with the collateral. The *migoo* cannot absolve the lender from taking an oath. Furthermore, it is an enactment of the Sages that a person may not retain an object that is not his for satisfaction of a debt without taking an oath. There is an opinion that holds that if the lender is not pressing the borrower to pay the debt, but merely wishes at this time to establish the amount of the debt, then the lender need not take an oath while holding a sacred object; a *hesseth* oath would be sufficient.

them the amount of the loan and that they had found no records that would indicate that the loan was for less than the value of the collateral.

In all of the foregoing situations, the beth din is under an obligation to ascertain the facts regarding the manner in which the collateral came into the hands of the lender. Did it come to him to secure a monetary obligation?

In situation 1, if the borrower takes a *hesseth* oath that the loan was for only $200, and he pays it, then the lender must return the collateral to the borrower. In situations 2 and 3, the lender can obtain a judgment up to the value of the collateral.

The lender alleges that the loan was for $400, and the borrower denies that there was a loan and claims that the lender is holding his object that he wants returned. Experts have appraised the object to be worth $200.[41] The lender agrees to take the collateral in full satisfaction of the debt, which is denied by the borrower. The borrower, seeing that the lender will obtain a judgment for the value of the collateral, asserts that he will pay the lender the $200 appraised value of the collateral and then he wants the collateral back. The codes provide two opinions. One holds that the borrower can obtain the collateral back. The theory is that the lender had accepted the collateral knowing that if the borrower did not pay, then he would receive only the collateral; thus the lender had resigned himself to the fact that he might obtain only $200 when the time for repayment arrived.[42] The other opinion holds that the lender can retain the collateral and must take an oath while holding a sacred object.[43]

An analogous situation arises when the parties agree on the amount

---

41. Any amount could have been used here. The amount used in the codes shows that the laws stated in this paragraph would apply even when there is a gross disproportion between the loan and the collateral security held by the lender.

42. There is the additional reason that the *migoo* claim of the lender applies only to the loan and establishes the loan, but does not address itself to the possession of the collateral. Since the loan has been repaid to whatever extent the lender can now anticipate on the strength of the *migoo*, the collateral should be returned to its owner.

43. The theory behind this opinion is that in situations 2 and 3, the lender could have alleged that he purchased the object. Therefore the *migoo* holds that the lender is believed when he alleges that the loan was for more than the value of the collateral and when he promises that he will return the collateral when the borrower pays him the difference between the value of the collateral and the amount of the loan (as alleged by the lender).

of the loan but dispute the giving of collateral: the lender alleges that he received no collateral and demands the full amount of the loan; while the borrower alleges that he gave the lender collateral that he wishes to deduct from the loan (or, if the collateral was worth more than the loan, that the lender should cancel the loan and return the overage to borrower). The borrower also states the value of the collateral.

For example, the loan was for $400 and the lender denies that he took collateral and demands the full $400. The borrower alleges that he gave collateral worth $500 and that the loan should be discharged and the lender should pay him $100. Both parties take oaths. The lender takes a *hesseth* oath that he did not receive any collateral, and the borrower takes a *hesseth* oath the lender is holding collateral worth $500. The result is that the borrower does not have to pay anything, since the lender has no proof and it is only the borrower's admission that establishes the loan; thus the borrower can take a *hesseth* oath that the loan is paid by dint of the collateral. The lender pays nothing because he has sworn that there was no collateral. The result would be the same if the borrower alleged that the value of the collateral was $400. However, if the borrower alleged that the collateral was worth $300 and that he still owed $100, then the borrower would have to take a Torah oath that he owed no more than the $100, and he would pay the $100.[44] If the borrower refuses to take the oath, he will pay the $400; and if the lender refuses to take the oath, he will pay the overage if the borrower alleges that the collateral was worth more than the amount of the loan.

The aforementioned procedure, whereby both the lender and the borrower take oaths, is followed in any similar situation in which one party claims something from the second party and the second party claims something from the first party. Another example would be a case in which the lender alleges that he loaned $400 to the borrower, who is the owner of the object that the lender is holding, and that the collateral given to him by the borrower was worth $300; thus, he says, there is still $100 due him, assuming that he is permitted to retain the collateral. The owner of the object, on the other hand, alleges that

---

44. The borrower takes a Torah oath because he admits part of the claim, and, as will be explained in Volume III, Chapter 87, if one admits part of a claim, he must take a Torah oath as to the part he denies.

there was no loan at all, and that the object was in fact sold to the lender for $300, which has not been paid; thus, he says, the lender owes him $300. Both parties take oaths to free themselves of liability. The lender takes an oath that the object that he is holding is collateral for a loan, and thus he will retain it.[45] The owner of the object takes an oath that there was a sale, and thus he will be free of the alleged obligation to pay.[46]

The borrower borrows money from the lender and deposits collateral with the lender. There was a witness present who saw the transaction, but he does not know the amount of the loan.[47] The lender alleges that he loaned the borrower $20, while the borrower alleges that it was only $10. If before the difference of opinion develops between the parties it becomes known to the beth din or to witnesses that the lender still has the collateral, then judgment will be rendered in favor of the borrower; he will have to pay $10 and will receive back his collateral. The borrower must take an oath regarding the $10, which he denies, and he will be free of paying it. But if the difference of opinion develops before the witnesses or beth din saw the collateral in the hands of the lender, then the lender could have claimed that he returned the collateral. Since it is the lender who has established the fact of the collateral held by him, the lender may take an oath holding a sacred object and collect the $20 before he has to give the collateral back to the borrower.

The borrower borrows $700 from the lender, with whom he deposits collateral. The borrower then alleges that he repaid $200 on one occasion, and another $200 on a second occasion, and $100 on a third occasion, and he now offers the final $200 and demands return of the collateral. The lender alleges that he remembers only the third payment of $100 and does not recollect whether the borrower made the other two payments. The borrower pays the $200 and receives the return of the collateral. The reason is that the collateral belongs to the borrower, and the lender is in doubt as to whether he has any further reason to hold it, since he does not *deny* payment of the $400;

---

45. The lender does not take an oath regarding the last $100, since he will not collect it.

46. The owner of the object does not take an oath that $300 is due him, since he will not receive it.

47. Some authorities contend that it would be no different if there were two witnesses present when the loan was made.

he states merely that he has no recollection. A person may not retain property belonging to another when there is a doubt as to whether he has the right to do so.

Ruven occupies realty that is known to have belonged to Shimon, and Ruven harvested the crops and benefited from them. Ruven alleges that he is occupying the land as a mortgagee in possession for a loan of $100 that he gave to Shimon, and Ruven is reducing the loan by the value of the crops. The instrument of mortgage was lost, and Shimon alleges that the loan was for $50, which has already been reduced. If Ruven had not occupied the realty for the necessary 3-year presumption in favor of occupiers, then Shimon takes a Torah oath and is believed, since the realty is his and he may, if he desires, evict Ruven from it, since Ruven has lost the instrument permitting him to occupy it. Shimon takes the Torah oath since he has admitted part of a claim and denies the balance of the claim. However, if Ruven had occupied the realty for the necessary 3 years and could have alleged that he purchased the realty and lost his deed and would have been believed, then, according to the foregoing facts, Ruven takes a *hesseth* oath and receives $100 less the value of the crops that he took.[48]

The lender and the borrower dispute the amount of the loan, and the lender is holding collateral. The borrower cannot prove that the lender is holding his collateral. In those instances where the lender will be believed if he states that he purchased the collateral, or that he returned the collateral to the borrower, or that he never took collateral, he will then be believed if he states the amount of the loan up to the value of the collateral he is holding.[49] This applies even if the collateral consists of something that the Torah prohibits the lender to take as collateral.[50] If there are witnesses to attest to the fact that the

---

48. See Chapter 140.

49. He is believed because he could have denied the holding of the collateral and thus he would have been repaid to the extent of the collateral. Thus when the borrower disputes the amount of the loan, the lender is believed as to the amount of the collateral if he takes an oath while holding a sacred object. The lender wants only to have returned what he alleges is the true amount of the loan.

50. For example, a lender may not take utensils from the borrower that are used for the preparation of food, nor may he take the clothing of a widow. It is not theorized that since the lender must return these items it is as if he does not have them, and therefore his statement of the extent of the collateral he is holding is not believed.

lender borrowed the collateral from the borrower, and that he still has the collateral in his possession,[51] then the lender does not have the benefit of the aforesaid rules, since he cannot say that he purchased the collateral. He also cannot say that he purchased the collateral if it is the type of thing that people borrow or lease.[52] But if the borrower can prove that the lender is holding the collateral and thus the lender is no longer in the position of being believed as just stated, then the borrower may take a *hesseth* oath as to the amount of the loan and will be believed; he may then pay the lender the amount he swears is due, and he will repossess the collateral.

If there are witnesses to the giving of the collateral but the witnesses do not know the amount of the loan, the borrower takes an oath as to the amount; he then pays that amount and the collateral is returned to him.[53] The same would hold true if there was only one witness and he saw the collateral being delivered but does not know the amount of the loan.

The lender alleges that the loan was in an amount greater than the value of the collateral as fixed by experts, and he will retain the collateral in full payment of the loan. The borrower alleges that the collateral was in excess of the loan, and he will pay the value of the collateral as fixed by the experts. The choice is the borrower's.

## Deterioration of the collateral

If the collateral deteriorated while in the hands of the lender, and the borrower pleads that he is certain that it deteriorated because of the lender's negligence, and the lender pleads that he took proper care of

---

51. If the witnesses do not know that he still has the borrowed collateral in his possession, then the lender may plead that he returned it. There would then no longer be proof that he has the collateral, and the lender would have the benefit of the laws to which this note refers.

52. According to Maimonides, things that are originally manufactured to be loaned or leased are things that are not manufactured for a person's own use; examples might include a large copper kettle that is used for cooking at a banquet hall, or gilded ornaments that are rented to brides for adornment. According to Alfasi and Rabbeinu Tam, however, the things that are likely to be loaned or leased include almost anything except things that a person is apt to refuse to loan or lease because they may be damaged.

53. There is also an opinion that the lender may take an oath and collect the amount to which he swore.

the collateral and that it deteriorated despite that proper care, then the lender takes a *hesseth* oath that he took proper care of the collateral, and he is absolved of liability for the deterioration.

If the borrower alleges that the collateral has depreciated in value due to the lender's letting it rot or rust or become moth-eaten, and the lender denies that the collateral has thus depreciated, then the lender takes a *hesseth* oath and is free of liability, and the borrower must repay the full amount of the loan. The result would be the same if the lender admits the depreciation but alleges that he took proper care of the collateral and states that the depreciation was not due to his negligence: he would take a *hesseth* oath and be free of liability for the depreciation.

If the lender admits that he did not take proper care of the collateral, then the lender must pay the borrower the amount of the depreciation. (Differences of opinion regarding the values are handled in a variety of ways.[54])

---

54. Differences of opinion may be handled in any of the following ways:
   1. The loan was for $20 and is about to be repaid. The collateral is now worth $10. The borrower alleges that it was worth $20 at the time of the loan, and the lender owes him $10 in reduction of the loan. The lender, on the other hand, alleges that the collateral was worth $15 and that he now owes just $5 in reduction of the loan. The lender proposes that the borrower authorize him to keep the collateral and pay him $5, which is the difference between the loan and what the lender alleges the collateral was worth; alternatively, the borrower should take back the collateral and pay the lender $15, which is the difference between the loan and the loss of value of the collateral according to the lender. The borrower may take a *hesseth* oath and the lender will have to give him a $10 credit.
   2. The borrower alleges that the collateral was worth $30, while the loan was for $20. The borrower contends that the collateral is now worth only $15, and he states that the lender may keep the collateral and pay the borrower $10 because he does not want the ruined collateral. (In essence, the borrower is proposing that the lender purchase the collateral for the original value and the loss, whatever it is, will fall on the lender.) The lender alleges that the collateral was worth only $25. The lender has two options. He may state that he will pay the borrower $5 and keep the collateral; in order to do so, he must take an oath while holding a sacred object that the collateral did not depreciate more than $10. The second option is for the lender to claim $10 (the difference between the original value and the current value is $10, which the lender admits should be reduced from the $20 loan) and take an oath while holding a sacred object that the collateral did not depreciate more than $10. The borrower would then have to take back the collateral and pay $10.

If the lender does not know whether the deterioration came about through his neglect or by *force majeure*, and he therefore cannot take an oath as to how it deteriorated, then he must pay the amount of the deterioration. If there is a disagreement as to the amount of the deterioration, then since the lender admits part of the value of the deterioration and denies part, he takes a Torah oath that the deterioration does not exceed the amount that he admits, and he pays only that amount.

If the lender admits that he did not take proper care of the collateral and thus it was his fault that it deteriorated, then the lender must pay for the amount of the deterioration.

In the last situation there may be a difference of opinion between the parties as to the extent to which the collateral had deteriorated. For example, the loan was for $20. The borrower alleges that the value of the collateral when the loan was made was $20, and it is now worth only $10, and thus the loan should be reduced by $10. The borrower wishes to pay the remaining $10 and have the collateral returned or, if both parties agree, to let the lender retain the collateral and cancel the loan. The lender alleges that the collateral was worth only $15 at the time the loan was made and is now worth $10, and thus there is a loss of only $5. Deducting the $5 from the $20 loan leaves a balance of $15. If the borrower would either give the lender $15 or give him $5 and let him keep the collateral, then the loan will be canceled. The law is that the borrower takes a *hesseth* oath and, if both parties agree, they can leave the collateral with the lender, and the borrower is absolved of any further liability on the loan. If both do not agree to leave the collateral with the lender, then the borrower must pay the $10 and the collateral will be returned to the borrower.

The borrower alleges that at the outset the collateral was worth $30, and the loan was for $20. Now, he says, the collateral is worth only $15. The borrower seeks to have the lender keep the collateral and pay him $10 (the $30 for the collateral less the amount of the loan). The lender alleges that the collateral was worth only $25 at the time the loan was made and thus the lender may retain the collateral and pay the borrower $5 ($25 for the value of the collateral less the $20 loan). The lender takes an oath that the collateral deteriorated by only $10 and pays the borrower $5. The reason that the lender prevails in this case is that the lender is believed if he takes an oath to the extent of the loan if the collateral is equal to or exceeds the amount of the loan.

Ruven gives the borrower his books to hold for safekeeping. The borrower subsequently has to borrow money, and he approaches the lender. The lender requires collateral, and the borrower gives him Ruven's books, informing him that the books belong to Ruven. When Ruven comes to redeem them from lender, he finds that they have deteriorated. The lender admits that the books have deteriorated while in his hands, but he alleges that he used them for study with the borrower's authority, and that they had agreed to reduce the loan by some small amount for the right of lender to use the books. Furthermore, the lender pleads that he had nothing to do with Ruven because there was no privity between them, since the lender had not received the books from Ruven. In this case it was held that lender had no right to use the books, since he knew that they did not belong to the person who had given him the authority to use them. The lender knew that he needed Ruven's permission to use the books. Therefore, the lender must pay Ruven the amount of the deterioration of the books. There are those who hold that even if Ruven had given the borrower authority to use the books, such authority would not extend to lender.[55] Others authorities hold that since Ruven gave authority to the borrower to use the books, such authority followed the books, and the lender could not be held liable for ordinary deterioration resulting from usual use. However, if the lender was not aware of the fact that the books did not belong to borrower, then he has no responsibility at all, since the borrower gave him authority to use the books.

## Cases wherein one of the parties died or wherein one of the parties is a Gentile

The lender dies and his heirs produce an instrument of indebtedness stating that their father loaned money to the borrower. The loan was secured by collateral given by the borrower to the lender.[56] The heirs

---

55. Ruven can claim that he knew that the borrower would take good care of the books while using them, but that his confidence did not extend to others.

56. The fact that the loan was secured with collateral was determined by its being disclosed in the instrument of indebtedness; alternatively, the heirs admit that they know that their father had held the collateral.

allege that they cannot find the collateral and suggest that perhaps the collateral was destroyed through *force majeure* while in the hands of the lender. The heirs thus demand the repayment of the loan. In such a case the instrument is canceled.[57] However, if the heirs plead with certainty that the collateral was lost through *force majeure*, they may take an oath to that effect and collect the amount of the loan.

The borrower deposits collateral with the lender. Thereafter the lender dies, leaving minor heirs. The borrower comes to retrieve the collateral from the heirs and to pay them $50, which he alleges was the amount of the loan. The heirs plead that their father had told them that the loan was for $100. The borrower must immediately pay to the heirs the $50 that he admits is due, and he deposits the other $50 into escrow until the heirs reach the age of majority. At that time, if the borrower demands it, the heirs will take the oath of heirs that they know nothing about the collateral and that their father told them nothing about it nor did they find any indications in their father's records regarding the collateral. The heirs may then receive the $50 deposited with the escrowee. The foregoing applies if the collateral is worth $100. If it is worth less than $100, however, the borrower pays the $50 that he admits to the heirs, and the value of the collateral over the $50 is deposited with the escrowee. The borrower takes a *hesseth* oath that the indebtedness did not exceed the value of the collateral. If the collateral was of a kind that was borrowed or hired, then the borrower pays only $50, even if the collateral was worth more than $50, since he could have pleaded that the lender was holding the collateral as a borrower or hirer. All of the foregoing assumes that the heirs are capable of understanding the events of the case and the information that their father had imparted. However, if they are too young to have an understanding of these matters, then the borrower must pay only the amount he admits; he takes a *hesseth* oath on the balance.

The borrower is a Jew, and the lender is a proselyte.[58] The

---

57. The instrument is cancelled because it has surely been redeemed by the loss of the collateral. Whether there is still a loan outstanding is doubtful, since the collateral is missing; this loss offsets the loan, since there is doubt as to whether the loss of the collateral came about because of *force majeure*.

58. See Volume I, Chapter 7, for a definition of the term *proselyte*.

proselyte dies without leaving heirs.[59] Thus, anyone who takes possession of his assets becomes the owner of those assets. If a person takes possession of the collateral that was deposited with the proselyte, such collateral must be returned to the borrower. The reason is that at the moment the proselyte died, the lien that he held on the collateral terminated.[60] The same would apply if the proselyte held a mortgage on realty belonging to the borrower and the proselyte had taken possession of the realty before he died. If another Jew seized the realty after the proselyte died, then the realty is taken from him and returned to the borrower, since in this case, too, the lien terminates upon the proselyte's death.

A Gentile loans money to a Jew and takes collateral as security. He then loses the collateral and another Jew finds it. The finder must return the collateral to the Jewish borrower since the collateral belongs to him, and the Gentile had only a lien on the collateral; when he lost the collateral, his lien was terminated.[61] The finder may not return the collateral to the Gentile even if his intention was to show the Gentile that Jews are kind, honest people who return lost property.[62] If the lender is Jewish and the borrower is a Gentile, and the Gentile loses the money he borrowed, then the finder need not return the money to the lender, since the money was loaned to the

---

59. In halachah there is almost no possibility of a Jew's dying without heirs. The search for collateral relatives goes back several generations. A proselyte is deemed to be a newborn from the moment of conversion, and his former relatives are no longer considered his legal relatives for the purpose of inheriting his assets. Thus his assets are upon his death considered ownerless unless he had a new family after his conversion.

60. The laws apply whether the collateral was given at the time of the making of the loan or subsequent thereto. In either case, the lender has only a lien on the collateral, which ceases upon his death, at which time the collateral is owned by the borrower free and clear of the lien.

61. If the collateral was worth less than the loan, there are those who hold that the finder can keep it because the Jewish borrower will not have to repay the loan, since the Gentile does not have the collateral to return to him. Thus the Jewish borrower will suffer no loss.

62. The finder's returning of the collateral to the Gentile may result in sanctification of the name of Heaven, for the Gentile might praise the God of the Jews for giving the Jews such excellent laws. However, a person cannot sanctify the name of Heaven by using property that belongs to someone else, and in this case the property belongs to the Jewish borrower.

Gentile to be spent. Dissenting opinion asserts, however, that the money should be returned to the Jewish lender.

The borrower is a proselyte and the lender a Jew. The borrower deposits collateral with the lender. The proselyte subsequently dies.[63] Another Jew seizes the collateral. The law is that the lender acquires an interest in the collateral to the extent of the loan, and the seizer acquires an interest in the collateral to the extent that the value of the collateral exceeds the amount of the loan. All this applies when the collateral is not under the lender's control. But if the collateral is under the lender's control, then the seizer acquires nothing of the collateral, and the entire collateral belongs to the lender.[64]

A Jewish lender loans money to a Gentile borrower, or to a proselyte who has no heirs, and receives collateral security for the loan. Thereafter the lender says to the borrower, "Pay back the loan and retake your collateral." The borrower tells the lender to transfer the collateral to another Jew who would lend the borrower money on the strength of the collateral, and the lender gives the collateral to the second lender, who pays the first lender the amount due on the loan. Thereafter the Gentile dies. The collateral is worth more than the loan. The collateral belongs to the second lender, since the first lender gave up all rights to the collateral when the loan was repaid. If the borrower dies before the first lender transfers the collateral to the second lender, then the first lender keeps the collateral even though he had already been instructed by the borrower to make the transfer. The second lender had not yet acquired any rights in the collateral.

However, if the first lender deposits the collateral for safekeeping with a bailee and then the borrower dies, there is a question as to whether the bailee acquires title to the collateral insofar as it exceeds the amount of the loan. Upon the borrower's death, the collateral became ownerless. The doubt arises for the following reason. It can be said that the bailee acquires title to the collateral, subject to the lien of the lender which the bailee must pay and he keeps the collateral, or

---

63. At the moment that the proselyte dies without heirs, his property becomes ownerless; presumably this would also include the collateral.

64. If the collateral is lying in the lender's house, then surely it is under his control. If, on the other hand, the collateral was lying in a field belonging to the lender, and the field was not fenced, and the lender was not in the field when the proselyte died, then this would be a situation in which the finder would obtain title to the overage.

else the bailee stands in the place of the lender and thus all of the collateral belongs to the lender. The majority opinion is that the bailee acquires title subject to the lien of the lender.

A Gentile has loaned money at interest to Ruven, a Jewish borrower. Shimon, a second Jewish borrower, also wishes to borrow money from the same Gentile lender and asks Ruven whether the collateral that he has deposited can also stand as collateral security for his own loan. Ruven agrees and the loan is made to Shimon. Thereafter, the collateral is burned while in the possession of the Gentile lender. Ruven demands that Shimon pay him the value of the collateral to the extent of Shimon's loan, which Shimon refuses to do. The holding was that Shimon need not pay anything to Ruven, since Ruven would have, in any event, lost the entire collateral, since the lender was holding the collateral as security for the original loan to Ruven. However, if the secular law of the land where the loan occurred was that the lender has to make good to the borrower any overage between the value of the collateral and the loan, then Shimon would have to pay Ruven such overage to the extent of his own loan.

It would be laudatory for the beth din to try to persuade Shimon to make some payment to Ruven on the grounds that he did benefit. In fact, the codes and responsa suggest that in all of the laws of this chapter, the beth din should endeavor to work out compromises and thereby avoid the taking of the many types of oaths mentioned herein.

## Return of the collateral

Upon payment of the loan, the borrower is entitled to the return of the collateral. Many of the questions dealing with differences of opinion between the parties as to the value of the collateral have already been discussed.

# Chapter 73

## TIME ALLOWED FOR REPAYMENT OF A LOAN

### INTRODUCTION

In this chapter, *Shulhan Aruch* takes up a variety of topics dealing with loans. What if a loan does not stipulate the time of repayment? How much time does the borrower have before he has to pay the loan? If the terms of payment are stated in the loan, then the agreement between the parties will be controlling. If the loan has time to run before it has to be repaid, then the lender may not demand payment from the borrower prior to expiration of that time. That which is stated herein regarding loans will also apply to other credit transactions.

This chapter also discusses some laws dealing with oaths—either oaths taken by a borrower so that he does not have to repay a loan, or oaths taken by either the lender or the borrower to bolster his allegations regarding a loan. In halachah, oaths are a solemn matter. The taker of the oath must invoke the Divine name and bears all of the attendant consequences if he fails to abide by the terms of the oath. With this in mind, many lenders insisted that a borrower take an oath that he would repay the loan by the time specified for repayment. Thus, if a borrower failed to repay on the date on which he had sworn to repay, then he not only still had to make repayment, but he was also guilty of transgressing an oath. As will be seen in Volume III, Chapter 87, there is a Torah oath placed upon the defendant if he admits part of the plaintiff's claim. For example, if the plaintiff is suing for $100 and the defendant admits that he owes the plaintiff only $40, and the plaintiff has no proof as to the remaining $60, the defendant may obtain a judgment dismissing the complaint for the remaining $60 by taking a Torah oath that he does not owe the plaintiff the $60, and the plaintiff will obtain a judgment for the $40 that the defendant admitted. This chapter also discusses a subject that is now theoretical: the administering of a beating to a recalcitrant borrower by the beth din for the oath that the borrower takes to refrain from selling any of his assets to repay the loan. Also discussed are the rights that the lender has if he believes that the borrower is dissipating or secreting his assets, or that the assets are wasting. Finally, there is discussed the sale of collateral held by the lender. This follows the topic of attaching the borrower's assets if he is dissipating them. That which applies to the borrower's assets will also apply to the collateral.

# TEXT

## Amount of time to repay a loan

If the loan was given for a certain term—that is, if the time for repayment was specified—then whether the loan was or was not evidenced by a note of indebtedness, the agreed-upon terms will be controlling.[1] The lender may not demand payment or sue for payment before the time specified.[2] He cannot demand prepayment, whether

---

1. The lender may insist that he will not make the loan unless a note of indebtedness is written and delivered to him. In the event that the lender gave the money to the borrower while the transaction was proceeding, and the borrower then refused to authorize the writing of a note, the lender may immediately demand the return of the money. There are those who state that this may be done if the borrower has agreed by a kinyan to have a note written. The laws of kinyan are discussed in Chapter 195.

2. This applies if the term was specified when the loan was made, and even if no kinyan was made. However, if the time was specified after the making of the loan, then there is an opinion that the lender will be bound by the time specified only if a kinyan was made. The majority opinion, however, treats this as a waiver of the lender's rights to collect his debt until the specified time, and as will be noted in Chapter 231, a waiver or relinquishing of rights does not require a kinyan.

or not the loan was evidenced by a note of indebtedness, whether or not there was collateral security given to secure the loan, and whether or not the lender or the debtor (or neither) is alive when the demand is made, provided, in the latter instance, that the debtor's heirs are in a position similar to the debtor's regarding the ability to repay the loan.[3] A *kinyan* need not be made, even if the time for repayment is more than 30 days. All that is stated regarding loans will also apply to other forms of extension of credit, such as credit for goods purchased. If the loan agreement states that the loan must be "repaid during the next 30 days," the intent is that it will be repaid in increments over the 30 days. However, if the borrower lacks the wherewithal to make payments during the 30-day period, then beth din will not issue a judgment for collection until that period has expired.

If the loan does not contain a time for repayment, then the community's custom, if any, will be followed.[4]

If the terms were not specified when the loan was made, and if there is no custom in the community to govern repayment, then it is deemed to be a 30-day loan. The lender cannot demand payment or institute suit to collect before the termination of the 30-day period.[5] This is true whether the loan is oral or is evidenced by a note of indebtedness, and whether or not collateral security is posted for the loan. If, however, the loan is payable upon demand, then the lender may demand the repayment even on the day the loan is made (or the credit extended).[6]

---

3. There are those who hold that the financial position of the debtor's heirs should not be taken into account, but that the lender can demand collateral from the heirs or a guarantor for the loan, and the heirs cannot be sued in such event nor demand made upon them before the time specified for the repayment of the loan.
4. The custom will be followed whether it is for 30 days or for a period less or more than 30 days.
5. This principle does not negate the fact that the borrower may prove that he repaid before the 30-day period had expired.
6. What has been said regarding loans and extensions of credit does not apply to borrowed objects. A lender may demand return of a borrowed object at any time. The difference between loans and borrowings of objects is that the money of the loan is intended to be spent by the borrower, and other moneys is to be used for repayment. In the case of the borrowing of an object, the same object is to be returned to the lender. A minority opinion holds that borrowed objects are also subject to the 30-day period. In all events, the lender cannot demand the return of the loaned object until the borrower has used it at least once.

## Dispute as to the term of the loan

If the lender alleges that the date for repayment of the loan has arrived, and the borrower alleges that there are still 10 more days before the loan is due, the borrower takes a *hesseth* oath and obtains another 10 days in his favor.[7] If it is the borrower who produces a witness to substantiate his allegations, then the borrower is believed without having to take an oath. If the lender has one witness who testifies to substantiate his allegation, then the borrower must take a Torah oath that there are 10 days remaining until the time of repayment.[8] If the lender alleges that there are only 5 days left before the loan is due, and the borrower alleges that there are still 10 days remaining, then the beth din will not give either party a declaratory judgment as to how much time remains, but will tell the parties to return on the fifth day, when the borrower will take a *hesseth* oath that there are still 5 more days left, and he will be given these 5 days in which to repay. All of this holds true if the loan was neither collateralized nor evidenced by a note of indebtedness. If the loan was

---

7. See Volume III, Chapter 87 regarding different types of oaths. The reason that the borrower takes a *hesseth* oath is that he denies an essential term of the transaction. Just as he would take a *hesseth* oath if he denied the loan, so does he take a *hesseth* oath when he denies that the loan is due.

8. The reason for the borrower's taking a Torah oath is that whenever there is one witness who substantiates the plaintiff's allegations, the defendant must take a Torah oath of denial of the plaintiff's allegations. If the defendant takes such an oath, then the plaintiff's complaint will be dismissed, since a case can be proved only if there are two witnesses to substantiate the plaintiff's claim. If the defendant fails to take such an oath, then judgment will be entered for the plaintiff on the strength of his pleading and the one witness who substantiates his allegations. If there are two witnesses, then the defendant does not have the option to swear. It is only if there is one witness that the burden of proof shifts from the plaintiff to the defendant. Similarly, if the defendant admits part of the plaintiff's claim and denies the balance, as noted in the Introduction, then the burden of proof shifts to the defendant regarding that balance, and his taking of a Torah oath will result in a judgment for the defendant, dismissing the plaintiff's complaint as to the amount not admitted by the defendant. It has been suggested that the laws of this chapter can be combined so that if the lender alleges that the time for repayment has arrived and that the debtor owes $100, and the debtor alleges that he owes only $60 and that there are still 10 days left before the due date, then the borrower can take a *hesseth* oath regarding the time and he will be given the additional 10 days. At the end of the 10 days, he will have to take a Torah oath regarding the remaining $40.

collateralized or was evidenced by a note, then the lender may take a *hesseth* oath that the time for repayment has arrived, or that the loan was a demand loan, and judgment will be entered in his favor.[9]

## Oaths taken by the borrower regarding the loan

The borrower takes an oath that he would under no circumstances sell any of his assets in order to have money to repay any money that he might borrow in the future.[10] He thereafter borrows money from a lender and swears to him that he will repay the loan on a certain date. On the due date, he alleges that he has no money with which to repay the loan, and in response to the demand for payment, he alleges that he had taken an oath to refrain from selling any assets to repay a loan. The borrower is beaten at the direction of the beth din until he states that he regrets having made the first oath.[11] He is then absolved of the first oath, and he then sells assets to repay the loan.[12] In all events, the beth din has the authority to sell the borrower's assets to repay the loan.[13] In modern times, since the entire concept of beating recalcitrant litigants does not apply, the authority of the beth din to sell the borrower's assets is controlling.

If the oath to repay predated the oath to refrain from selling assets, then the second oath is of no effect, and the borrower is beaten until he sells assets to pay the loan.[14]

If the borrower takes an oath to repay the loan on a certain date, then he must repay the loan on that date even if the lender does not

---

9. There are those who hold that if the loan is not evidenced by a note, but the lender is holding collateral, then he must take an oath while holding a sacred object regarding the time for repayment.

10. The oath is effective because at the time it was made the borrower owed no money and thus did not violate any obligation.

11. One of the methods of annulling an oath is for the maker of the oath to state that he regrets having made the oath and to give a reason that, had he known the consequences of the oath, he would not have made it.

12. The borrower is beaten because his second oath to the lender was a vain oath, since he had already sworn to refrain from selling assets to repay the loan. If the borrower seeks to annul his first oath, then he will not be beaten for making the second, vain oath.

13. The fact that the beth din is not bound by the borrower's oath to refrain from selling assets to repay the loan undermines some of the effect of the oath.

14. He is beaten because he is in violation of his first oath to repay the loan.

make a demand for repayment.[15] If the date mentioned in the oath for repayment turns out to be a Sabbath day, then the loan must be repaid before that day. If the loan is not repaid before the Sabbath, and if the lender demands repayment on or before the Sabbath, then the borrower must furnish the lender with collateral on the Sabbath.[16] If the borrower took an oath to repay on a certain date, and the Sabbatical year intervened,[17] or the lender forgave the repayment, then the oath is automatically rendered ineffective.[18] If the money that the borrower set aside to pay the loan is seized by government authorities for some other indebtedness, then the borrower is not in violation of his oath until he once again has the money to repay the loan.

If on the date specified in the borrower's oath for the repayment of the loan, the lender or his agent is not in the city in which he resided when the loan was made,[19] and is not in the city where the borrower resides, then the borrower need not fulfill his oath until the lender or his agent returns to either city and makes demand for repayment. The

---

15. Some authorities hold that there must be a demand by the lender for repayment, as is the case for all loans wherein a date of repayment is specified.

16. According to some authorities, the collateral may be appraised on the Sabbath and be deemed to be repayment of the loan. The giving of the collateral and the appraisal is permitted on the Sabbath because by repaying the loan by delivering an object that may be used on the Sabbath, he has not technically violated any of the laws of the Sabbath and has complied with the Torah commandment to fulfill his oaths. Other authorities hold that the collateral may not be appraised or even measured on the Sabbath, and that these tasks should be performed after the Sabbath. The best procedure would be to find some way to have the oath annulled before the Sabbath.

17. The laws relating to the cancellation of debts at the end of the Sabbatical year are discussed in Chapter 67.

18. The reason that the oath to repay is no longer effective is that if the borrower is free of his obligation to repay, he cannot be held liable for repayment.

19. The borrower is not authorized to return the money to the wife or children of the lender because, under ordinary circumstances, they are not knowledgeable in business matters. If the borrower does make payment to them and the lender does not receive the payment, the borrower is still liable to the lender. If the wife is involved in her husband's business affairs, then payment should be made to her. See Chapter 62. Also, the borrower is not required, except as stated in the text, to follow the lender to his new location, for that is required only in the case where a thief wants to make restitution to the victim of his theft who has moved to another location. There is also no provision in the law for the borrower to convene a beth din and make payment to the beth din.

borrower should, however, have the money available on the specified date; he is not permitted to spend it on the due date or at any time thereafter until he repays the lender. He must be ready to repay immediately when demand is made, and if he fails to repay at that time, then he transgresses the oath. Some authorities hold that if the lender moved to a place that is no more distant than the place where he resided when the loan was made, then the borrower must repay in the city where the lender is now located.[20]

If a person swears to make a wedding gift to his prospective son-in-law, and if quarrels have broken out between the son-in-law and the bride as a result of such proposed gift, then the father is absolved of the oath if it will lead to more bickering.[21]

If a person, aware of the fact that he owes nothing to a second person, nevertheless swears to make payment to that second person, then the oath is binding upon him.[22] However, if he mistakenly believed that he owed the second person money, then it is an oath made in error, and it is of no effect.

If a person takes an oath to pay on the first day of the month of Adar, and if the year in which payment is to be made has 2 months of Adar, then he must make the payment on the first day of the first Adar.[23] If a person takes an oath to repay a loan on the festival of

---

20. Some authorities hold that the oath is to be strictly construed and is not to be broadened to include the borrower's having to go to places not specified or intended when the oath was made.

21. Since the father is no longer obligated to make the gift, he is no longer bound by the oath because the oath is only in support of the obligation. Thus it is similar to the situation in which the Sabbatical year has intervened or the lender has forgiven the debt, in which events the oath to make the payment terminated with the forgiveness of the debt. The father would certainly not have made the oath had he thought it would lead to bickering between the bride and her husband.

22. This last-mentioned situation, in which a person can obligate himself by oath to make payment to another person, is not similar to the situation mentioned earlier, in which an oath is annulled if a lender forgives a debt that the debtor swore to pay. In the latter case, the obligation did not arise from the oath to pay. It was the loan that created the indebtedness, and the oath to pay gave comfort to the lender that the borrower would repay. In the former case, however, the debt arises out of the oath to pay even though the borrower knows that he owes the lender nothing, and thus the oath is binding.

23. The Jewish calendar is based on both solar and lunar calendars. The months are lunar months, so that each has either twenty-nine or thirty days. This is because the mean new moon comes out every twenty-nine days, twelve hours, forty-four minutes

Hanuka, then he may repay the loan during any of the eight days of the festival.[24]

In all cases, the borrower has not violated the oath by nonpayment until dusk of the day specified.

## The lender alleges that the borrower's assets are being dissipated

The lender alleges in beth din that he wants to attach the borrower's assets before the time for repayment of the loan because he fears that the borrower is dissipating them.[25] The result would be the same whether there is a time specified in the loan or there is no time specified and the parties are relying on the custom of the community or the 30-day rule of repayment. These laws apply only if the loan is evidenced by a note of indebtedness.[26] The matter should be investigated by the beth din, and if they find that the lender's fears are reasonable, then they should issue an order to prevent the borrower from dissipating his assets. The same would apply if the lender locates assets belonging to the borrower in the hands of a third party; he may obtain an order from the beth din to enjoin the third party from turning the assets over to the borrower until the lender is repaid. The same would apply if the lender fears that the borrower is about to depart from the jurisdiction of the beth din without repaying him. In all such instances, the beth din should investigate the matter upon such notice

---

and three and ⅓ seconds. The year would thus have approximately 354 days. But since the holidays must come out according to the seasons, an extra month of Adar, known as the second Adar, is inserted between the first Adar and the month of Nissan, the first spring month. (See the notes to Chapters 1 and 5 in Volume I.)

24. See Volume I, Chapter 5, regarding the festivals in the Jewish calendar.

25. If the borrower simply does not have sufficient assets, and whatever assets he has are diminishing in a normal manner without intent to defraud on his part, and the lender fears that the borrower will not have sufficient assets to pay when the loan becomes due, this is not ordinarily sufficient reason to attach the borrower's assets. Chapter 97, Volume IV, discusses the situation where the creditor applies to beth din for an order attaching assets of the borrower after the date set for repayment of the loan, but prior to the commencement of proceedings to enforce repayment.

26. If there is no note of indebtedness, the borrower can allege payment and take a *hesseth* oath that he has paid the loan, and that he will be prejudiced by the attachment.

to the borrower as it deems advisable and then issue its order. The beth din may require the borrower to post security or collateral or to provide a guarantor for the indebtedness. The beth din may order an attachment of the borrower's assets within its jurisdiction and issue any orders it deems proper, always remembering that in most instances it will be the lender who will be most prejudiced if his fears of the borrower's not being available or dissipating his assets are confirmed.[27] If the repayment is past due, the beth din should be very liberal in attaching the assets of the borrower in the hands of a third party or in enjoining the borrower from dissipating his assets.

There is also an opinion that the beth din may issue an order attaching the borrower's assets if a guarantor petitions the beth din that he fears that the borrower on whose behalf he gave the guarantee is dissipating his assets and that he will therefore have to pay the lender.

Ruven purchased real estate from Shimon. Levi sues Ruven to obtain the real estate on the allegation that the real estate belonged to Levi and not to Shimon. As soon as Ruven hears of Levi's claim, he may move to attach Shimon's assets in case Levi prevails in the lawsuit and shows that the real estate never belonged to Shimon.[28] Beth din will decide whether it is necessary to order an attachment of Shimon's assets.

As was stated in Volume I, Chapter 14, if the plaintiff finds property of the defendant in the city where the plaintiff resides, and it is not likely that the defendant will abide by the service of a summons or the decision of the beth din where he resides, then the plaintiff may obtain an order attaching the defendant's property, and the plaintiff must

---

27. If the borrower resides in another jurisdiction and his assets are found in the jurisdiction of the beth din, then beth din should attach those assets. If the beth din decides that the borrower is honorable and will pay his debts, and that in the event of a dispute the borrower will certainly appear before the beth din where he resides, then there is no reason to attach the borrower's assets just because he is not in the jurisdiction of the beth din where the assets are located. (The laws relating to seizing the borrower's collateral after the loan repayment is due will be found in Volume IV, Chapter 97.)

28. Ruven may ask that the beth din require Shimon to purchase a second parcel with the proceeds of the sale and that the second parcel be held until the lawsuit between himself and Levi is completed. If Ruven prevails, then the second parcel purchased by Shimon is his to do with whatever he desires, since Ruven will keep the land he bought from Shimon. If Levi wins the lawsuit, then Shimon shall turn the purchased land over to Ruven.

notify the defendant of the attachment. The plaintiff may have a summons served upon the defendant requiring the trial to be held in the city where the plaintiff resides.[29]

## Selling collateral security

If collateral is depreciating in value or is becoming ruined by the passage of time, beth din may grant an order to sell the collateral at any time, even before the due date of repayment. This may be done with or without notice, as beth din deems best in each case.[30]

If the parties by agreement provide for the sale of collateral held by the lender, such agreement is controlling. The laws that follow hold in those instances where there is no agreement.

If the borrower has not repaid the loan at the time specified for repayment, or if no time was specified, then at the end of 30 days, the lender may apply for a beth din order to sell whatever collateral security he is holding. The same would apply to attached assets of the borrower. If the borrower is in the city, he must be notified of the lender's application of the lender, and he must be informed that if he fails to repay, an order will be issued permitting the sale of the collateral. If the borrower is not in the city, then beth din may proceed without his presence, or upon such terms of notification as beth din shall deem advisable.[31] Some authorities contend that the beth din should refrain from issuing an order for the sale of the collateral until 30 days after demand for payment has been made.[32] There is also an opinion that the law of the land should be followed regarding the time

---

29. If the lender were always required to chase the borrower, people might be likely to borrow and then leave the jurisdiction, believing that lenders will not be inclined to chase them to a distant place.

30. If the collateral diminishes in value, the borrower also stands to lose, since at a sale of the collateral he will receive a smaller overage if the collateral is worth more than the loan, and if it is worth less, he will have to pay a larger deficiency.

31. In modern times, with the availability of telephones, telegraphs, telephoto copier machines, and facsimile machines, beth din should make appropriate terms of notification if the borrower's whereabouts are known.

32. The demand need not be made in beth din. It is preferable that the demand be made in the presence of witnesses so that the borrower cannot deny that the demand was made. Perhaps registered mail would suffice under circumstances where the letter's contents can be proven. If the borrower admits that the demand was made, then no external proof is necessary according to the view that beth din must wait until 30 days after demand of repayment.

that should elapse between default and sale, since the parties probably had this law in mind when the collateral was delivered.

That which has been stated regarding credit between individuals also applies to collateral given to secure a pledge to charity.

Unless provided for in the agreement between the parties, security may not be sold without an order of the beth din.[33] Beth din should appraise the collateral or should have it appraised by experts as to its market value. It is preferrable that the security should then be sold for that amount in the presence of witnesses.[34] If the sale was held without an appraisal by the beth din or its experts, then the sale is void, even if the price realized is a fair market value price. However, if the sale cannot be rescinded, then the borrower will be given credit for the value of the sold collateral at the time of the sale, as testified to by witnesses. If the collateral was worth more than the amount of the loan, then the lender must pay the overage to the borrower. If there were no witnesses, then the lender may swear as to the value of the sold collateral and then pay the overage to the borrower. If the lender does not want to take an oath, or states that he has no knowledge of the value at the time of the sale, then the borrower may take an oath as to its value, and the lender will pay the overage to the borrower.

Ordinarily, the lender may not purchase the collateral at the sale. There are also authorities who contend that if the sale is conducted by a beth din including at least one member who is expert as to the value of the collateral, then the lender may purchase at the sale. Many authorities dissent, however, contending that the lender may not purchase at the sale in any event, even if the loan agreement so provided.

Two parties agreed that if a loan was not paid by a certain date, the collateral would be sold and the lender would keep any overage as a retroactive gift. Such an agreement is not enforceable as to the overage, since it is in the nature of a penalty.[35] There is an opinion that

---

33. As is evident from some of the laws that follow, the lender who sells without the order and appraisal of beth din may be embarking upon a risky course of action.

34. The presence of witnesses is suggested so that the borrower cannot later allege that the sale of the collateral fetched a greater price than the appraised value and that the seller kept the overage for himself.

35. Such an agreement, known as *asmachta*, is an illusory promise, since the person who makes the promise does not want the terms ever to come into existence. (See Chapter 207 regarding agreements that contain penalty clauses disguised in

if the agreement states that the collateral belongs to the lender immediately upon receipt, then the overage would belong to the lender if the borrower does not subsequently redeem the collateral from the lender by paying the amount of the loan. If there is a difference of opinion as to whether the collateral is given as a present gift subject to defeasement if the loan is repaid, then the lender will be believed if he takes an oath. If the borrower authorized the lender to sell the collateral, then the lender may proceed with the sale unless the borrower has revoked the authority prior to the sale.[36] If the lender takes the collateral to another community and sells it for a higher price than could have been obtained in the lender's community, then the expenses of traveling to the other community may be deducted from the proceeds of the sale, and any overage in excess of the amount of the loan belongs to the borrower.

The borrower may not allege that the underlying loan was forgiven and that he is therefore entitled to the return of the collateral.[37]

Lender alleges the following facts: "On January 1 lender lent $100 to borrower to be repaid March 1. On January 1 borrower gave collateral to lender. On March 1 lender asked borrower to repay the loan and to take back the collateral. Borrower asked lender to take the collateral to a Gentile and borrow $100 from him. That $100 would be used to repay the $100 due to lender from borrower. Borrower on April 1 gave $100 to lender to give to the Gentile and repossess the collateral. Lender alleges that the Gentile demands interest on the $100 before he will return the collateral." Who is liable for the interest? The law in this case states that the instructions to repledge the collateral with the Gentile did not include the rights to pledge it to secure a loan with interest.

---

commercial terms.) If, however, the promise was to pay a sum to charity if the loan was not repaid on a timely basis, then this is not *asmachta* and the pledge to charity must be paid. Of course, the debt must also be repaid.

36. When the borrower authorizes the sale, the lender takes on the role of an agent of the borrower, and any agency may be revoked before the agent has undertaken the execution for the principal.

37. The same would apply if the lender is holding money security from the borrower that the lender is not authorized to use.

# Chaper 74

---

# PLACE AND MANNER
# OF LOAN REPAYMENT

## INTRODUCTION

This chapter, the last one dealing with loans, discusses the place where the loan should be repaid. Assuming that there are locations where the repayment of the loan would be a hardship for the lender or for the borrower, which of the parties has the right to name the place of payment? Are there differences if the loan is repaid before the due date or on or after the due date? It should be remembered that if there are too many difficulties for the lender or for the extender of credit in collecting the amount due to him, then he will be reluctant to extend credit, and therefore not only the borrower in this case but also other borrowers may suffer.

Many of the matters discussed in this chapter cause fewer problems today because of payment by checks, credit cards, wiring of funds, and other modern methods of communication and domestic and international payment. The question of prepayment of a loan, however, is relevant at all times. The lender or extender of credit may not want to be prepaid for any number of reasons. May the borrower insist that the lender accept prepayment?

# TEXT

## Place of repayment

If the time for repayment has arrived, the lender may demand repayment at any place where he can locate the borrower. It need not be the place where the loan was made. This holds true if demanding payment in the place where the borrower is now found will not cause undue hardship; however, if it is in the place where the loan was made, then the borrower's hardship claim will be of no avail. If the place of demand (other than the place where the loan was made) will cause undue hardship to the borrower, he will be given 30 days to repay the loan.[1] In addition, there must be enough money left for the borrower to travel home and to obtain food and shelter along the way.[2]

If the borrower does not have money in the place other than the place where the loan was made, then the lender may not insist that the borrower send for money from the place where it is kept. If there is a disagreement as to whether the borrower has sufficient funds with him—the lender claiming that the borrower can repay the loan without being prejudiced, and the borrower alleging that to repay the loan in this place would leave him without funds for the trip home—then if the borrower takes a *hesseth* oath, he need not repay until he returns home.

The borrower may not repay the loan in a place other than where the loan was made if it is inconvenient for the lender.[3] The borrower may repay at any location within the community where the loan was made, even if the place of repayment is not the exact place where the loan was made (or the credit extended).

---

1. For example, the loan was made in Jerusalem. Both the lender and the borrower are in Australia, and the borrower has money with him to repay the loan. However, he has funds in Jerusalem, and he requires the money that he has with him for business in Australia. Therefore, he will be disadvantaged if he does not have money available to conduct his business in Australia.

2. Thus, the lender must leave the borrower enough money not only for his business needs but also to travel back to Jerusalem and to obtain food, shelter, and other essentials until he returns home.

3. The example given in the codes is that loan was made in an urban area, and the borrower wishes to repay the loan in a desert.

## Prepayment of the loan

If the time for repayment has arrived, the lender must accept the repayment even if he claims that he will be prejudiced thereby because of an imminent devaluation. If the lender is not in the city to accept the timely payment, then the borrower may pay the money to beth din or to a trustee of the beth din according to the rules of the community. If the lender has refused to take possession of the repayment and the money is then stolen from the borrower, the borrower must still repay the loan.[4]

The borrower may prepay the loan at any time even if the lender objects, since the time of payment is for the benefit of the borrower.[5] If, however, there will be prejudice to the lender by accepting prepayment, such as an imminent devaluation of the currency,[6] or adverse tax results, then he need not accept such prepayment.[7]

If the borrower wishes to make partial prepayment, there is opinion that he may do so and also opinion that he may not do so.[8] If the loan is collateralized, then the lender does not have to accept prepayment if the borrower insists upon obtaining a proportional return of the collateral, whether personalty or realty. If the time for payment has arrived the lender need not accept partial payments.

---

4. In the case of a bailment, if the bailee offers to return the bailment to the bailor and the bailor refuses to accept it, and the bailment is then lost or stolen, the bailee is no longer responsible. If the time for the return of the bailment has not arrived, the bailor can refuse to accept the return of the bailment, and if the object is lost or stolen, the bailee is responsible.

5. If no time has been specified for repayment, then the loan is for thirty days. (See Chapter 73.)

6. For example, on January 1, 100 shekels are borrowed from a lender in Israel at a time when 1 shekel is equal to 1 dollar. Hearing that the shekel is about to be devalued, the borrower wishes to prepay the 100 shekels. The lender will be disadvantaged if the exchange drops to 2 shekels to the dollar. The 100 shekels are now worth only 50 dollars.

7. The lack of a place where the lender can safely store the money from the prepayment is not a sufficient prejudice to enable him to prevent prepayment.

8. The opinion that holds that he may not do is based on the theory that small sums of money cannot readily be put to use by the lender. If the loan was evidenced by a writing, then the lender may object to partial prepayment on the grounds that it will cause his note of indebtedness to be compromised, since he would have to either mark the prepayments on the note or admit that the note is now for a sum less than is stated therein.

The borrower gives his real estate to the lender under a mortgage arrangement whereby the lender has the use of the real estate.[9] If the custom of the community is not to permit prepayment, then the borrower may not prepay unless he also pays to the lender the anticipated profits that the lender would reap from the real estate, which the lender shall have commenced to work. If the custom in the community is to permit prepayment under mortgage arrangements, then the borrower may prepay without having to compensate the lender for the anticipated profits from the land.[10]

If a person invests money for a specified period and is promised a certain annual return, the investor may not be given his money back before the end of the period, unless he is given the anticipated return for the full period.

## Payment

If the lender is holding collateral that is worth more than the amount of the loan, the borrower cannot insist that the lender keep as much of the collateral as is necessary to repay the loan and remit the overage to the borrower. If the collateral is not worth more than the amount of the loan, the borrower may not insist that the lender keep the collateral and return the note of indebtedness to him. The lender may insist that he be paid in money.

If when the time for repayment arrives the borrower states that he has no money or personal property, and has only real estate with which he wishes to repay the loan, then the lender may insist that he does not want to be paid in real estate but will wait until the borrower has money with which to repay the loan.

---

9. Mortgages whereby the lender obtains the use of the real estate belonging to the borrower/mortgagor are generally of two kinds. The first is that wherein the lender/mortgagee has the use of the land for a fixed period, after which he will return the land to the borrower and the debt will be deemed satisfied. The second is that wherein the debt is reduced by the amount of the profits that the lender obtains from the land until the entire debt is paid off. Such a mortgage can either provide for prepayment or provide that the loan cannot be prepaid. Once the lender starts to work the land, it would prejudicial to him to permit the borrower to prepay the loan with the result that all of the lender's effort and potential profits would be lost to him.

10. The borrower will have to pay the lender for the amount of work he does on the land.

If the lender loans the money to the borrower and the agreement is to repay the loan in a certain currency, and thereafter the government invalidates that currency, then the lender must nevertheless accept the currency as it can be used in a country that is easily accessible, or so long as merchants from that other country are available to accept the currency.[11] If the lender has no access to a place where the currency is still in use, then the lender need not accept such currency in repayment. If the loan agreement was silent as to the type of currency to be used, then the type of currency that was loaned may be returned.

If the loan agreement provides for legal tender of the government, then the loan must be repaid in legal tender. In all events, if there are laws in the country stipulating the legal tender that is to be used for the payment of debts, then such currency must be used, since the law of the land governs in such matters.[12]

---

11. The lender must accept the currency unless it is a violation of the laws of the land to continue to accept such currency.

12. See Chapter 369 regarding the halachic requirement to follow the law of the land in certain commercial matters.

# GLOSSARY

**agov:** Literally, "along with." Personal property may be acquired only by certain acts of acquisition, such as lifting the object acquired (see Chapter 189). If realty is acquired by one of the accepted methods for acquisition of real estate, the parties may agree that certain personal property may be acquired "along with" the realty. In such a case, a separate act of acquisition need not be made for the personal property. Similarly, according to Talmudic law, if an instrument that creates a lien on real property of the debtor states that certain personal property of the borrower is also liened "along with" the real estate, then the lien attaches to such personal property of the debtor. (See Chapter 62 that states that this is no longer the law.)

**aleatory instrument:** A contract whereby the promise by one of the parties is conditioned upon a fortuitous event that he wishes will never come about and that he anticipates with confidence will never come about. It is usually hazardous for the party making the promise. Such a promise is known as *asmachta* and is generally unenforceable.

**along with:** See *agov*.

**asmachta:** See *aleatory instrument*.

**assignee:** The person to whom an assignment has been made. The assignor assigns his interest to the assignee, often called the *grantee*.

**assignment:** The transfer by the assignor to the assignee of all or part of his rights to some kind of property, usually intangible property such as rights in a lease, mortgage contract of sale or a partnership interest.

**assignor:** A person who assigns or transfers property or rights to another person, the assignee.

**attachment:** Two kinds of attachment are discussed in this volume. The first is that in which the goods or real estate of a party is seized before an action is started so that the owner of the attached property who is outside of the jurisdiction of the beth din will submit to its jurisdiction or will be prevented from moving the goods outside the jurisdiction. This type of attachment may also be used so that there will be property already seized on which the plaintiff can make a levy if he is successful in obtaining a judgment against the defendant. The second type of attachment is that in which the defendant's property is taken after the plaintiff has won the lawsuit and has a judgment against the defendant.

**authentication of a document:** A procedure by which the beth din affixes a statement that they have examined a document and the signatures of the witnesses and have ascertained that the document is genuine.

**bailee:** The person to whom goods are delivered for safekeeping for their bailor.

**bailment:** The goods that are delivered by the bailor to the bailee.

**bailor:** The person who delivers the bailment to the bailee.

**bearer:** The person in possession of an instrument or any other document of title or security endorsed in blank.

**bearer instrument:** An instrument is payable to the bearer when by its terms it is payable to (1) the bearer or the order of bearer; or (2) a specified person or bearer, or any other indication that does not purport to designate a specific payee.

**berrurin:** Two interpretations are given in the Talmud in defining instruments of *berrurin*. One interpretation is that they are the instruments whereby parties to a dispute agree to submit the dispute to arbitration; each party selects one arbitrator, and the two arbitrators select a third arbitrator. The instrument naming the arbitrators is an instrument of *berrurin*. Another interpretation is that they are the instruments containing a record of the pleadings of the parties.

**borrower:** The person or firm that is borrowing the money from the lender.

**commodatary:** The person to whom property (as distinguished from money) is loaned gratuitously by the owner for the sole benefit of the commodatary.

**credence agreement:** An agreement containing clauses wherein any party thereto agrees that if the other party presents the instrument then it shall be given credence; no proof need be presented. For example, a note will state that the seller, upon presenting the note of indebtedness, will be believed when he states that he delivered the goods to the buyer without having to present any other proof of delivery. Or, the note may state that a lender should be believed that a loan has not been paid in circumstances where he would otherwise have to present proof of nonpayment to win the case.

**credence clause:** This is the clause in the credence agreement that states who shall be believed, to what extent, and as to which matters.

**creditor:** The person to whom money is owed by another person, who is the debtor. In this volume the creditor is usually the lender.

**debtor:** The person owing the money to the creditor. In this volume the debtor is usually the borrower.

**draftsman:** A person who draws or frames a legal instrument, such as an instrument of indebtedness, deeds, wills, or mortgages.

**effecting a lien:** The documents, acts, and circumstances that makes a lien effective, such as the witnessing and delivering of an instrument of indebtedness, or the making of a kinyan establishing a lien.

The acts of the borrower whereby his realty becomes subject to a lien in favor of the lender. The lien puts the lender in the first position to take the property, even if the borrower has sold the realty subject to the lien to a third-party purchaser. The lien is usually effected if there is a note of indebtedness or a note of admission. The lien takes effect from the time the loan is reduced to writing and signed by the two subscribing witnesses, or from the time that a *kinyan* has been made. Neither a promissory note, nor certainly an oral loan, effects a lien. The authorities differ in their opinions as to whether the basis of the lien is of Torah origin and covered all of the property of the debtor, real and personal, or whether the lien is of Rabbinic origin and the decree was to cover only real property. In any event, the law is now that the lien extends to the real property in the debtor's hands at the time the lien was created, either by the *kinyan* or by the delivery to the creditor of the note of indebtedness. The lien does not exist in any of the other categories of loans, not even in that of the written note executed by the debtor if it is not signed by two witnesses. (Since it is not signed by two witnesses, there is no note of indebtedness to deliver to the creditor in the presence of witnesses.) It does not extend to a loan witnessed by two eligible witnesses but not reduced to writing as a note of indebtedness. The lien does not extend to personal property; if it did, it would be nearly impossible to sell anything, for the purchaser would always be fearful that there might be some lien of which he might be unaware. The parties may agree to insert into the note of indebtedness a clause stating that the lien extends to property acquired after the agreement. Any such real property sold or given away or levied upon by third parties for loans that arose after the note of indebtedness loan are subject to the superior lien of the note of indebtedness loan. The theory is that if there is a note of indebtedness loan, then the news of such debt will be publicized and all will be aware of the note of indebtedness loan and the lien that it has created; the indexing of such note of indebtedness loans will facilitate such awareness. There are several ways in which the law presumes that the public will be aware that a lien has been established on the debtor's realty. Those who witness the delivery of the note to the creditor establish such a lien. There is also an opinion that the witnesses establish such a lien merely by signing the note. This opinion usually is not followed unless there are also witnesses to the delivery. A *kinyan*, whereby the debtor receives the handkerchief from the creditor, establishes the lien. At the time of the making of the *kinyan*, the debtor accepts the lien on his realty. Say, for example, that the lender loaned money to the borrower on January 1, 1991, with repayment to be made on March 1, 1991. The loan was evidenced by a duly executed promissory note, and thus it effected a lien on all of the realty owned by the borrower on the date of the making of the loan. On January 1, the borrower owned parcel A, a piece of real property. On February 1, 1991, the borrower sold parcel A to the purchaser. On March 1, 1991, the borrower was not able to repay the loan. The lender may then trace the realty to the purchaser and demand repayment of the loan from the purchaser; alternatively, parcel A may be sold to satisfy the loan.

**escrow:** Property delivered by the depositor (the escrower) or depositors to a third person (the escrowee) to be held by him until the occurence of a certain event or contingency or performance of a condition. The property may consist of personal property or of intangibles, such as instruments of indebtedness, securities, money, or anything that the parties wish to deposit with the escrowee.

**escrowee:** The person who holds the escrowed property.

**escrower:** The person who has given property to the escrowee to hold.

**execute (or execution):** The signing of a document by the witnesses and/or the debtor.

**force majeure:** Usually, an act that takes place without human intervention or control, such as a storm, earthquake, or flood. The term may also denote unforeseen events that are out of the ordinary, such as a war or a labor strike.

**gifts causa mortis:** A gift from a dying person in contemplation of death, with the intent that the gift is to take effect at the time of giver's death.

**grantee:** The person who receives a thing, whether by a gift or by sale.

**grantor:** The person who gives or transfers a thing to another (the grantee), whether by gift or by sale.

**guarantor:** A person who binds himself to satisfy the obligation of another person. A guarantor differs from a surety, in that the guarantor is secondarily liable to the creditor. That is, the creditor cannot proceed against the guarantor in the first instance. He must attempt first to satisfy the debtor's debt, and failing that he may proceed against the guarantor. In the case of the surety, the creditor need not attempt to first satisfy the debt from the debtor.

**halizah:** If a husband dies without any children or issue of children surviving, then his wife, according to Torah law, is to be married to the deceased husband's brother (Deuteronomy 25:5–10.) This is known as *yibbum*. If the widow or the brother does not want to conclude the ceremony of *yibbum*, then they perform the ceremony of *halizah*, also described in Deuteronomy 25. After this, the widow is free to marry whomever she wishes.

**hanahah:** A benefit that flows to a person. The benefit may be tangible or intangible, such as the psychological benefit that accrues to someone who is trusted and relied upon.

**hesseth oath:** A post-Mishnaic oath instituted by the Rabbis of the Talmud. It is usually administered when the plaintiff has put forward a plea that he cannot prove; the plaintiff is then entitled to have the defendant take a hesseth oath to deny the claim of the plaintiff. The theory is that the plaintiff will not bring to litigation an unfounded lawsuit.

**holder:** The person who has in his possession an instrument, security, or other intangible property.

**instrument:** A written document such as a contract, note of indebtedness, negotiable instrument, or security.

**instrument of trust:** See *note of trust.*

**joint and several liability:** When one of at least two persons who are liable may be sued separately for the entire liability, or when the creditor may join all those who are liable in a lawsuit.

**kethubah:** A document in which the groom undertakes certain obligations to his bride. Besides general obligations of support, he undertakes to pay her the sum stipulated in the *kethubah* in the event that he divorces her. In the event of his death, his estate will pay the widow the same sum. The Rabbis have fixed the minimum sum. The wife cannot waive the *kethubah*. The *kethubah* places a lien on all of the real estate of the husband that remains, even if the real estate is sold, or until the death of the wife if she predeceases the husband.

**kinyan:** A *kinyan* is one of the methods by which property may be acquired, as will be explained in Chapter 195. A *kinyan* also acts to bind a person to his promise. In the case of a sale, the purchaser hands his handkerchief to the seller, which the seller holds for a moment. This symbolic handkerchief, as well as the money to be paid, are given in exchange for the sold article. Similarly, the person who undertakes to perform an act, such as repaying a loan and liening his real property for the promise to repay, takes from the obligee a handkerchief and in exchange for receiving the handkerchief obligates himself to perform the act agreed upon. A *kinyan* acts as an instruction to the witnesses that the debtor acquiesces to the fact that a note of indebtedness will be drawn, executed by the witnesses, and delivered to the creditor.

**lender:** The person or firm that lends the money to the borrower.

**lender's oath:** An oath taken by a lender who was holding collateral security that he alleges was lost or destroyed without his negligence; the oath states that the lender does not have possession or control over the collateral.

**lien clause:** An instrument that creates a lien on the real property of the borrower; it must be subscribed by at least two witnesses and given to the lender in the presence of witnesses. Thus, if the borrower owned real estate at the time the loan was made, all of the real estate then owned by him is subject to the lien of the lender. If the borrower thereafter sold any of such real estate, and the borrower does not have the means to pay the lender, then the lender may make a levy on the real estate that the borrower sold. The absence of a lien clause does not imply that the real estate of the borrower is free of the lien, since it is presumed that the lien was inadvertently omitted; thus the instrument will be treated as if the lien clause was in the instrument.

A lien clause may also be drawn in favor of a purchaser of real estate. If the seller warranteed good title to the real estate that he sold, then all of the remaining real estate owned by the seller at the time of the sale is liened to the purchaser to secure the warranty. If the purchaser then loses the real estate to someone who had superior title to the seller, then the purchaser may sue the seller on the warranty of title, and if the seller is not able to pay the purchaser, then the purchaser may levy on any real estate that the seller owned at the time of the sale to the first purchaser. Imagine, for example, that on January 1, 1991, the seller sold parcel A to purchaser A, at which time the seller warranteed title to purchaser A. When the sale was made, the seller also owned parcel B. On February 1, 1991, the seller sold parcel B to purchaser B. On March 1, 1991, Mr. X sued purchaser A to recover parcel A because it really belonged to him and had never belonged to the seller. Mr. X won the lawsuit, and purchaser A lost parcel A. He sues the seller on the warranty given on January 1, 1990, and wins the lawsuit against the seller. The seller now has no assets with which to pay purchaser A. Purchaser A may then levy on the property that the seller sold to purchaser B on February 1, 1990.

**liened property:** All of the real estate owned by the borrower at the time he borrows money provided that a note of indebtedness was executed and delivered to the lender. All of the real estate owned by the seller at the time he sells real estate with a warranty.

**loan:** Money that is loaned may fit into any one of the following four categories:

1. A loan made without witnesses and without any writing evidencing the loan. This is considered an oral loan.

2. A loan made in the presence of two or more witnesses, but without writing evidencing the loan. This is considered an oral loan.

3. A loan made with or without witnesses but evidenced by a writing signed by the borrower and/or one witness. This is considered an oral loan. The writing signed under this category shall be designated as a promissory note, as distinguished from a note of indebtedness (category 4).

4. A loan made in the presence of at least two witnesses who sign a writing evidencing the loan; the writing is then delivered to the lender in the presence of two witnesses, who need not be the witnesses who signed the writing. This is considered a loan with a writing, and the writing is designated as a note of indebtedness. Whether the borrower does or does not sign the note of indebtedness is of no legal significance.

**ma'amad sheloshton:** Literally, "the three persons standing." Ordinarily, as we see in Chapter 66, an instrument can be assigned only with a writing and transfer of the instrument. However, if the creditor, the borrower, and a third person are all present together, the lender may instruct the borrower to pay the debt to the third person. The debt is then deemed transferred.

**maaser:** Ten percent of the produce which the farmer must give to the Levite after he has given the *terumah* to the Kohen. (See Chapter 67.)

**maaser ani:** A second 10 percent of the produce which the farmer is commanded to give to the poor during the third and sixth year of the seven-year cycle, after he has given *terumah* and *maaser*. (See Chapter 67.)

**maaser sheni:** A second 10 percent of a farmer's produce that he is to take to eat in Jerusalem during the first, second, fourth and fifth years of the seven-year cycle. This is separated out after the giving of *terumah* and *maaser*. (See Chapter 67.)

**migoo:** Literally *since*. The term generally means that a person who makes a plea is believed, since he could have presented another, stronger plea that would have been believed. Say, for example, that a lender sues a borrower on an oral loan that the lender is not able to prove. The borrower pleads payment. He is believed *since* he could have pleaded that the loan never took place and the lender could not have proved otherwise.

**mi'un:** According to Torah law the father of a minor daughter had the right to betroth her to a husband. The Sages added certain situations where the mother or adult brothers of a minor girl whose father had died might betroth her to a husband. The enactment by the Sages provided that the girl could disaffirm that contract upon reaching her majority. Such a disaffirmation is known as *mi'un.*

**mortgage:** A security of a particular property, usually real estate, for the payment of a debt. If the borrower (mortgagor) does not pay off the loan, the lender (mortgagee) may levy on the real estate on which he holds the mortgage.

**mortgagee:** The person who holds a mortgage on the property of the owner, who is the mortgagor. When a bank lends money for the purchase of a home, the bank takes a mortgage on that home, thereby becoming the mortgagee. The home owner who borrowed the money and gave the mortgage on his home is the mortgagor.

**mortgagee in possession:** The lender who demands and receives a security interest in the real estate of the owner where the owner gives the mortgagee permission to enter upon the mortgaged land and to remain on the land until the land has given profits to the mortgagee sufficient to pay off the loan, at which time the mortgagee will leave the real estate and return it to the owner; the owner will then owe no more money to the lender. Alternatively, the parties may determine that the lender will take possession of the mortgaged real estate for a specified time and at the end of that time the loan will be considered fully repaid and the owner/borrower will retake possession of the land. The number of years must approximate the amount of time it would take to pay off the loan from the profits of the land, taking into account that in some years the lender may make a larger profit from the land, whereas in other years, such as years of drought, the lender may sustain losses from his operation of the real estate.

**mortgagor:** The owner of the property, who has borrowed money from the mortgagee and who gives a mortgage on his property to the mortgagee.

**note of admission:** A note written after the borrower has admitted in the presence of two persons that he owes money to the lender. The note must be signed by the witnesses who heard the admission.

**note of confession:** A note written by a person who owes no money to a certain person, and yet, in the presence of at least two witnesses, admits that he owes that certain person a specified sum; he instructs the witnesses to write a note stating that he confesses that he owes the money, and he authorizes the witnesses to deliver the note of confession to that certain person.

**note of indebtedness:** A note signed by two witnesses evidencing the loan and delivered to the lender in the presence of two witnesses, who need not be the same as the witnesses who signed the note. See category 4, under *loan*.

**note of indebtedness loan:** A loan that is evidenced by a note of indebtedness.

**note of trust:** A note of indebtedness that is signed by the subscribing witnesses and given to the lender to hold in trust until such time as he will actually lend the money to the borrower. (The loan was not yet made when the note of trust was written and delivered to the lender.)

**obligee:** The promissee, a person to whom an obligation or performance of an act is owed. If Ruven owes money to Shimon, then Ruven is the obligor and Shimon is the obligee.

**obligor:** The promissor; the person who owes money to another person or who owes performance of an act for the benefit of another person.

**operative clause:** The part of the instrument, regardless of type, that intends to create or transfer rights by which the main object of the instrument is carried into effect.

**oral loan:** A loan that is not witnessed by a note of indebtedness.

**payee:** The person to whom an instrument is made payable; for example, the person named on a check as the one to whom the money shall be paid.

**payor:** The person who will make the payment that is due on an instrument; for example, the person who writes a check to the payee.

**pithka d'latotah:** An authorization given by beth din to curse anyone who violates a ban about to be pronounced.

**postdated note:** An instrument that bears a date later than the date on which the transaction actually occurred. An example is a note of indebtedness dated February 1, 1991, for a loan made on January 1, 1991.

**predated note:** An instrument that bears a date preceding the date on which the transaction actually occurred. An example is a note of indebtedness dated January 1, 1991, for a loan made on February 1, 1991.

**promissory note:** A writing evidencing a loan and signed by the borrower and/or only one witness. See category 3 under *loan*.

**prosbul:** A creditor, fearing that a debt to him will be cancelled by *shemitah*, appears before beth din in person or through an agent and assigns the debt to beth din for collection. Once the debt is assigned to beth din it is no longer cancellable by *shemitah*. (See Chapter 67.)

**realty:** Real property, as distinguished from personalty, owned by a borrower; usually land and/or property attached to the land.

**reducing the loan to writing:** Providing written evidence of a transaction; usually refers to a note of indebtedness, a note of admission, or a promissory note.

**release:** The relinquishing of a right, claim, or privilege by the person who holds or held it to the person against whom it might have been demanded. A loan is released, for example, when a lender absolves a borrower from obligation to repay it.

**rules of construction:** The rules used by a beth din to determine the sense or accurate meaning of obscure or ambiguous terms in an instrument. The beth din will look to extraneous connected circumstances in an effort to ascertain the aim and purpose of the terms.

**scribe:** Writer of a document, nowadays usually a lawyer for one of the parties.

**shemitah:** The years in the Jewish calendar are divided into groups of seven. The number of the year determines which tithes and other agricultural dues would be given to the priests, the Levites, and the poor. The seventh year of each cycle marked a period when the fields would lie fallow and the poor could take whatever aftergrowth might occur. At the termination of the *shemitah* year, debts were usually forgiven unless there was a procedure followed to keep the debt alive. (See Chapter 67.)

**shop-book entry:** A merchant's present recollection of sales he made or merchandise he delivered, or of payments that were made to him. He may refresh his memory by examining his shop-books' entries. If they were kept in the regular course of business and beth din finds them to be reliable, they may be accepted as truth and beth din may grant a judgment in favor of the shopkeeper. (See Volume III, Chapter 91.)

**subscribing witness:** A witness, other than the borrower, who signs a writing.

**surety:** A person who binds himself to satisfy the obligation of another person. A surety has been distinguished from a guarantor, in that the surety is co-liable with the debtor. That is, the creditor can proceed against the surety in the first instance and need not attempt to satisfy first the debt from the debtor; while in the case of the guarantor, the creditor must first attempt to satisfy the debt from the debtor, and failing that, the creditor may proceed to sue the guarantor.

**tallit:** A prayer shawl used by men during morning prayers. There was a time when men wore the *tallit* and *tefillin* during the entire daylight hours.

**tefillin:** Two black leather boxes containing scriptural passages and bound by black leather straps worn on the left hand and on the head. They are worn for morning services except on the Sabbath and holy days. In times gone by, they were worn during the entire day, until nightfall. There are still some people who wear them all day.

**terumah:** A small percentage, approximately 2 percent, of the produce that the farmer must give to the Kohen before he may use it himself.

**testator:** A person who writes a will or dies leaving a will.

**tracing the assets:** If a borrower does not have assets with which to repay a loan, the lender may recover from the purchaser realty that is subject to the lien and that the purchaser purchased from the borrower. This usually applies only to realty that was owned by the borrower at the time when he borrowed the money.

**unsold property:** Any property in the hands of the debtor at the time the creditor comes to collect his debt.

**waiver:** The voluntary, intentional relinquishment of a known right.

**warranty:** A promise that certain facts are true as they are represented to be and, sometimes, that they will remain so. In sales, it may be a promise that the seller is the owner and has the right to sell the property without any restriction, and that no other person has rights in the property.

**witness:** A person who is eligible to be a witness in accordance with Volume I, Chapters 33–35. The witnesses may not be related to each other or to any of the parties.

**witness agreement:** An agreement, or a clause in an agreement, or instrument of indebtedness whereby one of the parties has the credibility of two witnesses.

**witness of delivery:** A witness who sees a note being delivered to the lender.

**writ of appraisal:** An instrument used by beth din to state the appraised value of the debtor's property that will be sold to satisfy the debt due the creditor.

# Index

311

## About the Author

Emanuel Quint is a rabbi and lawyer and a co-founder (with Rabbi Adin Steinsaltz) of the Jerusalem Institute of Jewish Law, where he is dean and *rosh kollel.* He wrote *Jewish Jurisprudence* and was a senior partner at Quint, Marx & Chill, a New York law firm. Rabbi Quint is married, has four children, and lives in Jerusalem.